MICROSOFT

WINDOWS 10

FOR BEGINNERS & POWER USERS

(MAY 2021 UPDATE)

The Concise Windows 10 A-Z Mastery Guide
for All Users

Tech Demystified

Copyright © 2021 *Tech Demystified Publishers*

All rights reserved. This book or any portion thereof may not be reproduced or used in any manner whatsoever without the express written permission of the publisher except for the use of brief quotations in a book review.

ISBN: 9798514658886

TABLE OF CONTENTS

INTRODUCTION ix

CHAPTER ONE 10

OVERVIEW OF MICROSOFT WINDOWS 10 10
- Brief Historical Background of Windows Operating System (OS) 10
- Windows Various Versions 10
- What is Windows 10? 11
- Importance of Installing Windows on your Computer 12
- What's New About Windows 10? 13
- Should you upgrade to Windows 10? 14
- Windows 10 Editions 15
- Essential Frameworks 17
- The Windows 10 Hardware Requirement 17

CHAPTER TWO 21

GETTING STARTED WITH WINDOWS 10 21
- Procedures for Downloading Windows 10 21
- Installing Windows 10 22
- Welcome to the World of Windows 31

CHAPTER THREE 32

WINDOWS 10 DESKTOP ENVIRONMENT 32
- Exploring Windows 10 Desktop Environment 32
- Inbuilt Apps on Windows 10 32
- Working with the Start Menu 40
- The Left Portion of the Start Screen 42
- The Right Portion of the Start Screen 42
- Pinning & Unpinning your Favourite Apps to the Taskbar & Start Menu 43
- Pin to Taskbar 43
- Unpin from Taskbar 44

iii

Working on Tiles 44
How to Rename Tiles Titles Bar 45
Resizing the Start Screen Tiles 46
Moving the Tiles Icon 47
Unpin Tiles Icon 47
Resizing the Tiles Icon 48
Turning Off Tiles 48
Launching Apps with the Start Menu 49
How to check all application programs? 50
How to Create A Tiles Group 51
How to hide the Apps list on the Start Menu 52
How to Display Apps List on the Start Menu 53
Go to "Start menu", type "Start settings" and double click on it. 53
Exploring Task View 54
How to Make Use of Task View 55
Working with Cortana 56
How to Enable Cortana 57
How to Disable Cortana 61
Configuring Cortana 63
Customizing Cortana 65
Setting up Cortana to be your Assistance 66

CHAPTER FOUR **68**

THE WINDOWS 10 STORAGE **68**
Exploring File Explorer 68
File Explorer Default Folders 76
What is Quick Access? 78
Renaming a Folder 79
Exploring OneDrive Storage 80
What are the Benefits of OneDrive? 80
Get OneDrive Cloud on PC 81
Using OneDrive Cloud in File Explorer 81
What is OneDrive Status Icon? 82

iv

OneDrive Cloud Storage Features 82
Accessing Your Files from Anywhere via the Web 85
Searching on OneDrive cloud storage 85
Creating Different Document Format.. 85
Uploading Content on OneDrive 86
Sorting of Files on OneDrive Cloud Storage 86
OneDrive Files & Folders Visualization 87
CD or DVD Drives 87
Difference between CD & DVD Drives.................................... 87
Types of CD or DVD drives 88
Process of Copying of Files & Folders to a CD or DVD............ 89
Using Flash Drive & Memory Card... 89
How to Ensure Windows Security is up to Date 90
What Should I Do When My PC Refuse to Give Me Latest Update?.. 92

CHAPTER FIVE 94

WINDOWS 10 ACTION CENTER USER 94
Toggling Between the Tablet Mode and Desktop Mode 99
The Power Key 104
All Apps 105
PC User Account Name 106
Changing Your Background Displayed Colour 106
How to Adjust the Screen Resolution................................... 109
Difference between Settings and Control Panel 111

CHAPTER SIX 113

HOW TO ADD A SHORTCUT INTO YOUR DESKTOP ENVIRONMENT 113
Windows 10 Shortcut Keys 115
How to Resize Your Desktop Application 122

v

CHAPTER SEVEN 123

UNDERSTANDING USER ACCOUNTS 123
- User Accounts 123
- Types of User Accounts 123
- User Account Settings 124
- Sign-in Options 126
- Types of Windows Security 127
- How to switch from Microsoft Account to Local Account ... 128
- How to switch from Local Account to Microsoft Account.... 130
- How to Create a New User 133
- How to Remove a User 136
- Changing an Account Type 137
- Managing User Accounts and Parental Controls 139
- How to Sign Out or Switch Users 144

CHAPTER EIGHT 146

EXPLORING SETTINGS FEATURES 146
- Settings Features 146
- Display settings 146
- Bluetooth & Other Devices' Settings 150
- Phone 153
- Network & Internet 154
- Personalization 156
- Apps & features 159
- Accounts Settings 160
- Privacy Settings 163

CHAPTER NINE 165

ENHANCING YOUR PC PERFORMANCE 165
- How to Speed Up Your Windows 10 165

CHAPTER TEN 188

TROUBLESHOOTING WINDOWS 10 188

How to Treat Windows Unexpected Issues 188
To Undo System Settings and Files to an Earlier State 192
Frequently Asked Questions about System Restore Point ... 201

CHAPTER ELEVEN 209

WINDOWS SECURITY 209
Windows Defender 209
Understanding Windows Defender Real-Time Protection ... 210
What is Spyware? 212
How to use Quick scan, Full scan, and Custom Scan 212
Types of Scanning 213
What is Firewall? 214
How to Locate Your Firewall 215
How to Block a Program With Windows Firewall 217

CHAPTER TWELVE 223

CONNECTIVITY 223
How to Connect Your Windows 10 PC to the Internet 223
Connecting to Another Computer 226
How to Add a Printer to Windows 10 228
How to Scan a Document or Image 237
Setting up Windows to Fax 238

CHAPTER THIRTEEN 241

INSTALLATION OF SOFTWARE ON WINDOWS 10 241
Applications Installation & Uninstallation of Software
Programs on PC 241
Steps on Uninstalling an Application 241
How to Recognize If an App Is Safe or Not 245
How to Download an App from Microsoft Store on Windows
10 247

CHAPTER FOURTEEN 254

WINDOWS 10 TIPS AND TRICKS **254**
Hiding of Desktop Items.. 254
Displaying Back All Hidden Items................................ 255
Enabling Clipboard History 256
How to Delete, Pin & Clear Clipboard History 260
Splitting Windows App on Windows 10 261
How To Make Use of Emojis on Windows 10 263
Speeding up Windows Start time 264
Customizing Your Search Box 266
How to Hide Your Search Box 267
How to Display Your Search Box 268
How to Display Only Your Search Icon 268
How to Show File Name Extension 269
Minimize All Opened Applications.............................. 271
Activating Dark Mode 272
Determining What Your File Explorer Opens First 274
How to Switch and Determine What File Explorer Should Open By Default.. 275
Factory Reset 276
Turn On & Off Background Apps 278
Dictation 280
God Mode 281
Snip & Sketch 283
Windows Sandbox 285
Sandbox Requirements 285
Launching Sandbox 286
Calculator 289
Storage Sense... 290
How to Use Inbuilt Video Editor to Edit Videos........... 292
Magnifier and Read Aloud 295
Windows Insider 295

CONCLUSION **298**

INTRODUCTION

Over time, the evolution of human beings has always moved around health and technology. The primary reason for technology is for simplicity which is the aim of Microsoft Corporation which leads to the development of Microsoft products such as Windows. For this very reason, Microsoft has been an undefeated product ever in human history.

As long as a computer system, be it desktop, laptop, tablet, or smartphone is concerned in the human race for simplicity of life, windows can never go out of demand.

Windows has been user-friendly right from its existence till date, but all of its features are useless without a proper guide on how to make use of them. It has been verified that every and anything can be learned only if an individual is willing and able to pay the price for it.

I, therefore, introduce to you Windows 10 operating system that businesses, students, professionals, and other fields cannot do without. This is a practically simple step-by-step guide on the in and out of Windows 10 operating system which has never and can never be out of demand; it has been in existence since 1985 and it's still relevant to date.

There is no operating system that can ever compete with Microsoft Windows. Follow me as I show you how to efficiently and effectively operate your Windows 10 operating system.

CHAPTER ONE

OVERVIEW OF MICROSOFT WINDOWS 10

Brief Historical Background of Windows Operating System (OS)

The historical background of Windows can be dated back to 1981 when Microsoft being the company name commenced work on a program called "Interface Manager" by Bill Gates who happens to be its founder. It was publicized in November 1983 under the name "Windows", however, the first version of Windows known as Windows 1.0 was not released until November 1985. Since 1985 till date, there have been dramatic changes in its upgrade due to security reasons against hackers looking for Windows vulnerability to exploit its users. For every product, there is always a symbol of identification as for Microsoft.

There have been different kinds of operating systems, also known as "OS" but when it comes to user-friendliness, right from Windows' launching date till now; there has not been any operating system that ever surpasses Windows. It has been proved flexible, reliable, friendly, and accessible.

Windows Various Versions

Version	Date
Windows 1.0	November 20, 1985
Windows 2.0 Windows 2.01 Windows 2.03	December 9, 1987
Windows 3.0	

Windows NT 3.5	May 22, 1990
Windows NT 4.0	
Windows 95	August 24, 1995
Windows 98	June 25, 1998,
Windows 2000	May 17, 2000
Windows Me	September 14, 2000
Windows Vista	November 30, 2006
Windows 7	October 22, 2009
Windows 8	August 26, 2012
Windows 8.1	October 17, 2013
Windows 10	July 15, 2015

Windows 10 is the best version ever, which was released on July 15, 2015, but was made available on July 29, 2015. Since then till date, Windows 10 has not been replaced due to its reliability, accessibility, and flexibility.

What is Windows 10?

Windows 10 is an operating system that manages all the hardware and software on a computer, which makes the hardware useful from a state of emptiness into a state of usefulness. Windows 10 is the most recent version of the Microsoft Windows operating system that was released on July 15, 2015, and was generally released to the public on July 29, 2015. It is built on the Windows NT kernel.

Windows 10 was programmed with C, C++, and C# programming language. Microsoft decided to name the 2015 released version as Windows 10 and skipped Windows 9 because the operating system is framed to be a new pathway for Microsoft. One of the aims of Windows10 is to merge the Windows experiences across multiple devices, such as desktop computers, laptops, tablets, and smartphones. Windows 10 also introduced the Microsoft Edge web browser, personal assistance called Cortana, a new window and desktop management feature called Task View, virtual desktop system, support for fingerprint and face recognition login, new security features for enterprise environments, excellent virus protection against attacks such as Cyber Attacks, Viruses, Worms, Trojan Horses, Spyware, Adware, Ransomware, a Microsoft store and so on.

There have been many different versions of Windows over the years, including **Windows 8.1, Windows 8, Windows 7, Windows Vista,** and **Windows XP**. While older versions of Windows mostly ran on **desktop** and **laptop computers**, Windows 10 is also structured to run equally well on **tablets** and **smartphones**.

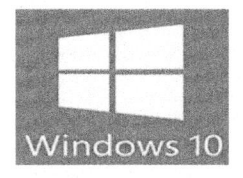

Importance of Installing Windows on your Computer

Windows operating system is one among thousands that have no competition when it comes to user-friendliness, reliability, flexibility, and availability. Some of the importance of installing Windows on your computer are:

- Windows operating system comes with auto-fix features.
- Windows 10 comes with a personal assistant called "Cortana".
- Windows comes with its store for downloading and security purposes.
- Windows has auto-update features.

- With Windows 10, you can now work on multiple desktop environments, which is known as "task view" without interfering with other applications.
- A higher level of security privacy.
- Windows 10 makes it possible to monitor your privacy anywhere around the world by creating a Microsoft account that enables synchronization on smartphones and laptops.
- Windows 10 is structured in such a way that every item has its folders by default e.g., Music, Videos, Pictures, and Documents.
- Windows 10 gives room for parental control dashboard.
- Windows 10 comes with a lot of inbuilt features such as Sticky Note, Snipping Tool, Microsoft Edge, and a lot more.
- With Windows 10, you can toggle in-between desktop mode and tablet mode.
- Understanding hardware has been a complex task that gives room for only programmers to comprehend but with Windows, you don't need such stress and worry, windows interact with your hardware without any complication and gives its users friendly feedback.

What's New About Windows 10?

Windows 10 has been the best of its kind; the previous version comes with a lot of critics which has led to the replacement with another version, but Windows 10 comes with lesser critics; since 2015 till date, Windows 10 is still much more very relevant. Windows 10 comes with a lot of flexibility and reliability such as personal assistance, toggling in-between tablet and desktop mode, Bluetooth support, and synchronization of devices. With Windows 10 auto-update, you are secured from fear of vulnerability and threat from attackers. Windows have no issue with your screen resolution (size), all that is required is for your system to meet up with Windows specification for its installation, which will be covered soon.

Should you upgrade to Windows 10?

The question is for those who don't know the adventure in Windows 10. People complained about Windows 10 high rate of data consumption which discourages many to upgrade from the old version to Windows 10 (been the latest version), others say Windows 7 is far better than any other version of Windows including Windows 10. But I am telling you Windows 10 is far better than all other versions of Microsoft Windows in security updates, flexibility, and simplicity of built-in features such as Cortana, Microsoft Edge, Tiles, and so on. In time past, the level of attack on Microsoft Windows was very high, but since Windows 10 was released; this issue of insecurity has dropped drastically.

Windows 10 has been framed for its users to control the totality of its features which makes data consumption monitored. Windows 10 was framed out of previous version experiences which makes it more flexible for tablets and smartphone users to also make use of it.

If your PC is running Windows 7, Windows 8, or Windows 8.1, you can purchase the Windows 10 update from the Microsoft website *https://www.microsoft.com*.

If you're using an older version, such as Windows 95, Windows Vista, or Windows XP, your computer most likely won't meet the hardware requirements to upgrade to Windows 10. If you're thinking about upgrading an older computer, I recommend purchasing a new computer that already has Windows 10 OS installed. System requirements will be fully explained in the next section of this book.

Windows 10 Editions

Windows 10 appears in various editions, which are divided into two segments: desktop/laptop edition and mobile edition. Three of the major editions are available in 32-bit and 64-bit embodiments. Fortunately, contemplating the 32-bit issue may exercise a few extra gloomy cells, but with a little help, you can probably figure it out easily. Using 4GB memory into your computer with a 32-bit operating system is out of reach due to its configuration to acquire a maximum of 3.5GB RAM, anything above it becomes unused, except it is a 64-bit operating system that can accommodate more RAM storage.

Features	Details
Windows 10 Home	Windows 10 Home as the name implies is mostly designed to suit in-home usage. Windows 10 Home has built-in security features including firewall, antivirus, internet protections, and other accessories used to edit photos, scan your face, fingerprint for those whose system has the hardware features. Those on the previous version are given the privilege to automatically auto-upgrade without paying

Windows 10 S	Windows 10 S is framed for the benefit of control which makes it more secure, reliable, and stable. You can only be permitted to download from the Windows Store, which means you can't install regular programs from other sources due to security reasons.
Windows 10 Pro	Windows 10 Pro which is an abbreviation of Professional, offers all of the same features as the Home version. Features in Windows 10 Pro include a Remote Desktop feature, BitLocker, and more in-depth access to the cloud.
Windows 10 Mobile	Windows 10 Mobile is designed for smartphones; it also gives complete access as it were on a computer.
Windows 10 Mobile Enterprise	It is similar to Windows 10 Enterprise; the difference is the tablet movable handle and the sizes of displayed icons.
Windows 10 Enterprise	It is designed for organization usage due to its make-up for organization suit. Enterprise is available only to companies that buy into Microsoft's Software Assurance program.
Windows 10 Education	Windows 10 Education is structured for students. Windows 10 Education is Microsoft's most healthy edition and students at participating schools through a program called Academic Volume Licensing.

Based on the dynamics of Windows' operating system, Microsoft was able to come up with various editions of selectivity on what is best suitable for an individual. The editions explanation will enable individuals to know what is best suitable for them.

Essential Frameworks

It is very important to be fully aware of operating system essential structures which are hardware and software.

- **Software:** Software is the opposite of hardware; it can be seen but can't be touched. They are in form of icon applications such as chrome, Microsoft Office Suite, Windows, and so on. Anything you install on your operating system is known as software as long as it is on your Windows because even Windows is software on its own.

- **Hardware:** Hardware is anything that can be seen and touched such as a computer screen, keyboard, mouse, hard drive, DVD drive, etc.

These two fundamental parts make up a system to function without any complication. Hardware can't function without software, likewise, software can't function without hardware.

The Windows 10 Hardware Requirement

It is important to notice that for every installation, there is always a requirement necessarily needed to execute its installation, due to its embedded files and directories compressed in its setup. Never disregard this significant requirement when getting a system or installing Windows 10 setups. Below are the requirements needed to properly install windows 10:

Features	Details
RAM - Random Access Memory	It is a form of computer memory typically used for machine code and working data in reading and allocating data from one end to the other end. RAM determines the volume of applications to be processed per milliseconds. It is known as a convener that runs errands between hardware and software codes. It switches quickly among multiple applications but it does not save any data. Windows 10 requirement for RAM capacity must be at least 1gigabyte (1GB) for 32-bit and 2gigabyte (2GB) for 64-bit. **Note:** RAM is an unstable memory that temporarily stores the files you are currently working on.
ROM – Read-Only Memory	It provides permanent storage for instructions needed during the process of turning on the computer. It does so by storing the BIOS and other firmware for the computer hardware. This firmware rarely needs updating.
Display	Screen resolution should not be below 800 x 600.

Graphics Card	Graphics card also known as "video card" renders an image to your system because it enhances graphics user interface (GUI) resolution and every other visual aid. The quality of your graphics card controls the standard of your image enrichment. It also communicates image data to the monitor. The Graphics card might be DirectX 9 or later WDDM 1.0, driver.
Hard disk drive	It is a data storage device that lives inside the computer. It has spinning disks inside where data is stored magnetically. It is one of the important requirements for running an operating system. This is part of the major requirements needed to make use of the Windows operating system. A hard disk consists of file storage such as videos, images, music, and documents. 16GB is needed for 32bit while 20GB is needed for 64bit for smooth running of the windows operating system in order not to slow down the system operation.
Processor	A processor (CPU) is the logic circuitry that responds to and processes the basic instructions that drive a computer. 1gigahertz and above is highly recommended as the requirement for windows 10 installation; anything below might lead to deadly disruption.

What's New in Windows 10 may 2021 Update?

- **Windows Hello Multicamera Support**: When you have both an external and internal Windows Hello camera on your PC, you can now set the default camera as your external camera. Windows Hello is used for signing into PCs.
- **Windows Defender Application Guard Performance**: Microsoft has sped up **WDAG**, a feature that lets administrators configure applications to run in an isolated, virtualized container for security. Microsoft says opening documents, in particular, should be faster.
- **WMI Group Policy Performance**: Microsoft has improved Windows Management Instrumentation (WMI) Group Policy Service (GPSVC) and made it perform more quickly "to support remote work scenarios."

CHAPTER TWO

GETTING STARTED WITH WINDOWS 10

Procedures for Downloading Windows 10

In this section, I will be showing you how you can download and install Windows 10 on your computer system, but before that, there is a need to understand that windows installation setup can be downloaded from the Microsoft website and it can also be purchased through disc or flash format. Based on this guide, we are going to be using the Microsoft website to illustrate it.

Microsoft Windows 10 comes with a different edition which has been explained in detail in the previous chapter.

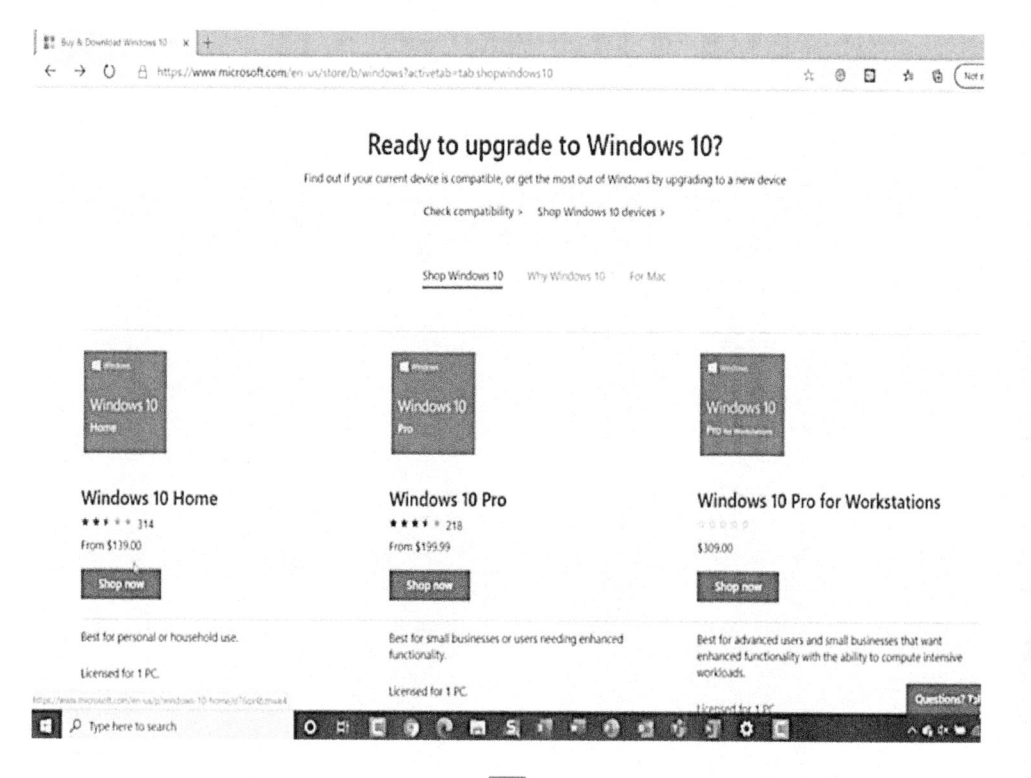

Installing Windows 10

i. Select your preferred language, time, and keyboard format, then click "next"

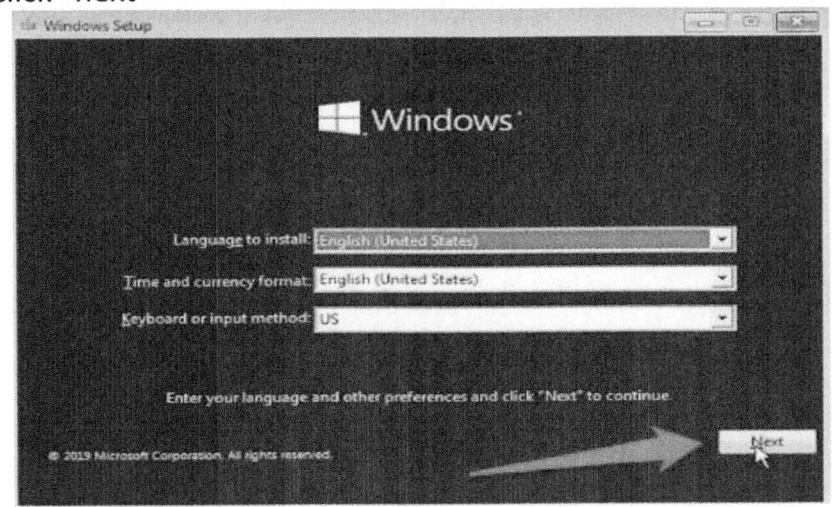

ii. Proceed and click "Install now".

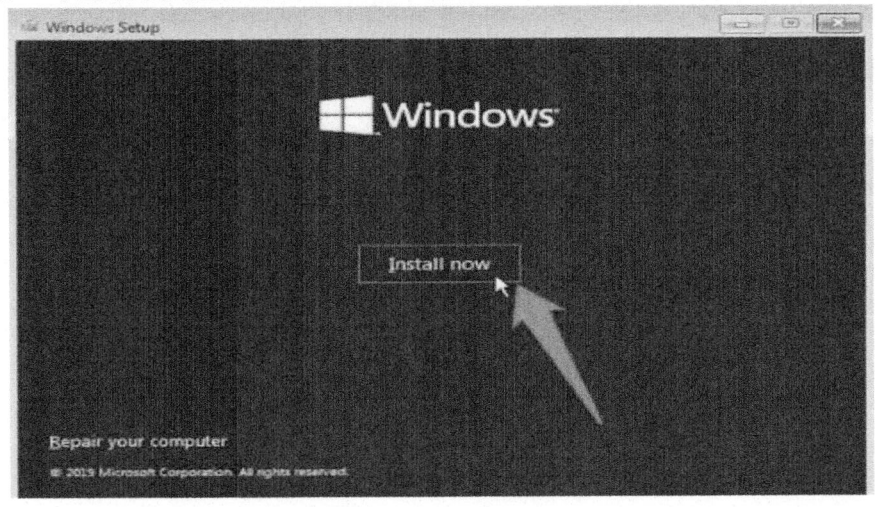

iii. Insert your Windows product key or click "I don't have a product key" if you don't have it. Then click on "next" to proceed.

22

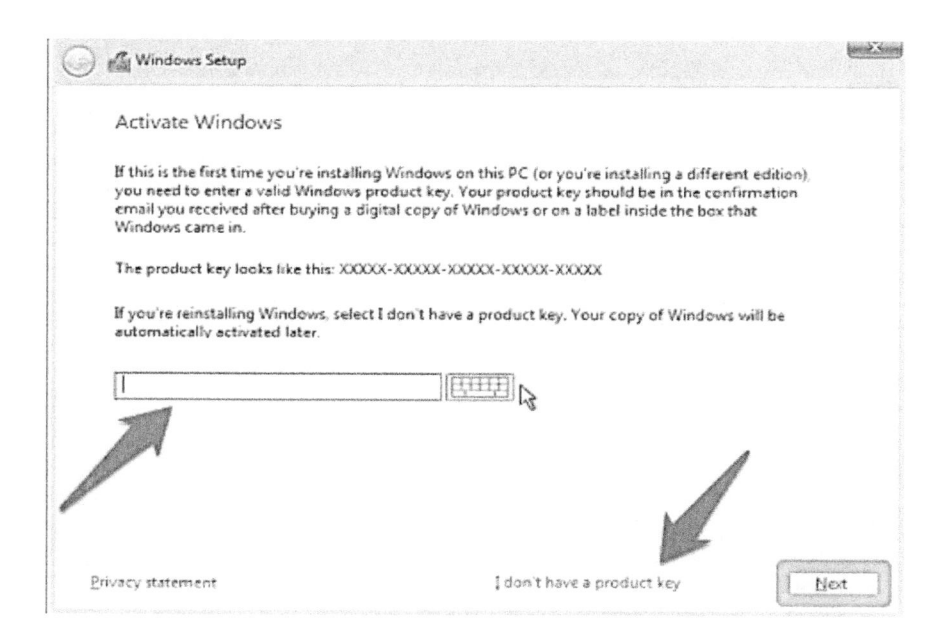

[Screenshot: Windows Setup — Activate Windows screen with product key entry field and "I don't have a product key" option]

iv. As shown earlier, choose the edition that best suits your specialization usage, then click "Next" below to continue.

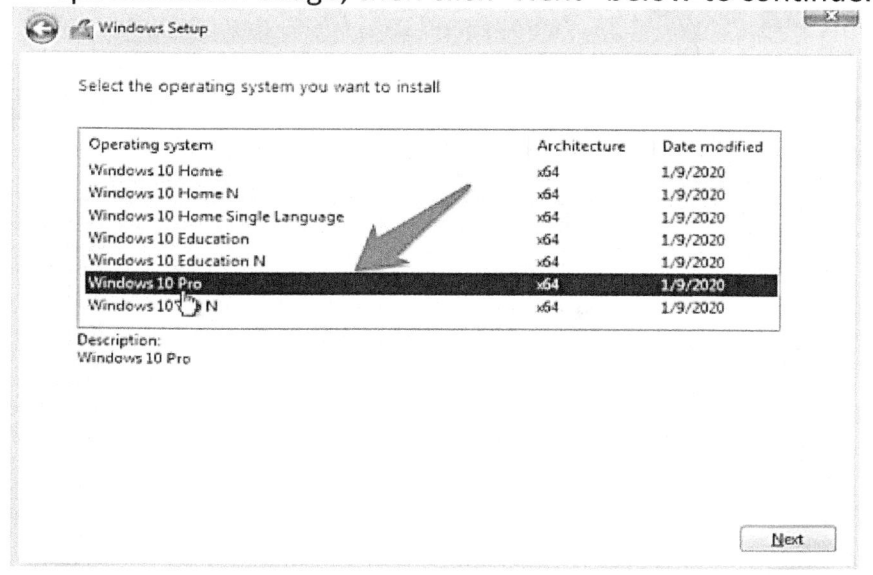

[Screenshot: Windows Setup — Select the operating system you want to install, with Windows 10 Pro highlighted]

v. Accept the license terms which are Microsoft terms and conditions, then click on "Next".

23

ix. Initiating Windows 10 desktop interface.

x. The first information Windows 10 setup will require from you is your region and keyboard layout. Be careful in your installation settings.

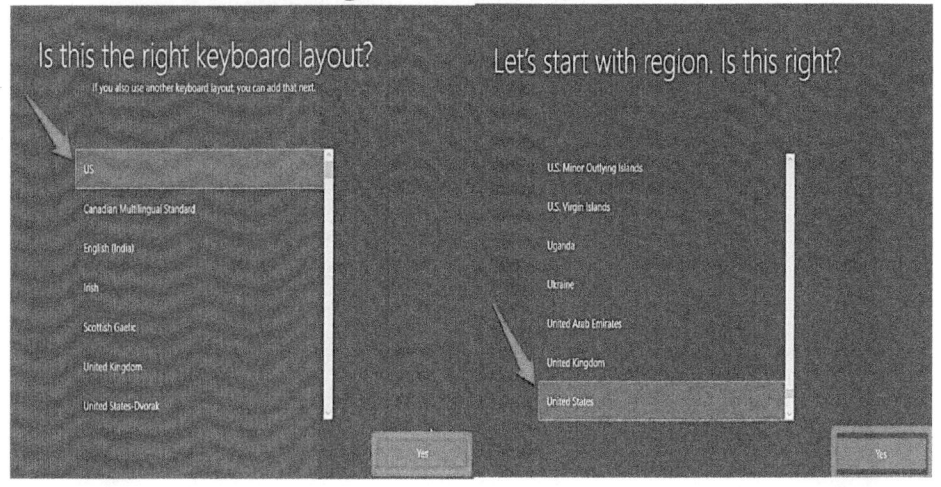

xi. Next is a piece of information about the usage purpose; is it for personal use or organizational use for a better experience.

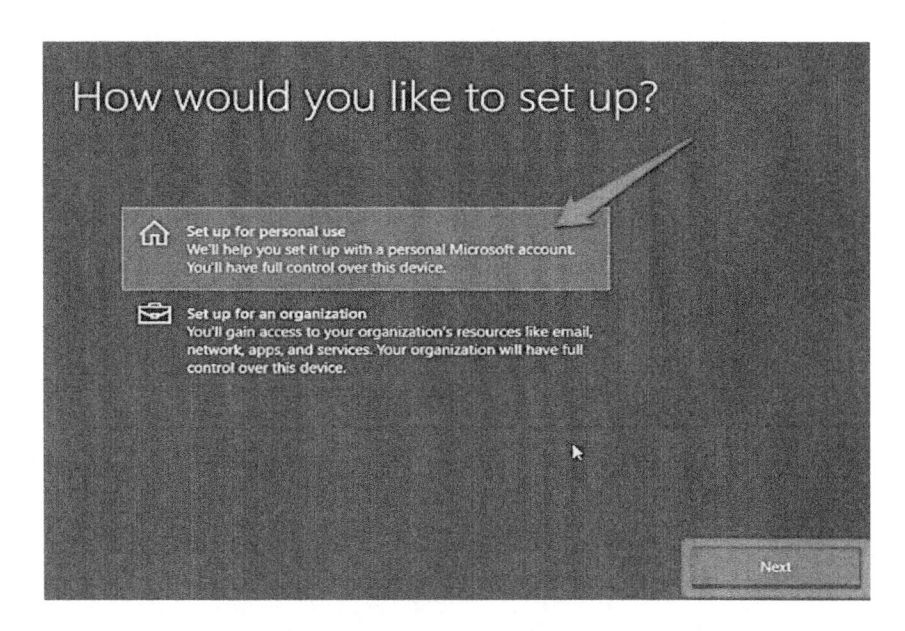

xii. You are required to create an account for yourself so that not everyone will have access to your PC. It is optional.

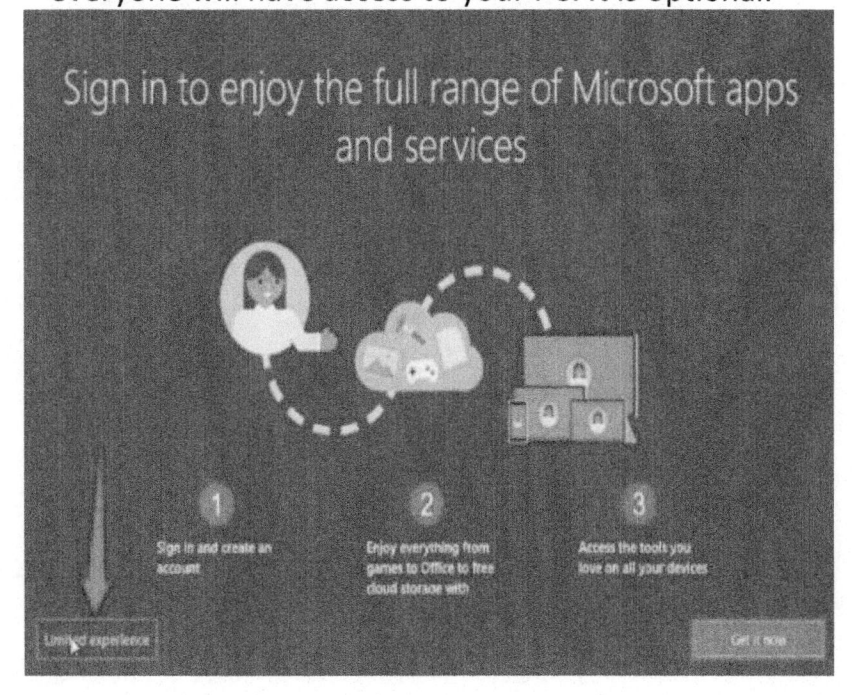

27

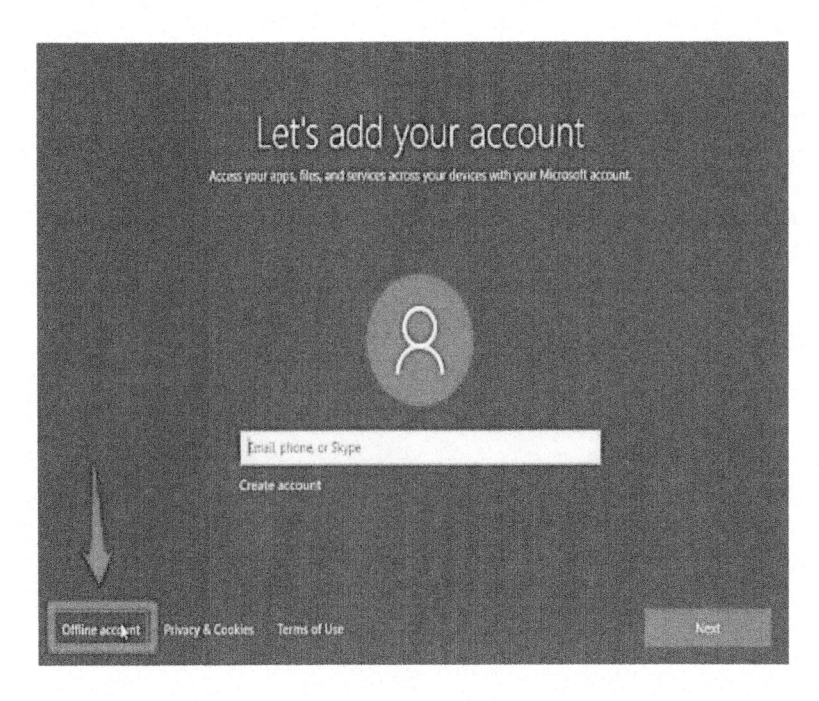

xiii. Create the name and password you want to use to access your PC.

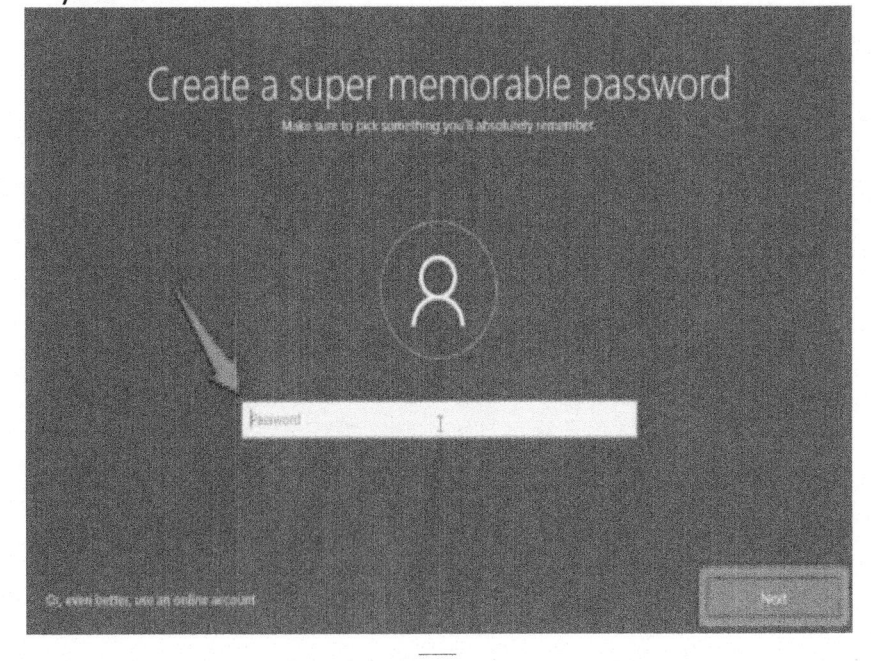

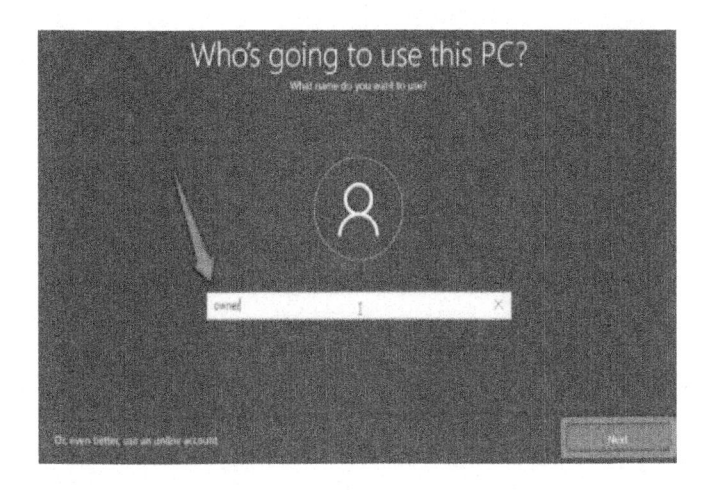

Note: Your password must be carefully decided because Windows 10 makeup is very sensitive to information. For example, using "STEV" during setup and typing "stev" while trying to login will lead to access denial; so be careful with the use of uppercase and lowercase as well as the use of numbers. Password on Windows doesn't do auto-correct or password suggestions on your behalf.

xiv. Next, you will be required to accept or decline Cortana service. It is optional.

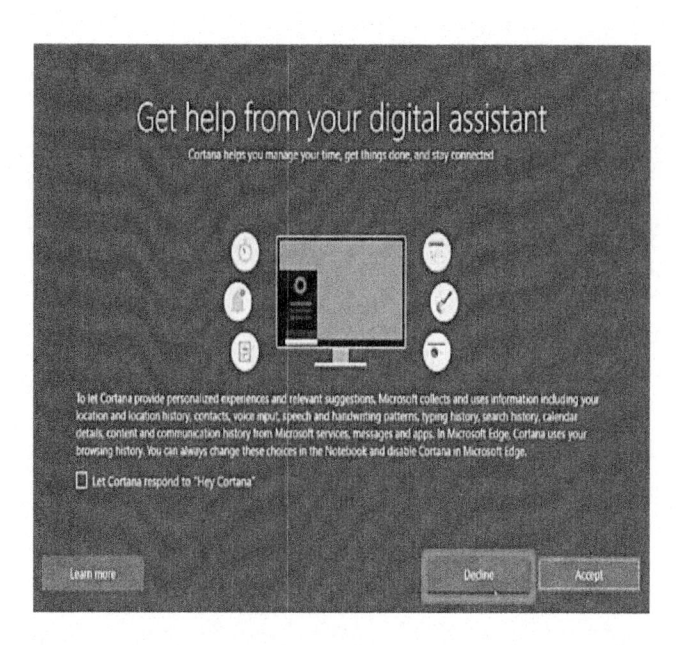

xv. Kindly tick and untick your settings configuration. If you know what you want, select it and, if you don't just leave it the way it is. Accept or click on learn more for more info.

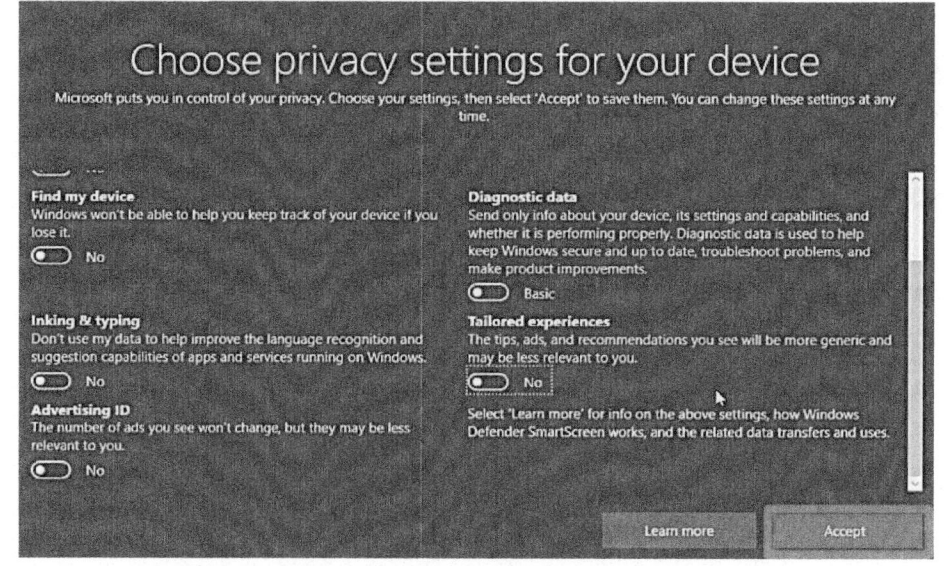

xvi. Wait for a minute for your desktop interface to come up.

xvii. This is how your desktop environment will look like when it is fully loaded.

Welcome to the World of Windows

Welcome to the world of windows. The picture above is your home screen by default. This home screen which is also known as a desktop interface is a hosting environment that helps to navigate through other tools and features. Hovering on any icon will by default tell you what such an icon means and represent.

CHAPTER THREE

WINDOWS 10 DESKTOP ENVIRONMENT

Exploring Windows 10 Desktop Environment

The desktop environment which is also known as the "graphical user interface" has been the hosting or an entry point into other parts of windows features. For every software, usage comes with a friendly environment for easy navigation which the desktop environment is serving such as:

Inbuilt Apps on Windows 10

With time, Windows has proved its software secured and reliable; this makes the corporation make more efforts by having some built-in applications that can't be uninstalled to download software online. Microsoft is already developing its environment for its users to download from to reduce Windows vulnerability and increase its security. Some of its built-in applications are:

- **Notepad:** Notepad is a built-in application that enables all sorts of text format. Its main aim is for plain text only.

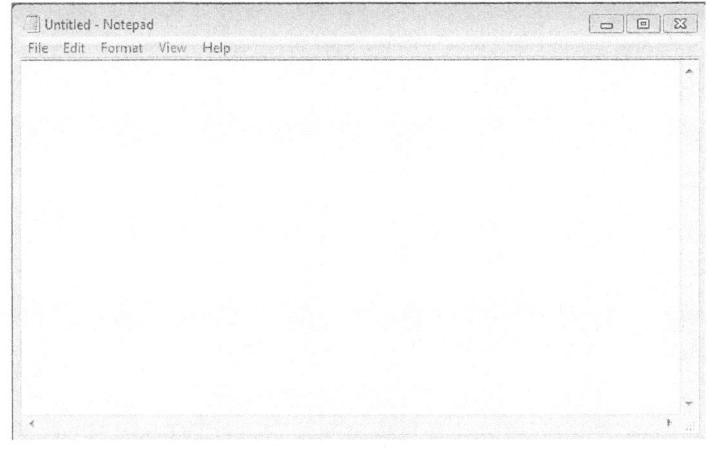

- **WordPad:** WordPad is similar in function to notepad but a little higher than notepad. WordPad deals with text, color, shape, image, and different fonts style and sizes.

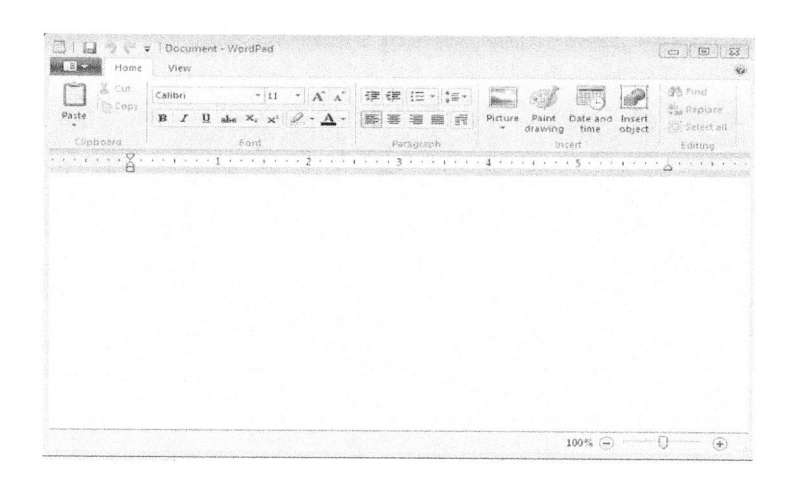

- **Sticky Notes:** Sticky Notes serve as a prompt notice of scheduled activities to be done or carried out. It can be called a To-do list. It also enables multiple creating of documentation.

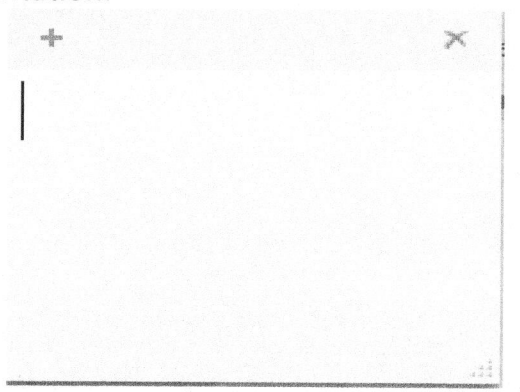

- **Microsoft Store:** Microsoft Store is a platform specially structured for windows users to download securely without any vulnerability to attack. Every application is thoroughly scrutinized by Microsoft.

- **Microsoft Edge:** Microsoft Edge is the latest built-in browser for windows 10; before it was internet explorer. By default, Microsoft Edge is Windows 10 recommended browser that enables its users to access the web, and all that is needed is an internet connection to utilize it.

- **Xbox:** The name Xbox was traceable from DirectX Box; Xbox was formerly known as xCloud. Xbox was first released in 2005. The Microsoft Xbox One system comes with a lot of features such as a gaming console, television & movie, music, and also interaction with other apps. It also has a live version known as Xbox Live.

- **Paint:** Paint is the opposite of Notepad, it is used mainly to design, edit an image, resize an object, import, draw, crop, add and edit colors, zoom. It has a lot more features embedded inside; it is similar to WordPad but higher than WordPad.

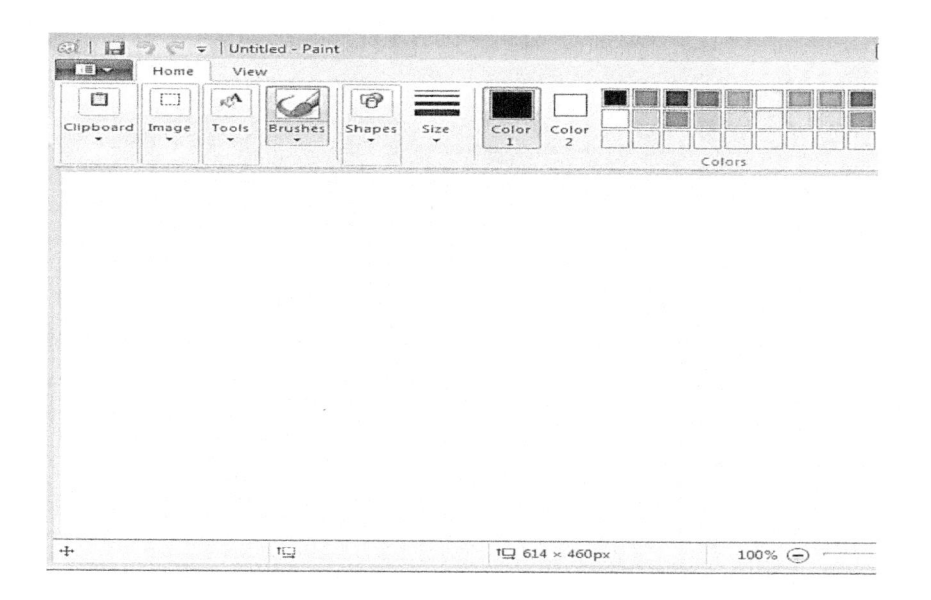

- **Mail:** Mail is an application specially framed to host multiple email account together such as **Google mail**, **Hotmail**, **Outlook mail, Live mail, Office365, Yahoo mail, iCloud, POP, IMAP.** There is also a place for additional options known as **Advanced setup**.

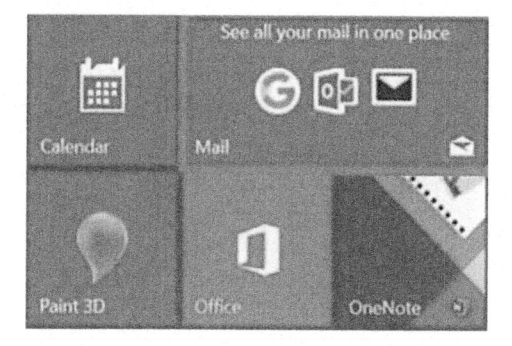

- **Weather:** Weather is used to verify or predict the weather of an environment and other location(s) you want to inspect more about, many researchers make use of it, depending on your purpose of usage, it is free to use.

- **Snipping tool:** The snipping tool is used to screenshot any part of the Windows interface, which is also used for description.

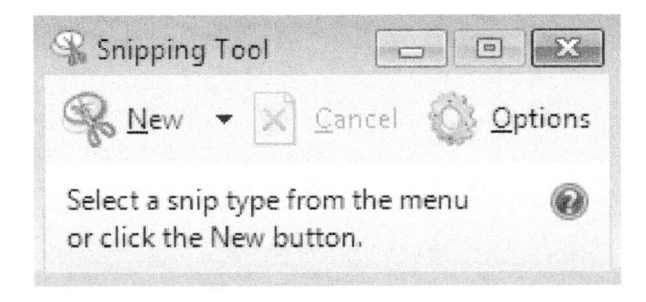

- **Voice Recorder:** Voice recorder is an audio recorder that enables virtual recognition of speech recording which captures every scene you click on and its meaning attached with it.

- **Windows Speech Recognition:** Windows Speech Recognition allows you to control your system by voice. Using only your voice, you can start a program, dictate text into the document,

- click buttons, open menus, and lots more. It works the same as you make use of your mouse and keyboard. Making use of it requires its users to select its preference Headset Microphone, Desktop Microphone, and Other Microphone devices. You select your preferred choice; fill other required procedures by windows to setup your Windows Speech Recognition. Windows Speech Recognition will take you through its procedures and will be activated once its requirement has been responded to.

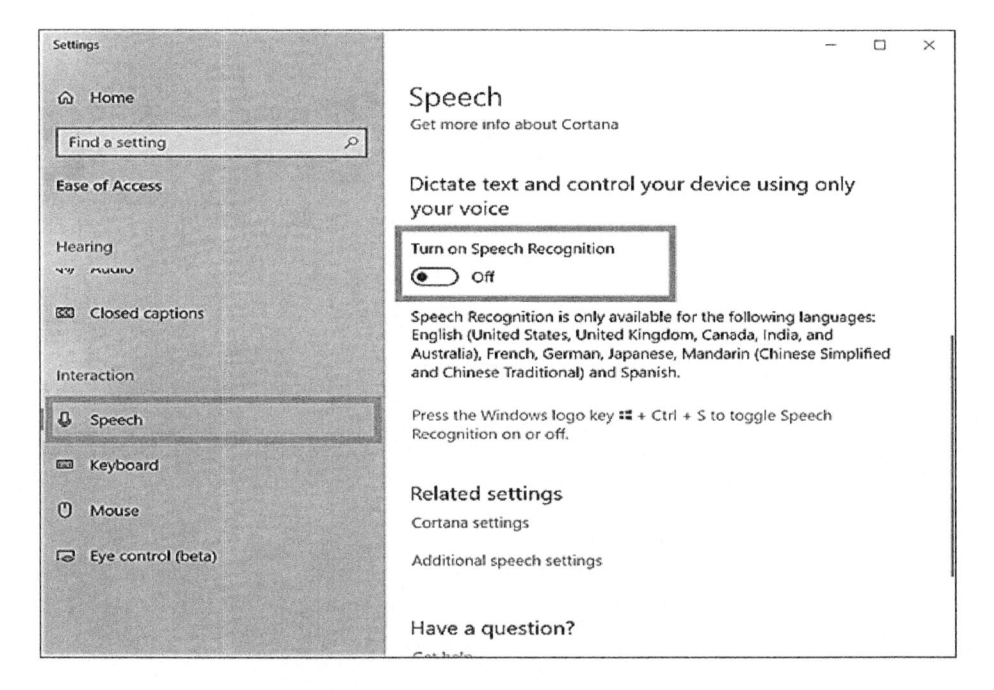

- **Task manager:** The task manager is specifically designed to monitor the activities on the windows interface. It is one of the most powerful built-in tools by windows to oversee the happenings of every activity going on, performances, application history, users' details, and services. With a task manager, you can control any active program. It is majorly used when an application refuses to close or slows down the windows interface.

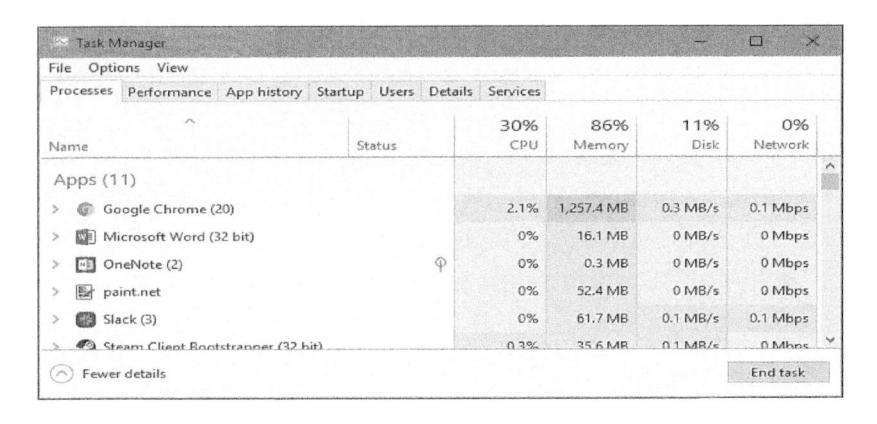

- **Calculator:** "Calculator" is constructed for the mathematical calculation of figures. It comes with the operator for multiplying, dividing, adding, and subtracting (+, x, -, /), etc. The built-in calculator comes in with a lot of features for the scientific method, standard method, programmer method, and statistics method. It functions in various ways depending on individual taste.

- **Calendar:** Calendar gives a direct illustration of days, months, and years.
- **Clock:** Clock and calendar are interwoven in the same position. Windows comes with an inbuilt clock with an alert for notice which is only active when your system is turned on.

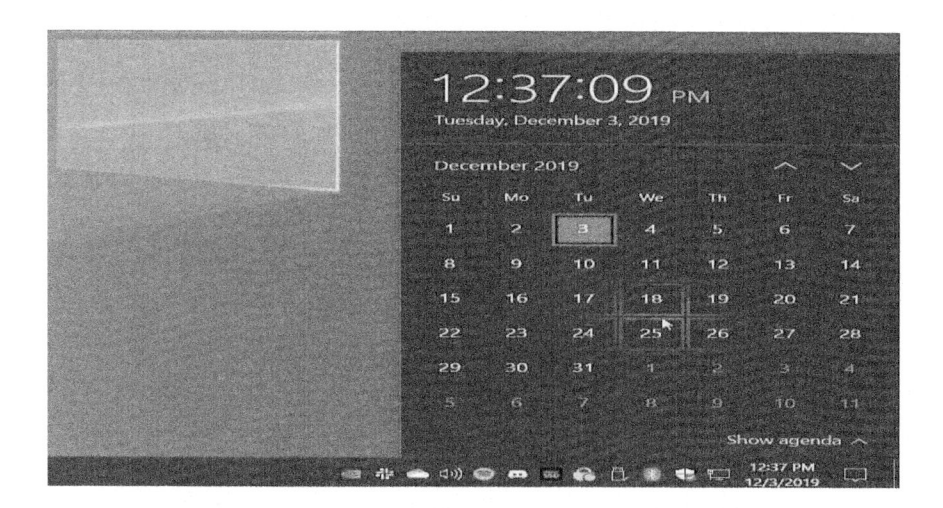

- **Cortana:** This is an inbuilt personal assistant. It is used primarily for getting things done by scheduling, reminding, finding facts, and lots more. With Cortana you can accomplish anything; all that is required is to speak.

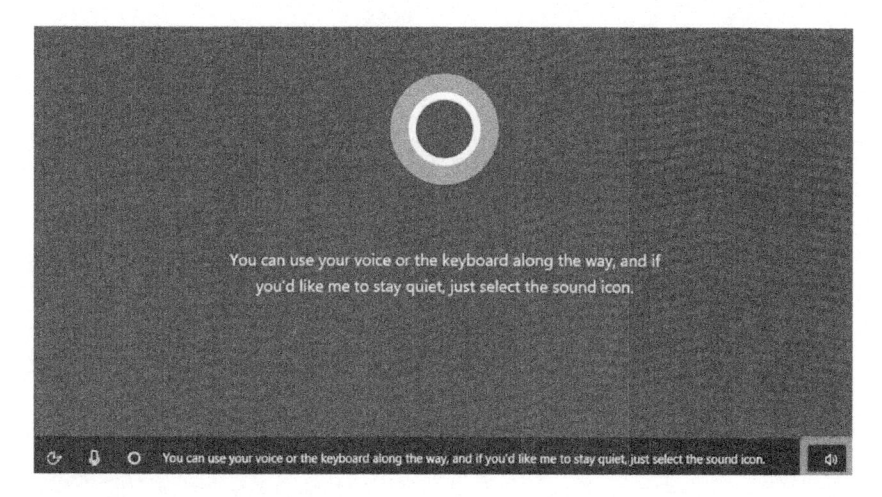

- **OneDrive:** OneDrive is built-in cloud storage specifically designed to accommodate data online to free up space on the PC. To make use of this tool, the user must sign up to fully make use of it. If you understand google drive using OneDrive won't be an issue.

Working with the Start Menu

The "Start Menu" is part of Windows features from Windows 95 till Windows 10, the only difference in the start menu button has been changes in its color and shape but the windows logo symbol remains unaltered. The start menu enables its users to see a multitude of options such as recently added applications, most used applications and search specifically on what the user needs and so on.

Some of the installed application has an indication arrow as seen in the illustration below by the left which indicates some dropdown folders and applications in itself depending on its purpose.

Note: All applications are arranged alphabetically.

The below arrow by the right-hand side shows the movement of the scroll bar mostly used to search.

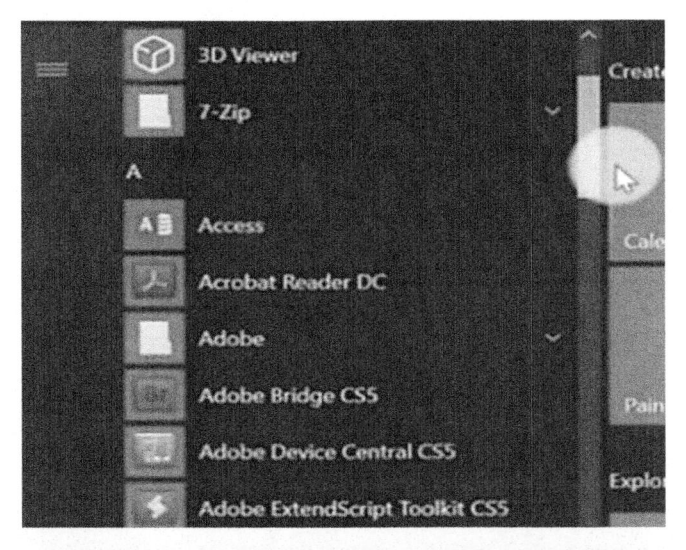

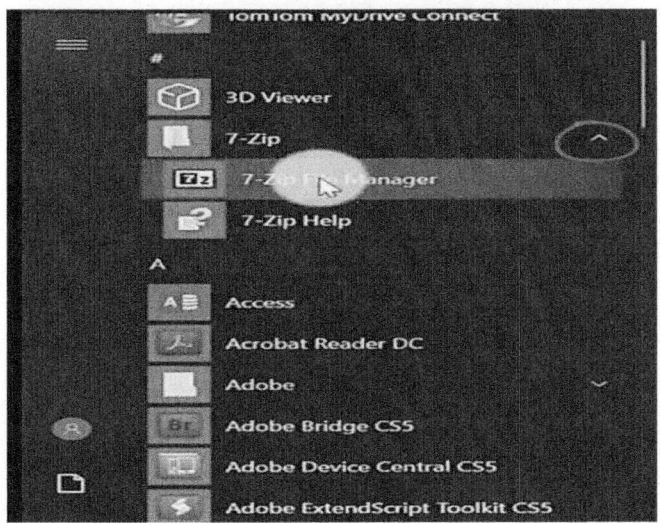

Next is the frequently used functions that are available where users can easily switch between **often-used applications** and **permanently used functions** which are **settings, shut down, restart, or sleep power buttons** depending on the user preference.

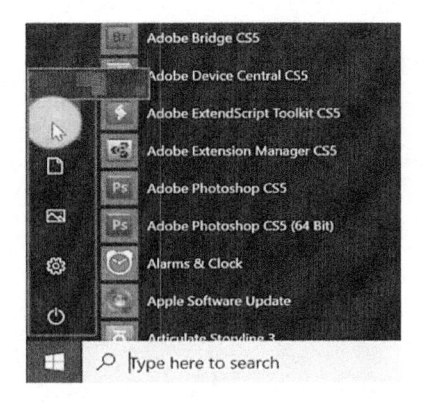

The Left Portion of the Start Screen

Clicking on the Windows icon at the left-hand side; below gives an overview of Windows world features where you can see *"Most used"*, *"Recently added"*, *"Search bar"* to locate files on your computer, and also *"task view"* to clip through multiple Windows.

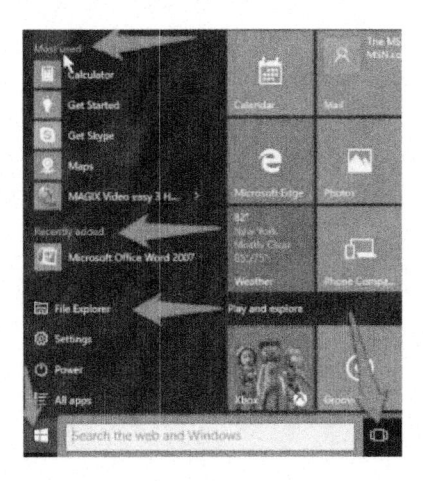

The Right Portion of the Start Screen

The right side portion of the start screen displays the tiles icons for quick access purposes. Tiles also give room for customization, adding new icons, resizing, and dragging icons to a preferred location.

42

Pinning & Unpinning your Favourite Apps to the Taskbar & Start Menu

With Windows 10 you can pin down applications into your start menu or your taskbar. For example, to pin down the "calculator", kindly right-click on "**calculator**" then select pin to the taskbar to pin it into your taskbar.

Pin to Taskbar

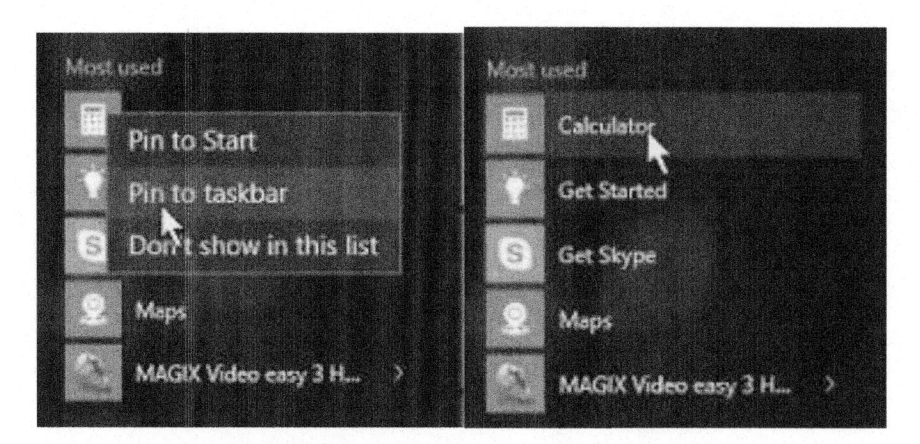

Immediately it will be added to the taskbar as illustrated below.

Unpin from Taskbar

You can also unpin it if need be from the list.

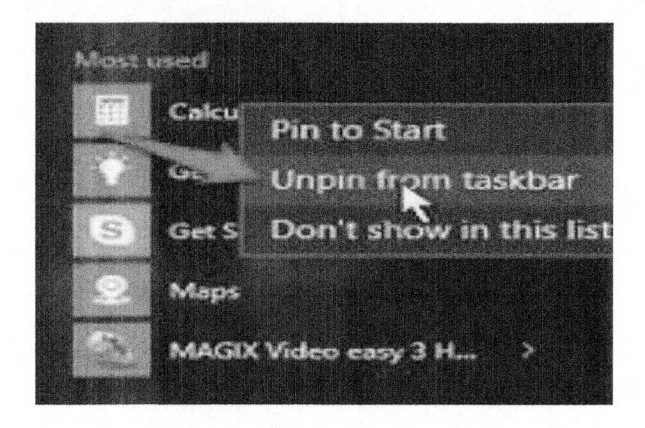

Working on Tiles

Tiles Menu is mostly used for 'touch screen' which are divided into three segments "Create", "Play" and "Explore". They are much useful for those using a touchscreen.

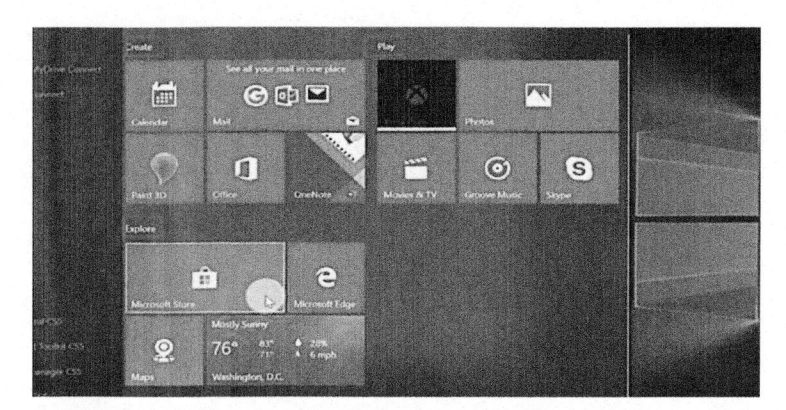

This tiles menu can be customized by resizing it into four different categories; small, medium, wide and large, removing it from the pinning down tiles menu, and more which entails turning live tile off, app settings, and share options.

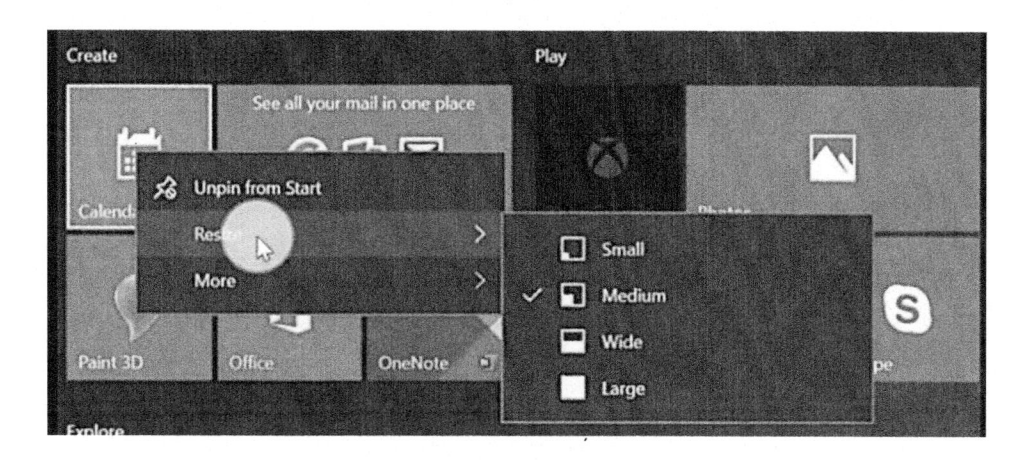

How to Rename Tiles Titles Bar

Click on "Start menu", on your right-hand side you will see your tiles which are subtitle. Click on the dropdown button beside the tile's title to rename "Life at a Glance"

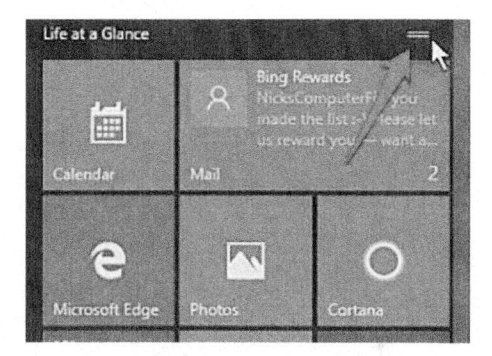

Then you can rename it to your preferred choice.

You can also do the same to "Play and explore".

45

You can also scroll up and down to see other features under tiles.

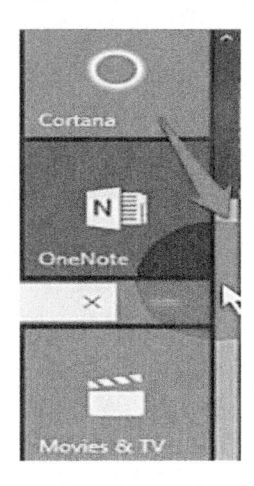

Resizing the Start Screen Tiles

Tiles can be resized vertically and horizontally. You can grab it at the edge horizontally to stretch it depending on how you want it.

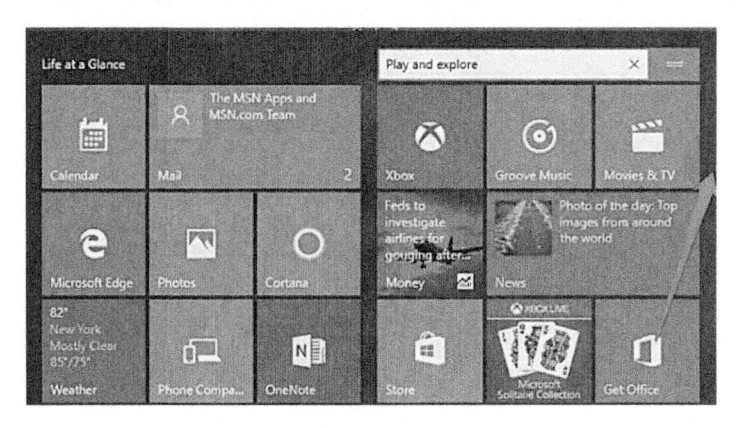

And also, vertically you can stretch it.

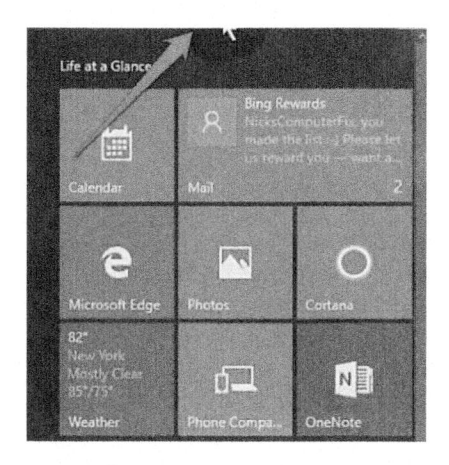

Moving the Tiles Icon

You can also move the tiles icon from one place to another by clicking on it, then drag it to your preferred location.

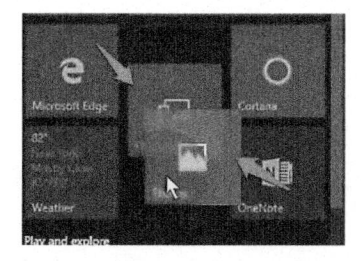

Unpin Tiles Icon

You can also right-click on any icon from your tiles to "Unpin from Start menu".

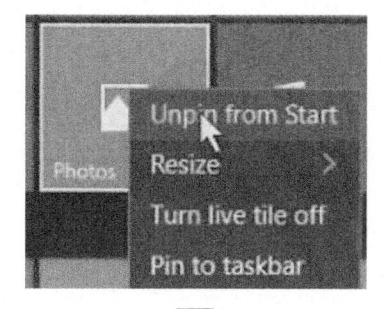

Resizing the Tiles Icon

You can resize the tiles icon by right-clicking on any of your preferred icons, click "resize" then choose among the list "small", "medium", "wide", or "large".

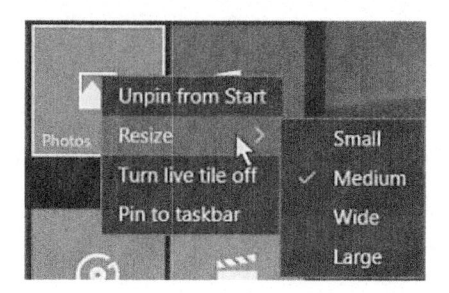

Turning Off Tiles

You can turn off tiles from displaying by right-clicking any icon from your tiles then click on "turn live tile off"

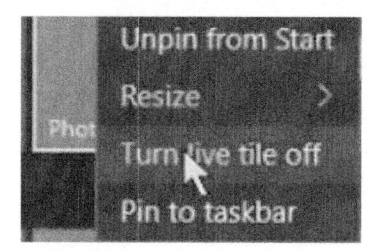

You can also pin to the taskbar by clicking on "pin to taskbar".

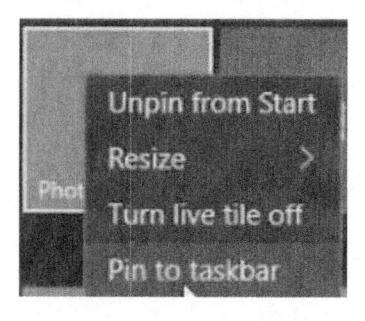

Launching Apps with the Start Menu

First of all, click on "Start menu", there you have your *"Most used"* applications and *"frequently used"* applications which will appear as you keep using your favorite apps.

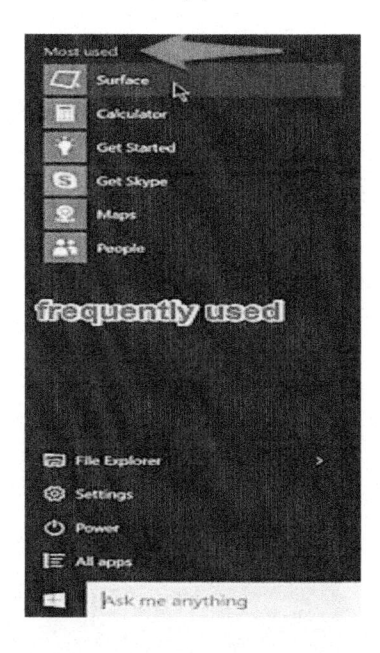

You can launch file explorer from the start menu or click on the little greater than symbol (">") to view pinned folders and frequently used items and then launch any of your preferred items from your file explorer.

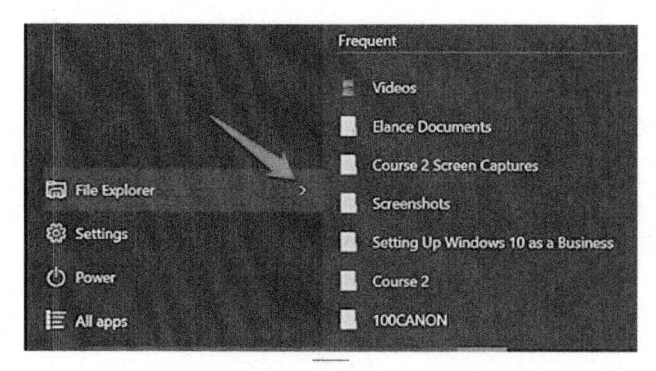

How to check all application programs?

You can also click on "all apps" to view all applications.

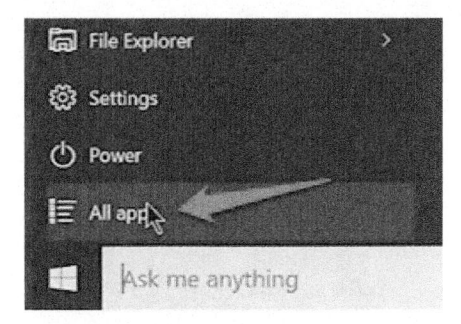

By default, all apps are arranged alphabetically in a vertical way with a vertical scrolling roll.

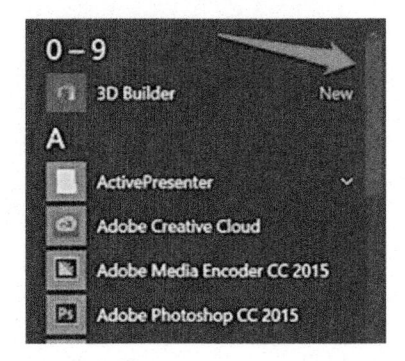

You can also click on a letter or number at a time to jump into any items alphabetically or numerically.

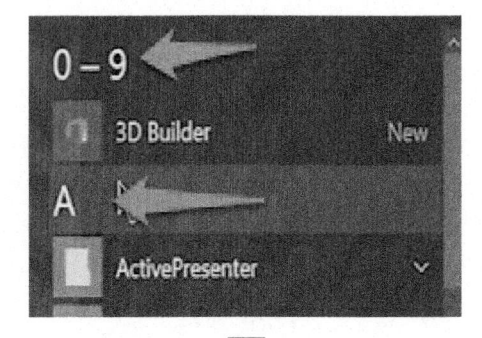

This is useful for quick access.

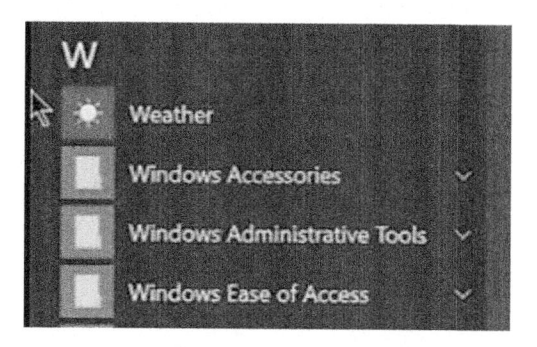

You can also launch an application from the live tiles area. In a situation where the *"Start menu"* is not viewing an item for you and it is not also reflecting on live tiles, just click on *"Ask me anything"* which is known as the search bar to automatically locate it.

How to Create A Tiles Group

Go to "Start menu".

On the tiles icon, simply click a tile, drag it on another tile which in return will create a group of tiles.

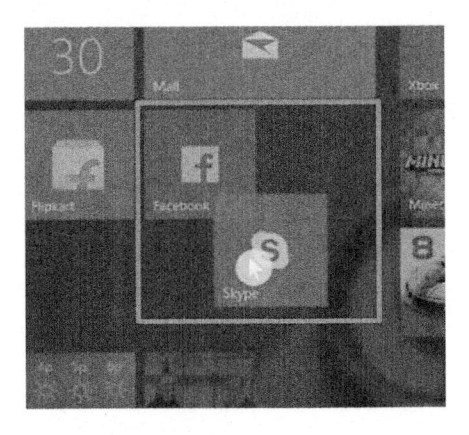

A tile will be created automatically.

It will be grouped as one tile.

How to hide the Apps list on the Start Menu

Go to your "Start menu", type "Start settings" on your search bar. Once it displays **Start settings** double click on it.

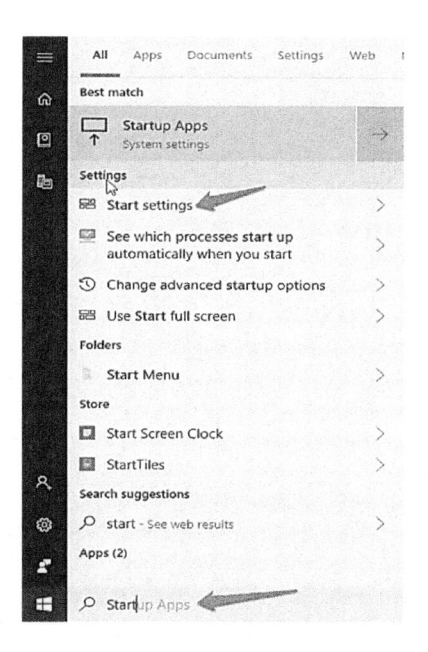

Look for "Show app list in the Start menu", turn it off.

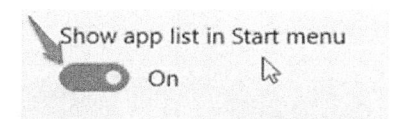

How to Display Apps List on the Start Menu

Go to "Start menu", type "Start settings" and double click on it.

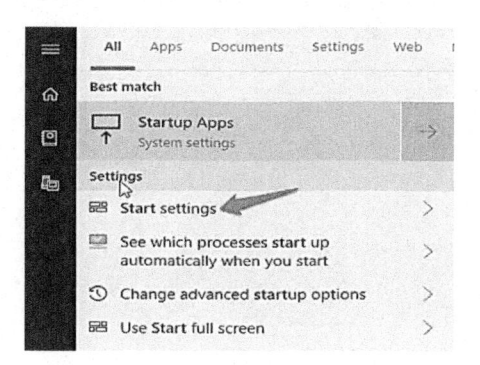

Look for "Show app list in the Start menu", turn it on.

53

Exploring Task View

Windows 10 task view shows you all your opened Windows in a permanent view until you dismiss it or make it to be in the foreground by clicking on it. Task view is designed as three little windows.

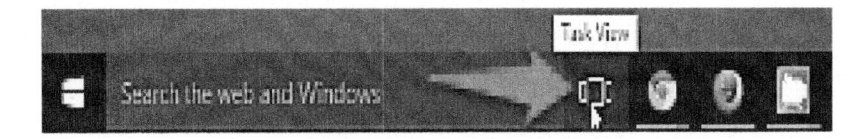

Task view is a new feature introduced to Windows 10 that gives the privilege to switch from one desktop Windows into another without any complication toggle.

It gives room for multiple desktop interfaces.

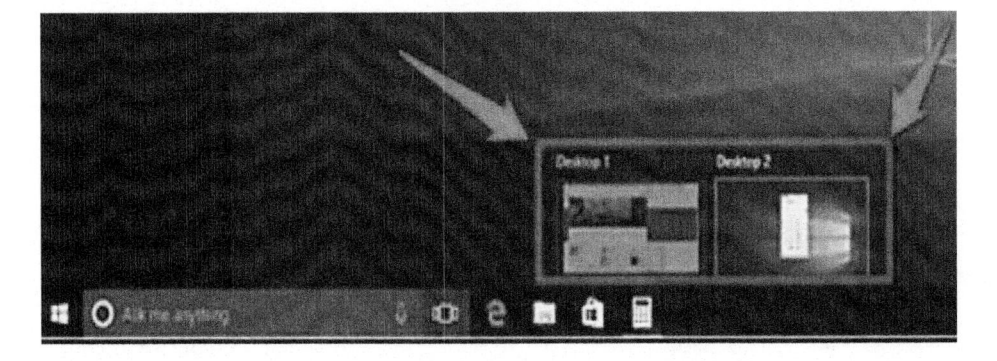

How to Make Use of Task View

Task View was primarily structured to make it flexible to understand and switch quickly between opened desktop interface and running applications. Although, the feature has been progressing ever since it was first introduced and now, you can also resume activities you were working with, as well as use virtual desktops to organize related tasks. Task View is located on your taskbar beside the Microsoft Edge browser, click on it as illustrated below.

Once you click on "Task view", you will be given an option to add a new desktop if need be.

When you click on "New desktop", you will see Desktop 1 and Desktop 2.

55

You can also see what is opened in each desktop interface, desktop 1 shows opened Microsoft store and browser while desktop 2 shows opened calculator (this depends on what you open on your desktop).

You can add as many as possible to your Task view.

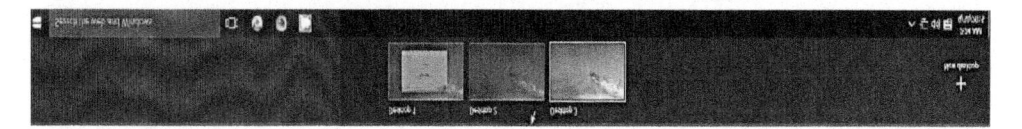

There are at least two (2) ways to access task view. You can click the Task View button in the taskbar and you can also use the **Windows key + Tab** on your keyboard as a shortcut to quickly access it.

Working with Cortana

One of the biggest new features in Windows 10 is Cortana. Cortana is virtual assistance used to search on your computer or the internet. Cortana works in two ways:

i. You can assign a task on your PC to Cortana
ii. And asking a question online while Cortana gets the answer back to you.

Cortana uses voice recognition to process assigned tasks or questions online and offline. With Cortana, you can accomplish anything; all that is required is to speak.

How to Enable Cortana

- Go to your "Start menu" and click on the "settings" icon.

- Under "Settings" click on "Privacy".

- Under "Privacy" at your left-hand side, select "Speech, inking & typing".

57

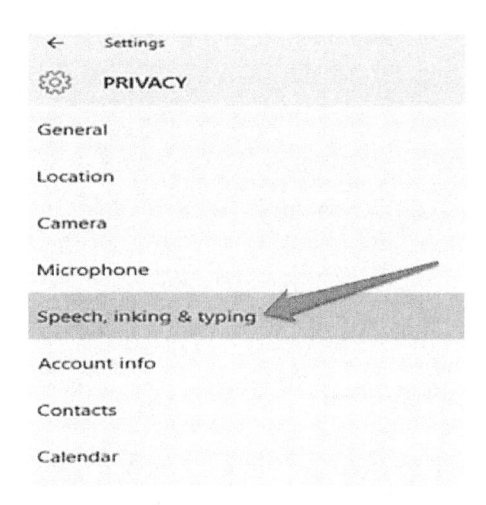

- A dialog box will appear at your right-hand side titled "Getting to know you", below it is a button titled *"Get to know me"* if your PC is showing "get to know me", it means Cortana is turned off on your PC.

- Click on the "Get to know me" button to enable Cortana; a dialog box will appear to confirm your activation by asking your permission to turn Cortana on.

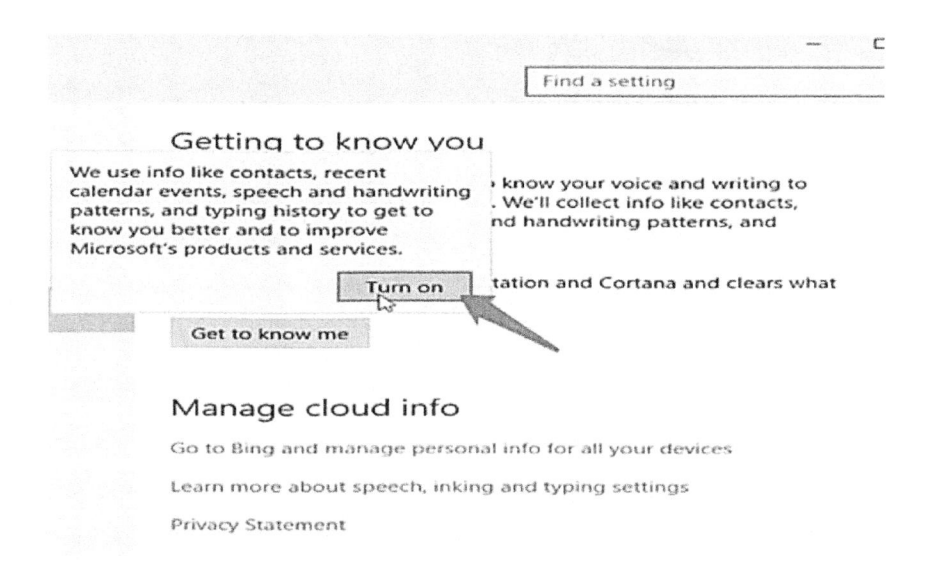

- Go to your desktop interface to confirm Cortana activation. Click on the "Search box" and Cortana will pop up itself, by welcoming you back.

- For Cortana to give you a better experience, you must give Cortana full access.

59

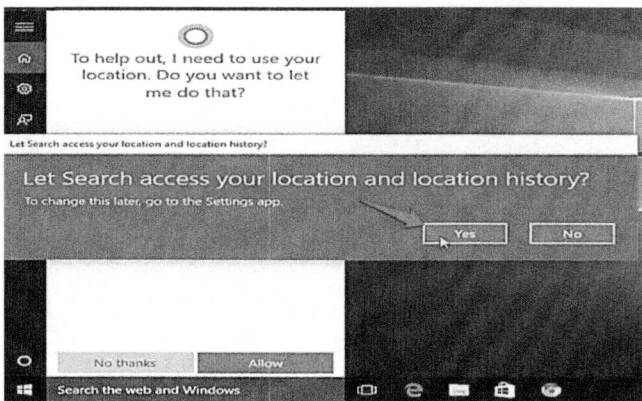

- Finally, you must sign in with your Microsoft account to enable Cortana to serve you better.

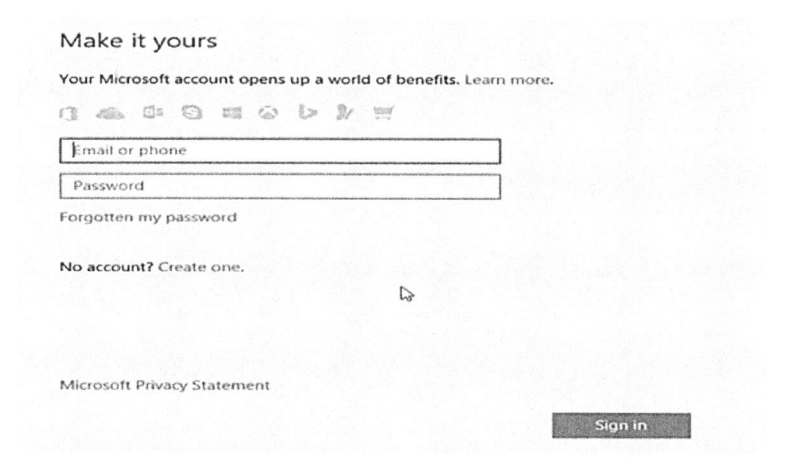

How to Disable Cortana

- Go to your "Start menu" and click on the settings icon.

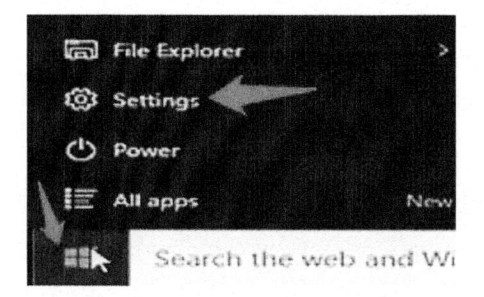

- Under "Settings" click on "Privacy".

- Under "Privacy" at your left-hand side, select "Speech, inking & typing".

> Settings
> ⚙ **PRIVACY**
> General
> Location
> Camera
> Microphone
> **Speech, inking & typing**
> Account info
> Contacts
> Calendar

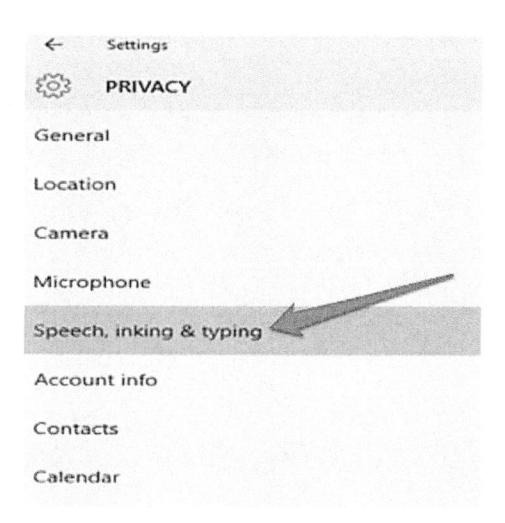

- A dialog box will appear at your right-hand side titled "Getting to know you", below is a button titled *"Stop getting to know me"* if your PC is showing stop "getting to know me", it means Cortana is enabled on your PC.

> **Getting to know you**
>
> Windows and Cortana can get to know your voice and writing to make better suggestions for you. We'll collect info like contacts, recent calendar events, speech and handwriting patterns, and typing history.
>
> Turning this off also turns off dictation and Cortana and clears what this device knows about you.
>
> Stop getting to know me
>
> **Manage cloud info**
>
> Go to Bing and manage personal info for all your devices
>
> Learn more about speech, inking and typing settings
>
> Privacy Statement

- Finally, a dialog box will appear to confirm your decision.

Getting to know you

This will turn off dictation and Cortana and will clear info on your device that Windows uses to make better suggestions for you.

w your voice and writing to
ll collect info like contacts,
andwriting patterns, and

Turn off

n and Cortana and clears what

Stop getting to know me

Manage cloud info

Go to Bing and manage personal info for all your devices

Learn more about speech, inking and typing settings

Privacy Statement

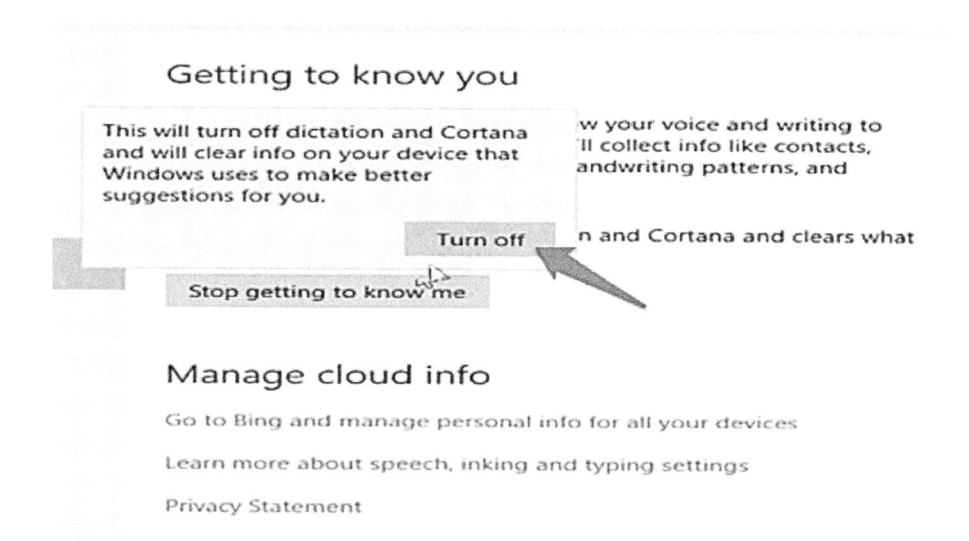

Configuring Cortana

The first thing to note is that Cortana needs your permission to help by default. Cortana does not listen to your command until Cortana gains permission to do so.

- Click inside your "Search box", double click on "settings" to open it.

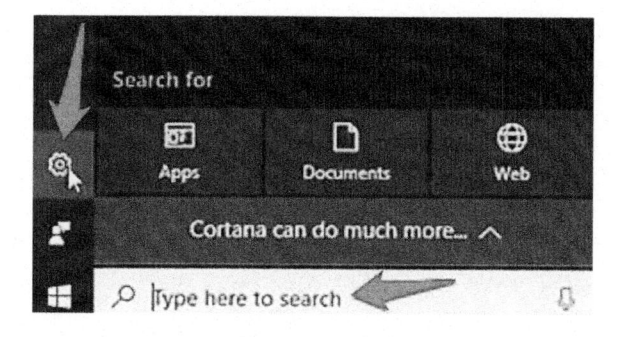

- Check the microphone to know if Cortana can hear you; Cortana dialog box will appear asking for your permission to turn on "Cortana", click on "Sure".

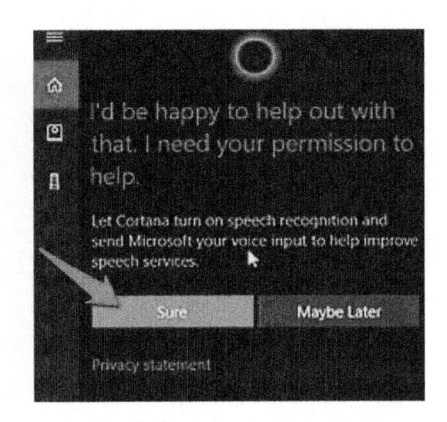

- Scroll down to enable "Let Cortana respond to Hey Cortana" by turning the button on.

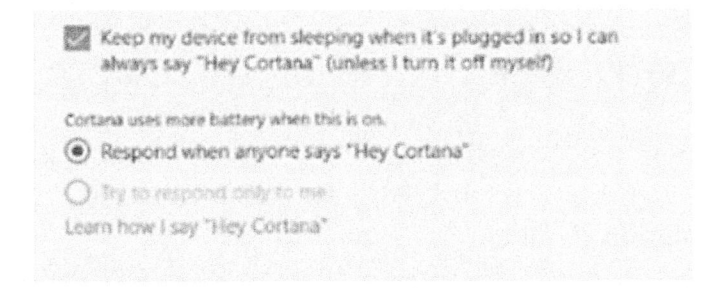

- You can also enable *"use Cortana even when my device is locked"* if you want Cortana to respond to you even when your PC is locked.

- Enable Cortana to access your calendar, email, messages, etc.

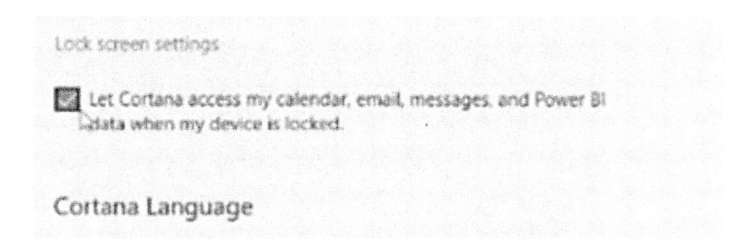

- Select your preferred language that Cortana can use to communicate with you.

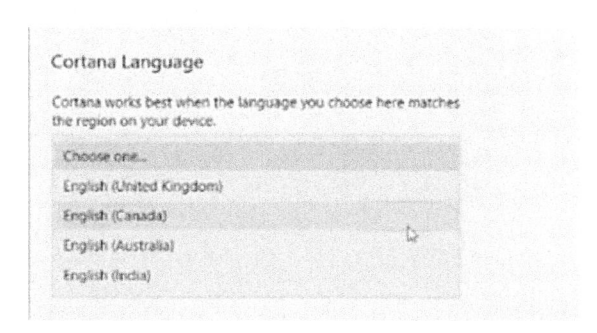

Customizing Cortana

- Click on the "Search box" at the left-hand side; double click on the "Notebook icon". Under Organizer, you can "Add to your To-Do list", "Create a reminder", "Check on suggested tasks".

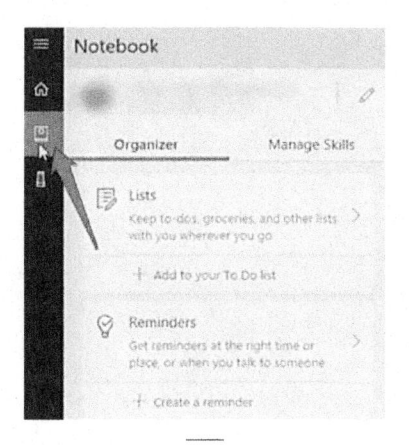

- Also click on "Manage Skills" to access an array of customization options such as connecting multiple services, linking your Music, connecting your home appliance, and also managing your family members' accounts.

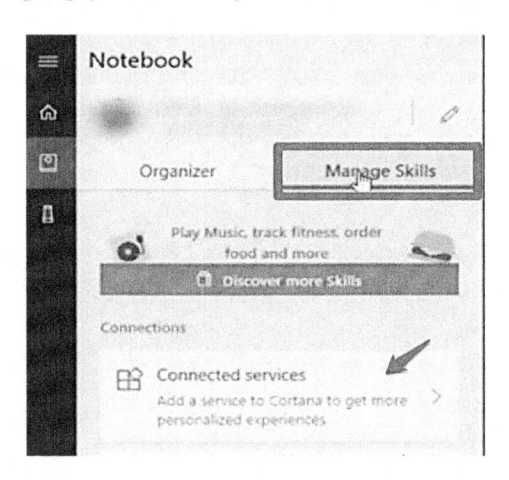

For a better experience, you need to sign in with your account.

Setting up Cortana to be your Assistance

- Click on "Search box" on the left-hand side click on "Notebook". A notebook dialog box will appear showing "Organizer & Manage Skills" click on "Manage Skills".

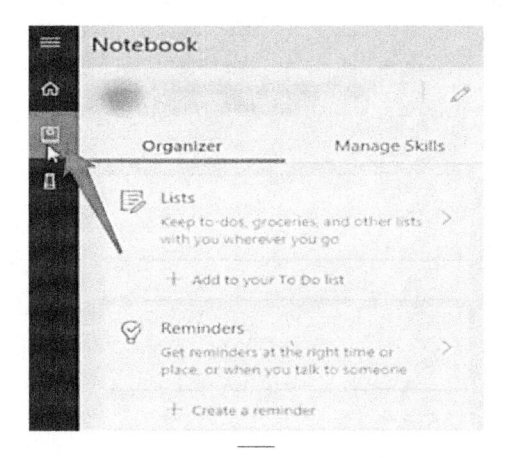

- Setup your Finance, reminder lists & tasks, flight direction, news, sports, weather, and lots more.

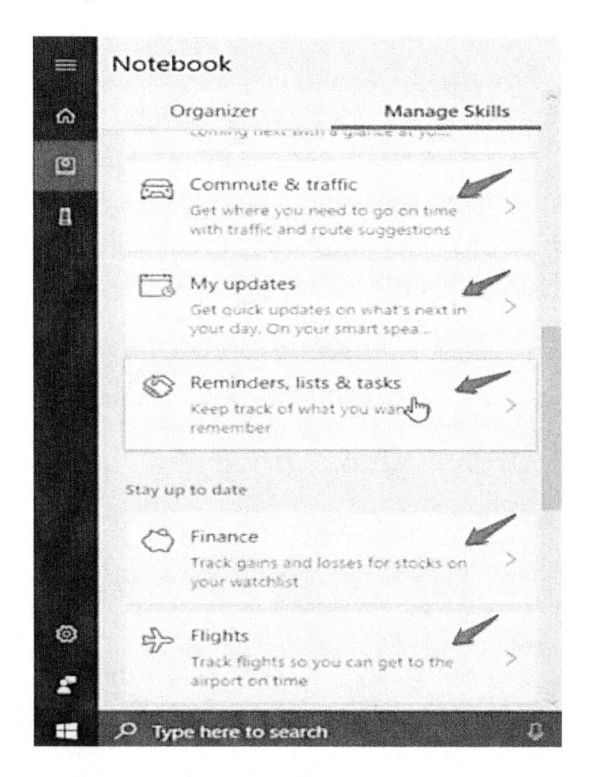

Whatsoever you want, Cortana can be setup to deliver it to you.

CHAPTER FOUR

THE WINDOWS 10 STORAGE

Exploring File Explorer

File Explorer is also known as Management Application used by Windows operating system to browse folders and files. It provides a user the interface to navigate and access folders. By default, file explorer is attached with the taskbar.

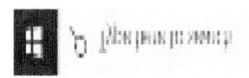

Alternatively, if you don't have file explorer on your taskbar you can search for it on your search bar.

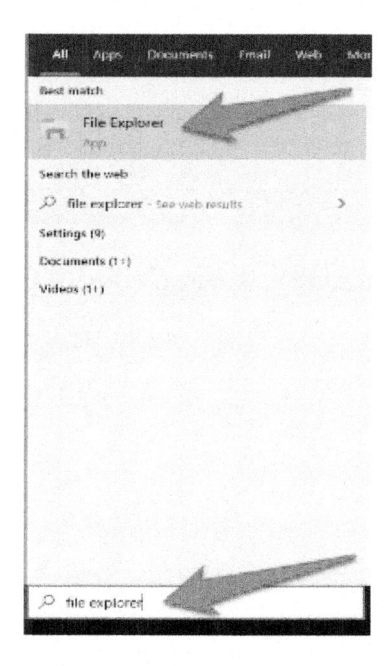

At the top of File Explorer is the ribbon that shows the features in File Explorer.

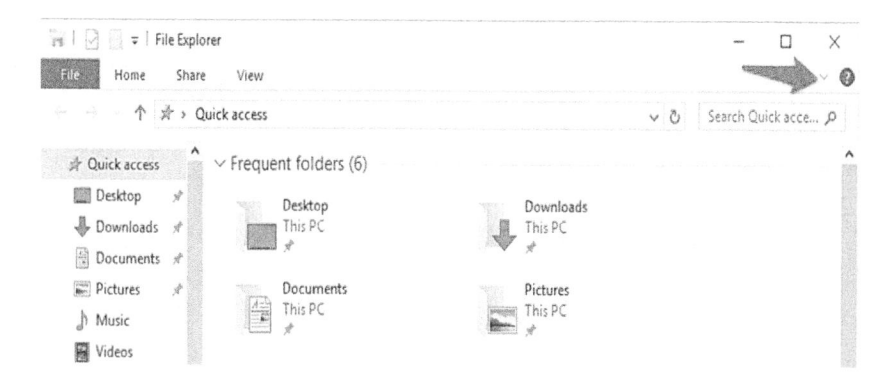

The enlargement ribbon shows dropdown features on your display screen.

There are four tabs available on the file explorer ribbon bar. The first tab available is the *"file tab"*, under the file option, you'll see "Open new Window" which also mean open new file explorer or you press *"Ctrl + N"* which is a shortcut for opening a new file explorer; to learn more click on *"Help"*.

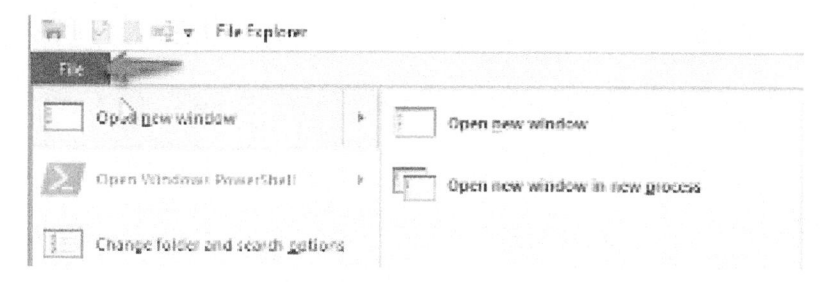

The second tab is the *"Home tab"* as its name implies, it is the host of all used features for copying, pasting, cutting, moving, renaming items with other features.

69

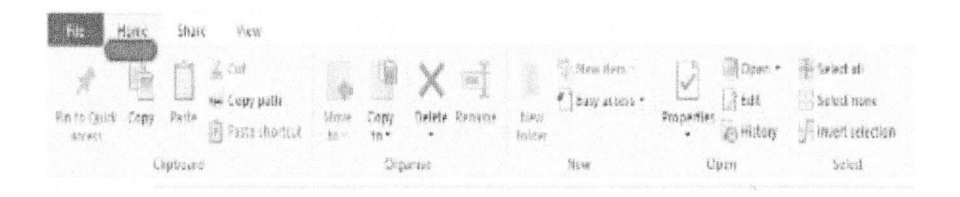

You can also perform various tasks such as "move to another location", "copy to another location", deleting an item, renaming an item, creating a new folder, and lots more.

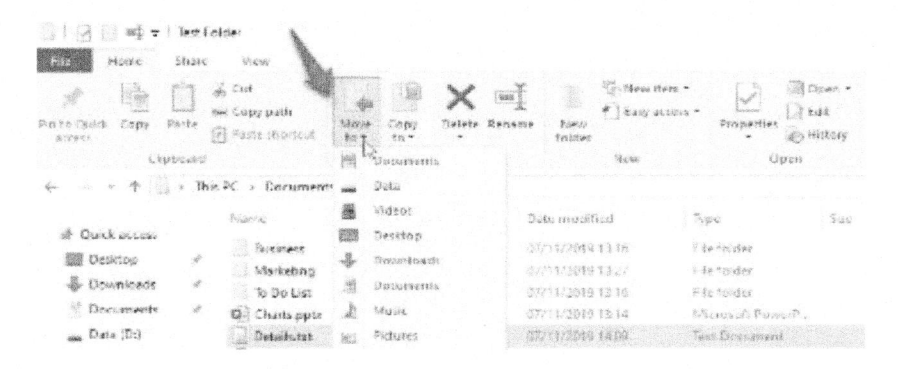

For example, to create a new folder, select "New folder" and click on Folder or if it is a shortcut you want to create, there are options for it in "New folder" also.

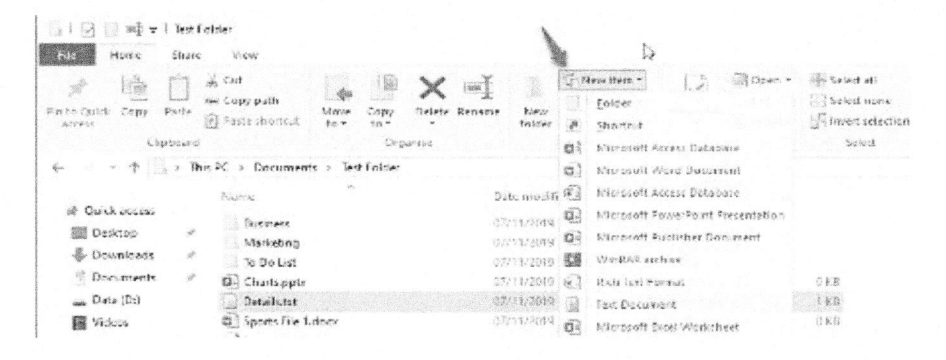

The third option available is the *"share tab"*. This is specifically designed to share items through various mediums with OneNote, mail, Outlook, Skype, and other online service applications.

70

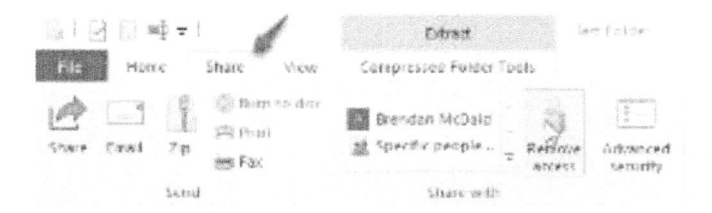

You can also use "Email" to share items.

You can decide to "Zip" an item and many other options available under "share".

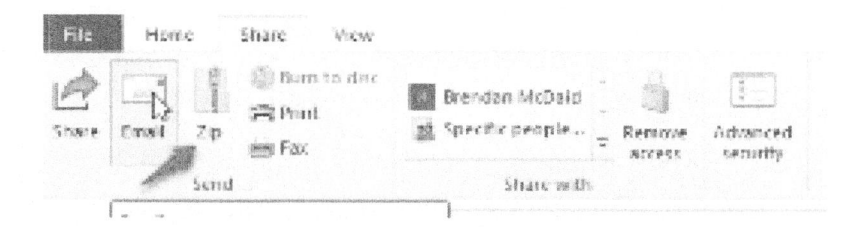

You can also click on "remove access" to stop sharing or change permission access.

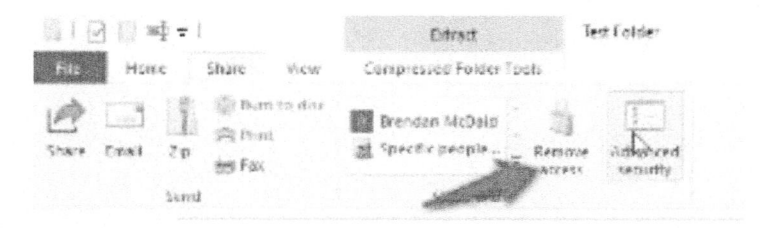

You can also click on "Advanced security" which will give you different options so that you can add other users to your local machine.

71

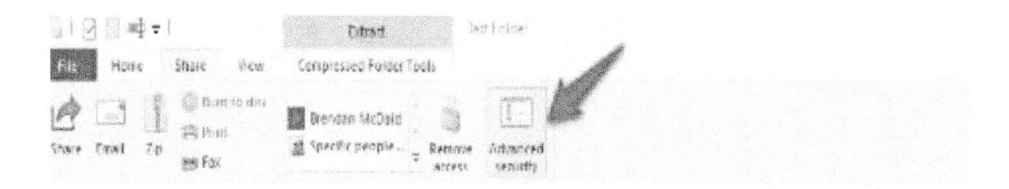

And lastly, is the **_"View tab"_** which allows you to change the way windows display your files and folders.

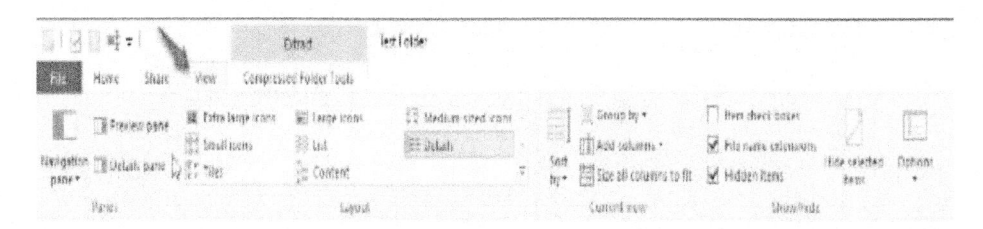

For instance, selecting an item and checking the "Preview pane" gives you the privilege to know what kind of item you selected. The illustration below at the right-hand side indicates that the item is a document. Below is the "details pane" which will give you the modification date of the file and the size of the file with its creation date.

There are many options you can play around with.

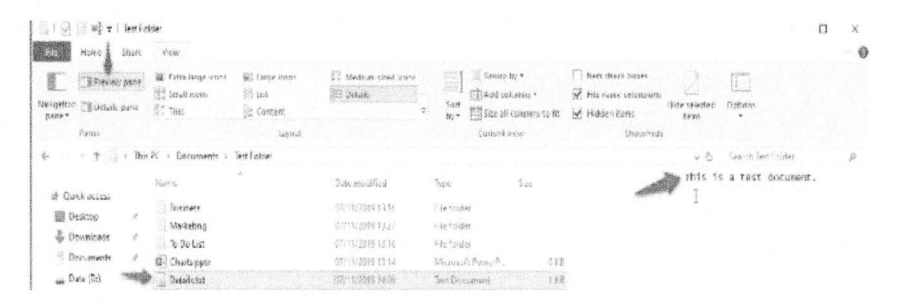

You can also decide to make every item extra-large icon, large icons, small icons, and so on, depending on your preferred choice. You also have the privilege to modify the type, size, date, and other options such as ascending and descending order.

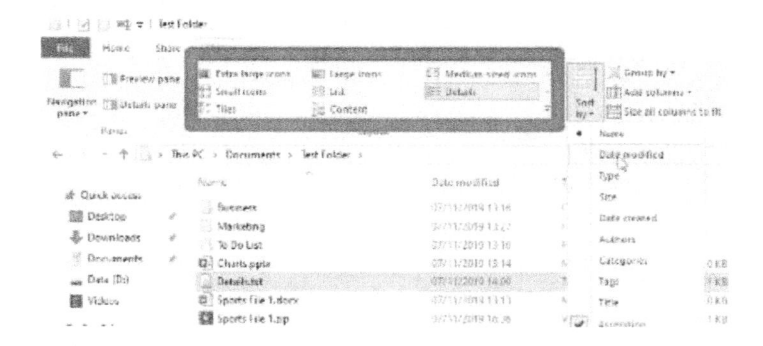

Coming to the top you will see a little arrow that represents your quick access toolbar; access to command what you frequently use such as undo, redo, delete, and other features. Once they are shown as ticked it will reflect beside the "quick access toolbar" if not ticked it will be hidden by default.

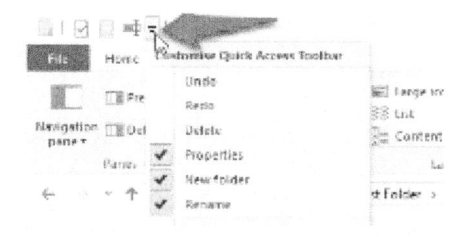

On the left-hand side is the navigation bar which gives access to your libraries of documents, pictures, as well as your storage devices. It also features frequently used folders, recent files, and documents you opened recently.

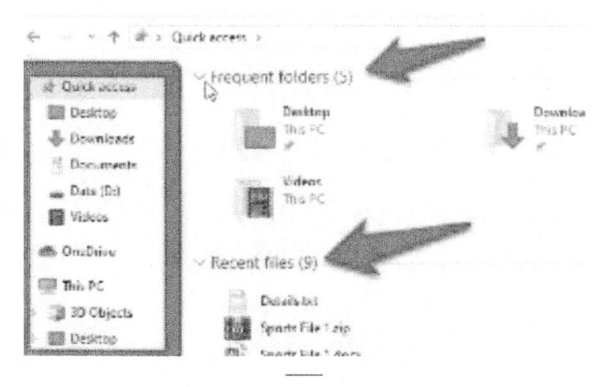

73

To locate your file source, kindly select the item, right-click on your mouse or system cursor; below is a dialog box that will appear, check below and you will see **"Open file location"** which will bring you to the folder that the file is in as well.

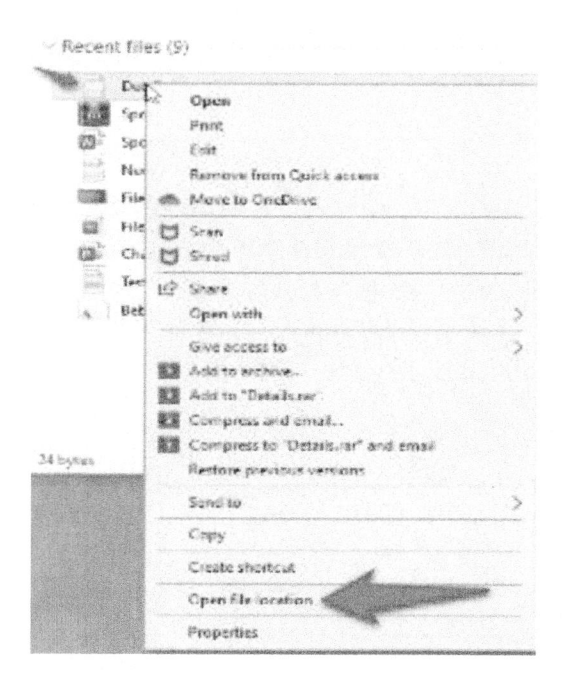

Clicking on "This PC" shows you every connected port such as USB, Hard drive, DVD, and any device storage that connects to the PC.

By default, OneDrive has been added into the file explorer which grants access to online storage. OneDrive storage only works for Microsoft users who have active email.

74

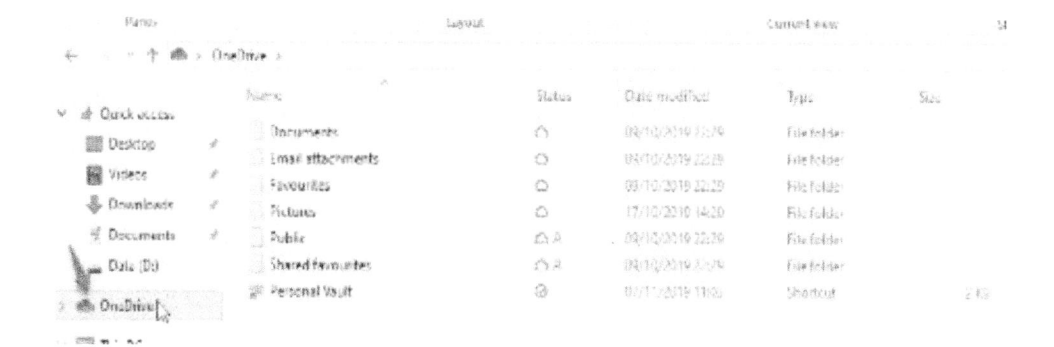

To change settings and learn more about OneDrive storage, kindly click on OneDrive from your taskbar panel and select your preferred options.

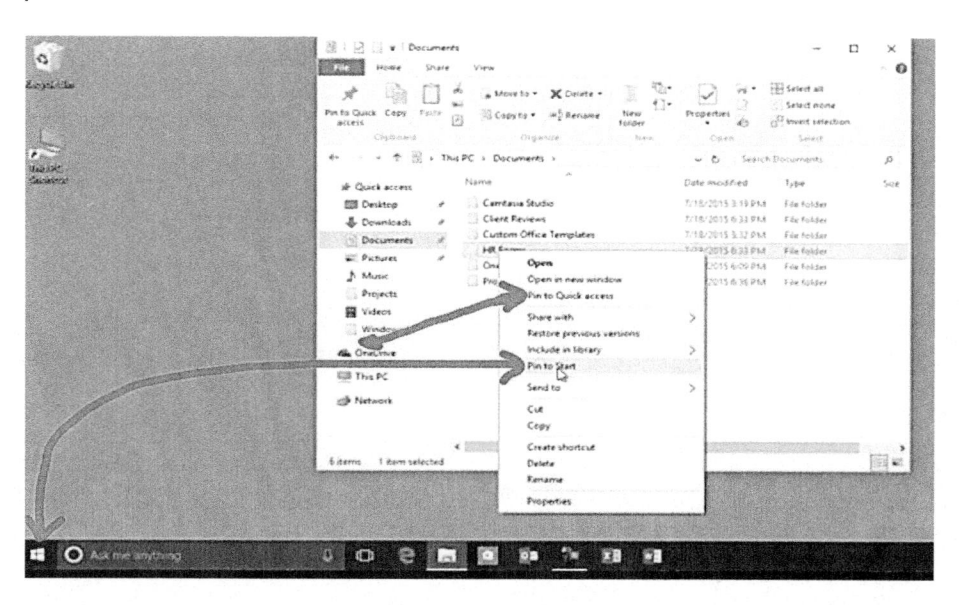

To pin any folder of your choice, specifically, frequently used folders, right-click on the folder and you will see "Pin to Quick access" and "Pin to start".

Quick access will be seen on the left-hand side of the file explorer page. "Start" represents the "Start menu" where your folder will be pinned depending on the user's choice.

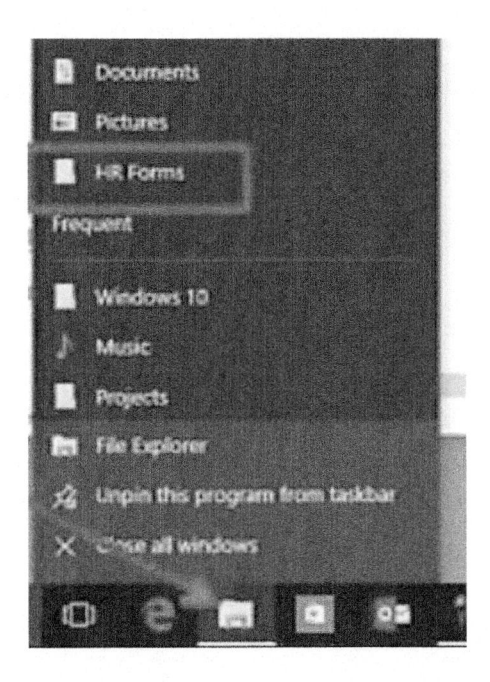

You can also drag your folder into "file explorer" and right-click on file explorer in your taskbar to see what you pinned.

File Explorer Default Folders

File Explorer represents the managing host of all folders. These folders are into seven (7) categories by default which are: Desktop, Downloads, Documents, Pictures, Music, and Videos. Subsequent adding of folders can be done by the user.

Desktop folder

Specifically, the desktop is purposely designed for installed applications and other items its user wishes to drop in it.

Downloads folder

Downloads

Download by default is a directory for downloaded items by the browser. This is not limited to items downloaded by the browser alone; its user can also add items into it at wish.

Documents folder

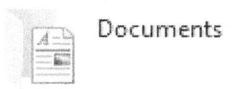

Documents

By default, all applications store in the document folder, but you can move it or manually add whatsoever item you want to store in it.

Pictures folder

Pictures

A picture is the same as an image. This deals with a static object. Windows make it possible to change its purpose and store other items into it and create subfolders into it if need be.

Music folder

Music

The music folder is specifically created by Microsoft for orderliness. It is advisable to let each folder represent its item.

Videos folder

Videos

This is specifically designed for motion objects known as video. It also has the capacity of receiving subfolders.

3D Object

3D Objects

3D Object is a newly added feature of Windows 10. It is used to store 3D graphics items. Just like 'download folder' is framed by default to store downloaded items, 3D object folders are designed to accommodate 3D graphics items for orderliness.

Kindly note that all these default folders are not fixed folders for only specific items, you can restructure it into your taste; it is only designed for orderliness and friendly usage.

What is Quick Access?

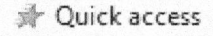

Quick access

Quick access is one of the file explorer features that is responsible for frequently used items such as pictures, videos, documents, and other stored data.

Renaming a Folder

"Select" the folder to be renamed; let's assume it is the document folder that you want to change.

Right-click on it; a dialog box will be shown as illustrated below:

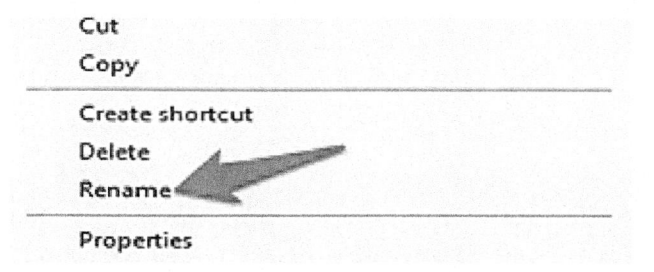

The "document" will be shown for editing; let's assume the name to be inserted is "Renamed"

Immediately you type "Renamed", click the "Enter" key on the keyboard.

Exploring OneDrive Storage

OneDrive is Microsoft technology that allows you to store and exchange information. It comes with a 15gigabyte capacity for you to make use of; you must have an active account with Microsoft or sign up to make use of it.

What are the Benefits of OneDrive?

- **File Backup:** Microsoft OneDrive gives the possibility of external backup without the need of getting an external hard disk drive. Whenever damage occurs or your PC was stolen, whatsoever the case may be, as long as you store your personal information on Microsoft OneDrive storage you can retrieve it back.

- **You can access your files anywhere:** When it comes to accessing your personal information on Microsoft OneDrive, time and space are not barriers; you can access your files anytime, anywhere with your OneDrive login details.

- **You can share & collaborate with others:** Microsoft OneDrive makes it possible to share a link of any document from your OneDrive storage without the need to start mailing it. With OneDrive shared link you can easily give others access to a specific document at wish.

Get OneDrive Cloud on PC

By default, OneDrive storage comes preinstalled with Windows 10. If you have a PC with an older version of Windows, you can easily download it from the Microsoft website.

Using OneDrive Cloud in File Explorer

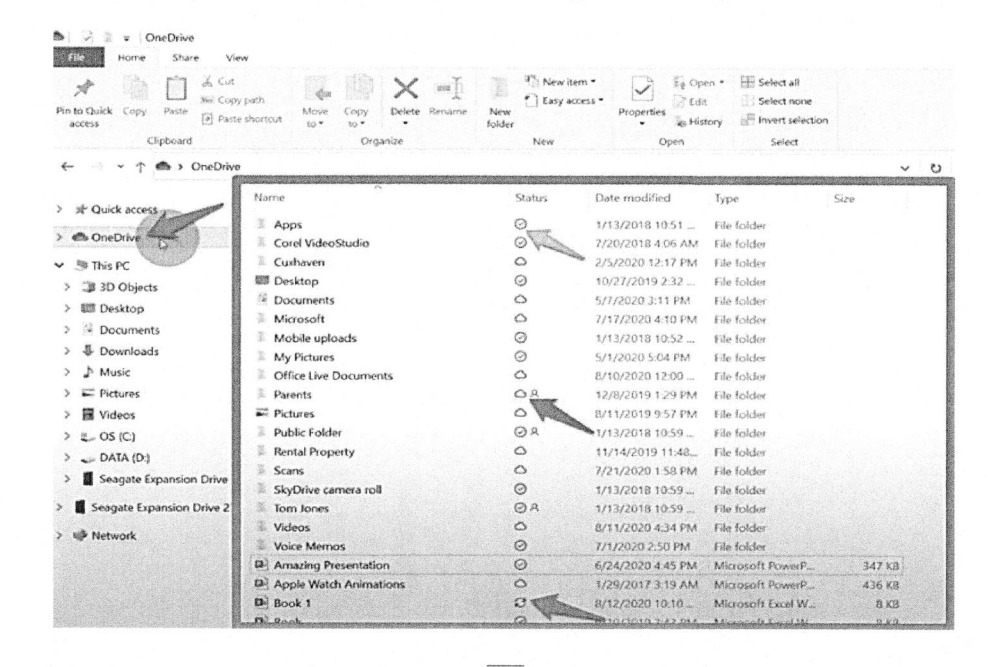

Microsoft OneDrive storage is only for those who have a Microsoft account. Above is an illustration of backup files on "OneDrive cloud".

What is OneDrive Status Icon?

OneDrive status icon is a symbol used for different files' statuses.

- **Blue cloud icons:** These are files that are stored on the cloud without a duplicate of themselves on your PC.

- **Green marked icons:** These are files that are stored both on the cloud and on your PC.

- **Sync icons (two blue circled arrow icons):** Sync icons symbolize synchronizing documents between your PC and OneDrive storage.

- **A person icon:** An icon that is attached with an image of a person indicates a shared document with others.

OneDrive Cloud Storage Features

Right-clicking on "OneDrive" gives many privileges such as:

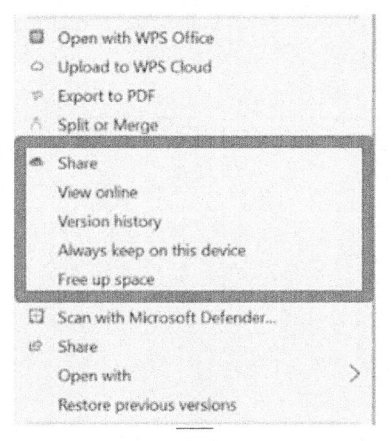

- **Share:** "Share" is framed to duplicate an item with others via a link with an edit privilege.

- **View online:** 'View online' makes the OneDrive document visible to preview.

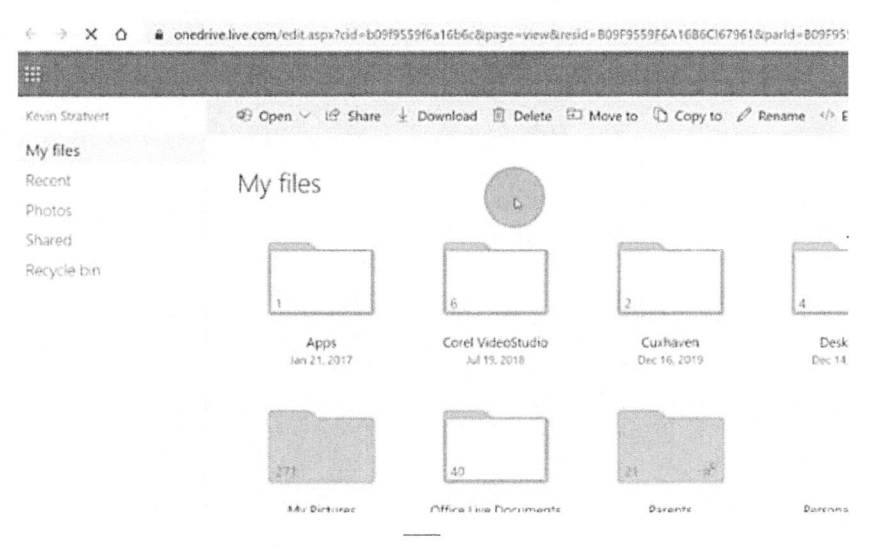

- **Version History:** Version history enables users to view the previous version of an item.

- **Always keep on this device:** This feature makes it possible to quickly drop an item on your PC.

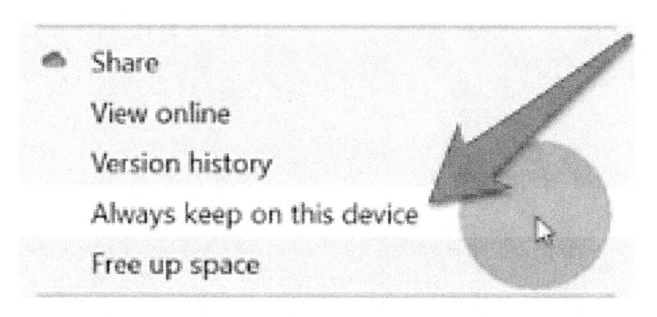

- **Free up space:** It is a feature that gives its users access to free up space by previewing items on the OneDrive cloud.

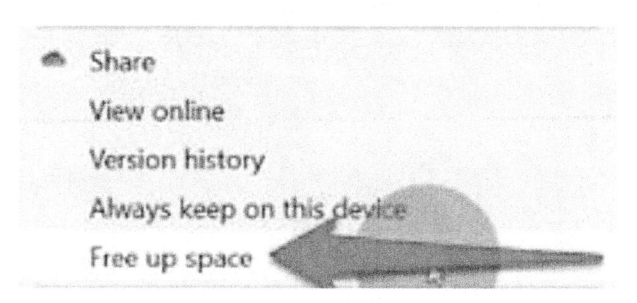

All these features are specifically designed for OneDrive cloud storage.

Accessing Your Files from Anywhere via the Web

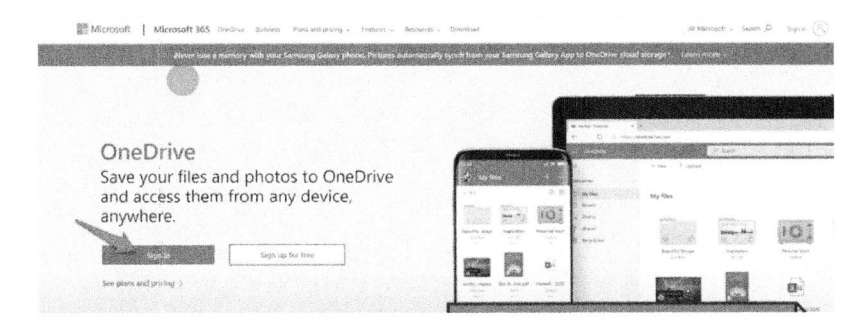

It is important to note that OneDrive cloud storage is not only limited to Microsoft Windows operating system; you can also download your files on Microsoft web by visiting www.onedrive.com and login into your account to perform any task directly from your OneDrive cloud storage.

Searching on OneDrive cloud storage

Microsoft OneDrive cloud storage also comes with the flexibility privilege of searching for any item from your OneDrive cloud storage after signing in to your OneDrive account.

Creating Different Document Format

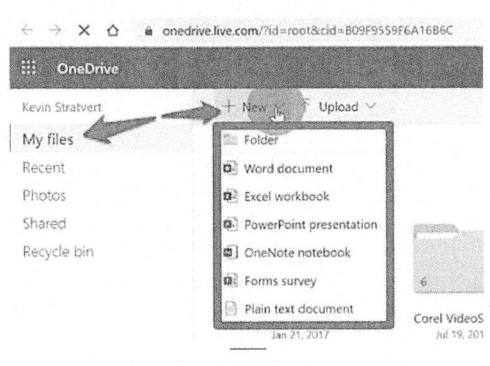

85

On your OneDrive account, you are also given the privilege to create different kinds of document format such as:

- A folder.
- Word document.
- Excel workbook.
- PowerPoint presentation.
- OneNote notebook and lots more.

Uploading Content on OneDrive

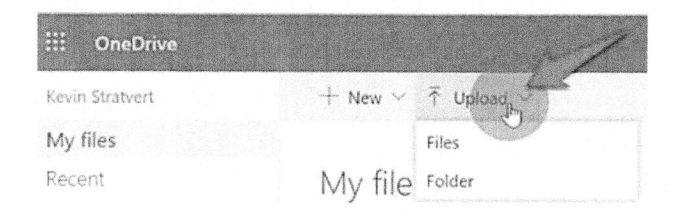

You can also upload content into your OneDrive account by clicking on "Upload"; and then choose your option either files or folder you want to upload.

Sorting of Files on OneDrive Cloud Storage

The sorting of files is specifically framed to ease the stress of sorting out documents by choosing Ascending or Descending order with other features to simplify your task.

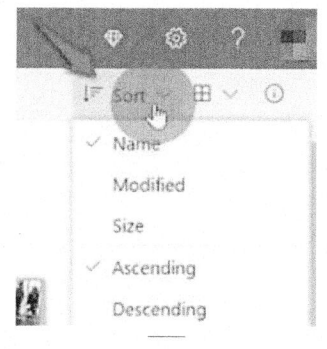

OneDrive Files & Folders Visualization

You can also rearrange the outlook of your files and folders by selecting:

- List
- Compact list
- Tiles
- Photo

CD or DVD Drives

CD or DVD drives is another part of the Microsoft Windows feature that is located on your file explorer. Only a PC with internal or external CD or DVD drives can make use of it. This is also another way of storing data.

Difference between CD & DVD Drives

- CD reads CDs, while DVD reads both CDs & DVDs.
- CD is majorly designed for audio storage, while DVD is designed for universal storage.
- CD is 700 Megabytes in size, while DVD is 4.7 Gigabytes in size.
- CD stands for Compact disk, while DVD stands for Digital versatile disk.

- CD transfer rate speed is 1.5 Megabytes per sec while DVD transfer rate speed is 11 Megabytes per sec.

Types of CD or DVD drives

- **Internal drive**

The internal drive comes with the PC. Due to the modernization and flexibility of PC, most of them do not come with an inbuilt feature for CD or DVD drive which gives room for an external drive.

- **External drive**

An external drive is a substitute for an internal CD or DVD drive which serves the same purpose. It is also used to store data. The only difference between internal and external is the detachable feature on an external drive.

Process of Copying of Files & Folders to a CD or DVD

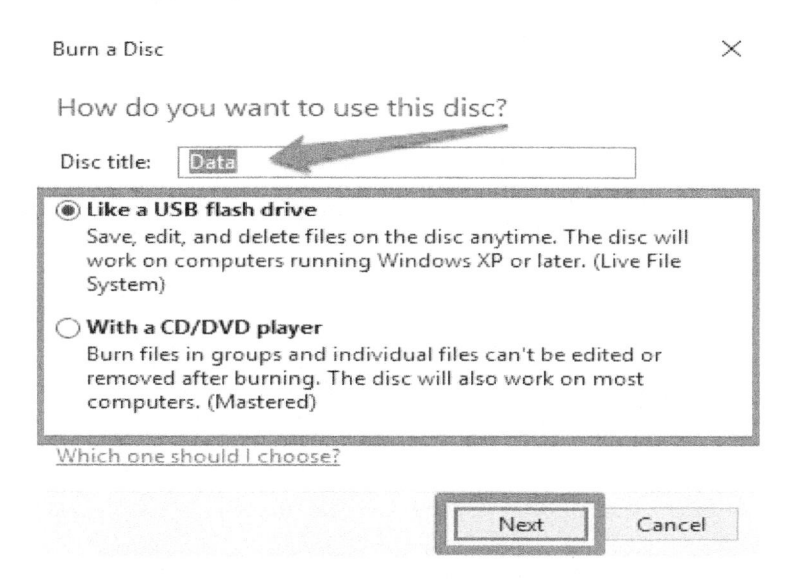

> Burn a Disc   ✕
>
> How do you want to use this disc?
>
> Disc title: [Data]
>
> ● **Like a USB flash drive**
>   Save, edit, and delete files on the disc anytime. The disc will work on computers running Windows XP or later. (Live File System)
>
> ○ **With a CD/DVD player**
>   Burn files in groups and individual files can't be edited or removed after burning. The disc will also work on most computers. (Mastered)
>
> Which one should I choose?
>
> [Next]   [Cancel]

- Get a CD or DVD.
- Insert it into your internal or external drive.
- You will receive the above message. If your purpose is to copy a temporary file, choose the first option-*"Like a USB flash drive"*; but if it is for permanent storage, make use of the second option-*"With a CD/DVD player"*.
- The CD or DVD will format the disc.
- Then you can copy and paste or drag down your files.
- Once completely copied, eject it and you are good to go.

Using Flash Drive & Memory Card

Flash drive and memory card are both external storages mostly used for quick storing and transferring of files.

Flash drive: Flash is a portable data storage device used to store & transfer data. Flash drive is detachable.

Memory card: A memory card is similar to a flash drive, but it's mostly used on digital cameras and smartphones. A memory card is mostly kept inside a gadget.

How to Ensure Windows Security is up to Date

As long as technology is concerned, security will never be an outdated demand. Microsoft Windows update helps the system to be equipped against attacks and software crashes. To update your PC,

i. Make sure you have an active internet connection.

ii. Search for Windows Update on your "Start menu bar"; you will see "Check for Updates" as illustrated below; double click on it.

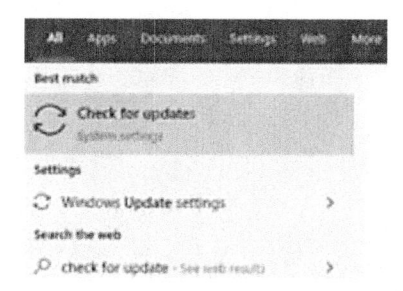

iii. Windows Update will be checking for recent updates,

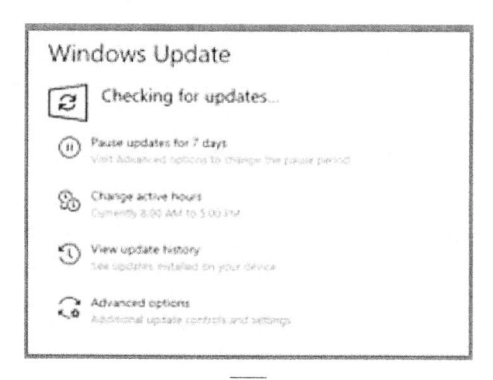

iv. Once updates are identified, Windows will start downloading automatically.

Windows Update

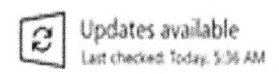

Updates available
Last checked: Today, 5:36 AM

Security Intelligence Update for Windows Defender Antivirus - KB2267602 (Version 1.307.1520.0)
Status: Installing - 0%

2019-12 Cumulative Update for .NET Framework 3.5 and 4.8 for Windows 10 Version 1909 for x64 (KB4533002)
Status: Pending download

2019-09 Security Update for Adobe Flash Player for Windows 10 Version 1909 for x64-based Systems (KB4516115)
Status: Pending download

v. Immediately Windows update has been fully installed, system configuration and restart will take place.

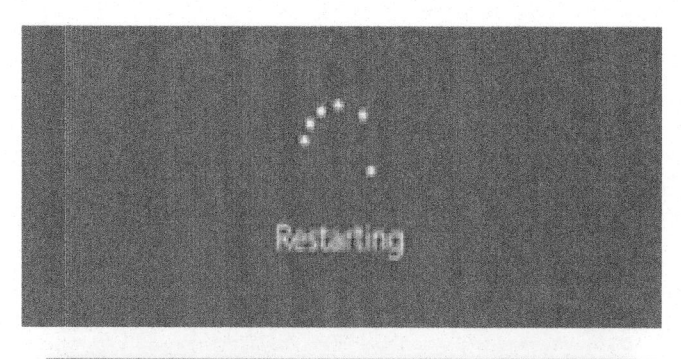

What Should I Do When My PC Refuse to Give Me Latest Update?

Kindly note that Windows update only works with an internet connection, else, you won't be granted access for an update.

As long as technology is concerned, there will always be a possibility of unexpected issues. In a situation where your Windows update refuses to give you an update, below is an alternative means of getting it fixed up.

Go to your *"browser"* and search for *"media creation tool"*; make sure the URL (the link) is directed to Microsoft website for security reasons. Then click on Microsoft website from your Google search

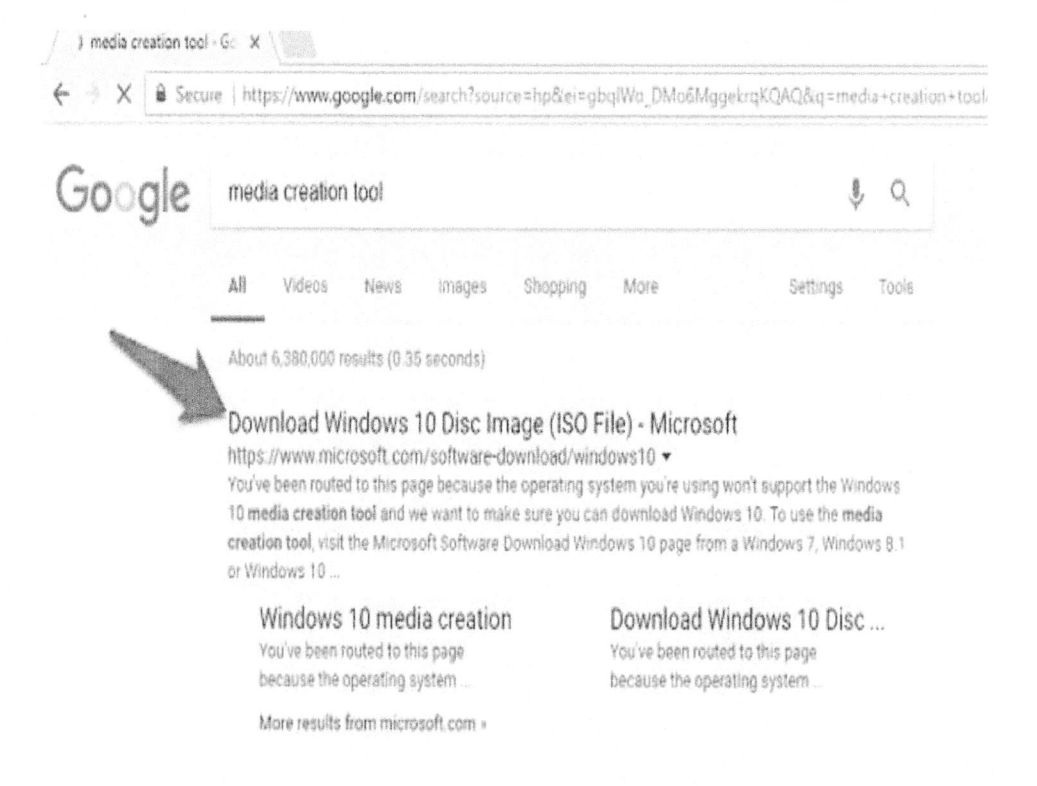

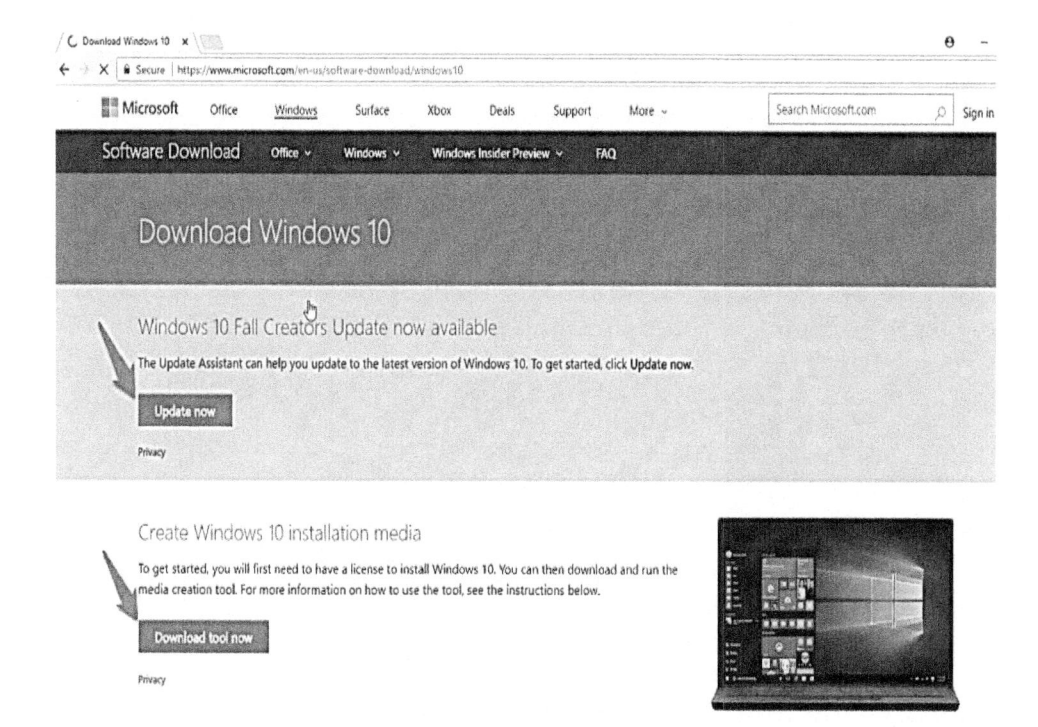

The first arrow indicates *"Update now"* which allows you to auto-update your PC, while the second option indicates *"Download tool now"*; it's also an updating tool that is only applicable for license users. To avoid long requirements and processes, it is advisable to choose the first option which is *"Update now"*.

93

CHAPTER FIVE

WINDOWS 10 ACTION CENTER USER

Action Center is a central place to view notifications and take actions that can help to keep Windows running smoothly. The action center is located at the taskbar right-hand corner known as the *"system tray"* where volume, battery, and Wi-Fi are located.

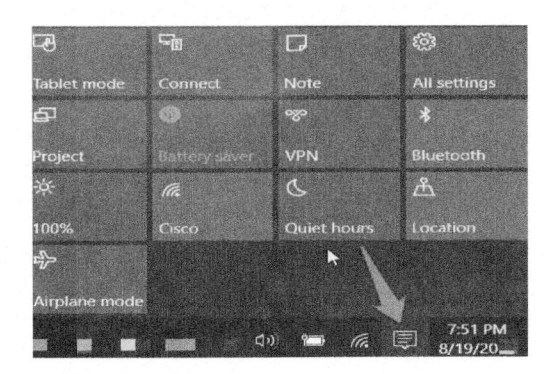

Action Center lists important messages about security and maintenance settings that need your attention. Red items in Action Center are labeled "Important" and indicates significant issues that should be addressed soon, such as an outdated antivirus program that needs updating. Yellow items are suggested tasks that you should consider addressing, like recommended maintenance tasks.
You can expand the Action center

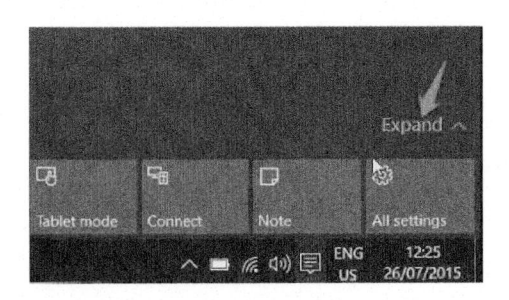

You can also collapse the Action center

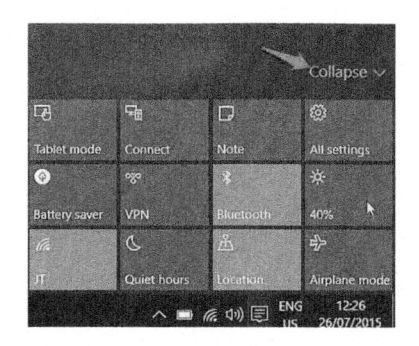

Windows 10 Action center has come to replace Windows 8 and Windows 8.1 *charms bar* which is a vertical panel that reflects itself at the right-hand side of the screen irrespective of what you are doing on your PC.

You can quickly see whether there are new messages in Action Center by placing your mouse over the Action Center icon in the notification area on the taskbar.

Click the icon to view more detail and click a message to address the issue or open Action Center to view the message in it entirely.

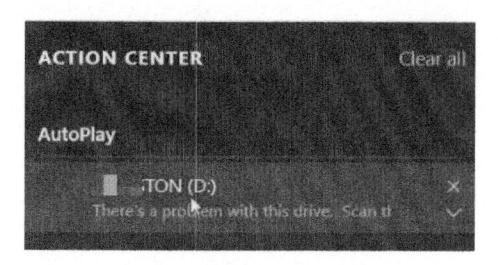

If you're having a problem with your computer, check Action Center to see if the issue has been identified. If it hasn't, you can also find helpful links to troubleshooters and other tools that can help fix problems.

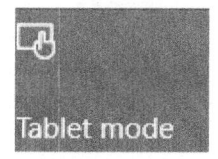

First of all, Action Center will have **tablet mode** which is used to switch between desktop mode & tablet mode.

Secondly is the *"connect"*; this is one of the Action Center features responsible for wireless display module and wireless audio devices connection.

The "note" option brings up 'OneNote' which is a nice note taking tool; traditionally, it's being part of Office. It gathers users' notes, screen clippings, inserted images, and drawings. It also gives room for notes sharing with other OneNote users over the Internet.

All settings

"All settings" have to do with the overall configuration of your operating system. The traditional control panel is still available which is called the "control panel", but everything is moving gradually into settings.

Battery saver

Battery saver shows the level of your battery capacity and screen brightness adjustment. Turning on battery saver settings enhances battery life and reduces consumption features.

VPN

VPN is a virtual private network that provides privacy while browsing through the internet.

Bluetooth

Bluetooth is one of the Action Center features that give a quick switch between the on & off button. It's majorly used to transfer items such as pictures, documents, and other items without the need for a USB connection.

Here is the screen brightness icon for increasing or decreasing your PC display screen brightness.

This has to do with your Network & Internet connection which gives access when connected to the world wide web.

Quiet hour is designed to silent all popping up notification alerts.

Location is framed to turn on & off. When on, it makes your PC location accessible by a third party.

Airplane mode disables all wireless connections such as Wi-Fi, Bluetooth, and other wireless connections.

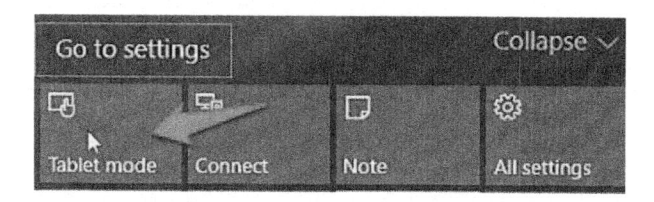

Note

To go into these entire breakdown features, kindly *right-click* on any of the Action Center features, this will take you into its features in detail.

Toggling Between the Tablet Mode and Desktop Mode

Tablet mode and desktop mode make the operating system friendlier in its usage. It gives room for flexibility in switching mode from tablet mode to desktop mode; when one is active the other one goes inactive in order not to cause a crash. It is purposely designed for users' choice preferences. There are two methods for turning on/off tablet mode and desktop mode.

Method 1

Go to your taskbar on the right-hand side, you will see "notification icon", click it as illustrated below:

You will notice a multiple option, kindly select "tablet mode".

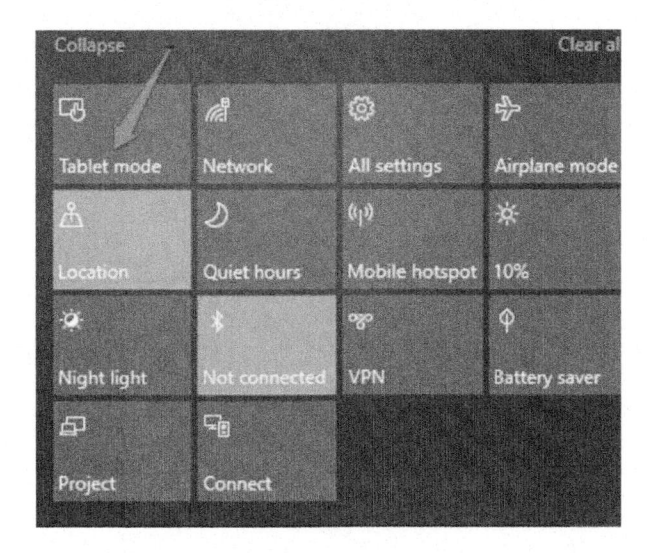

By default, you will be in tablet mode.

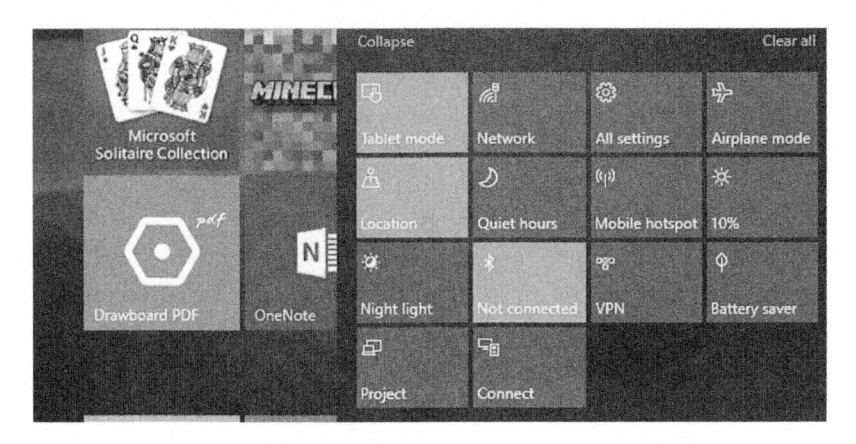

In case you want to reverse it back, kindly repeat the same process by going back to the notification bar.

And, click on tablet mode the second time to switch out of "tablet mode".

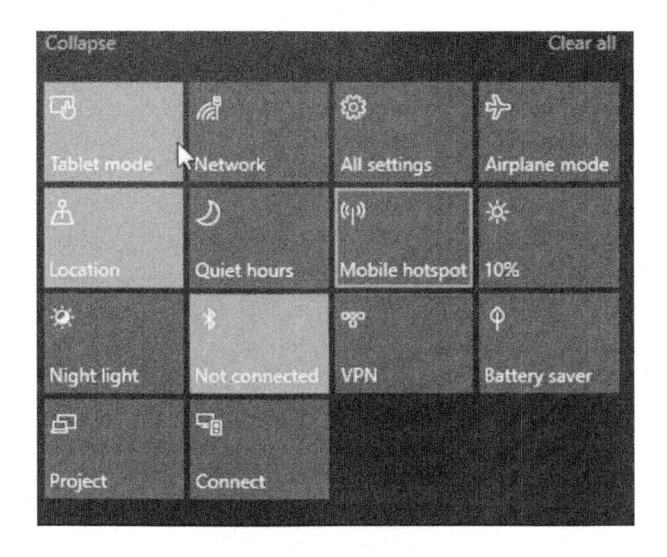

Method 2
Click on "Start menu", go to "Settings icon".

Click on the System option.

101

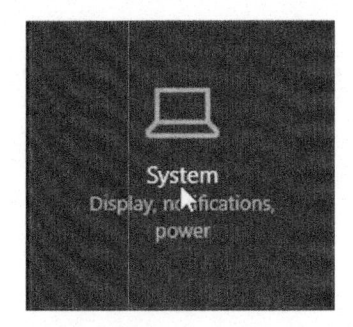

On your right-hand side, you will see "Tablet mode" click it.

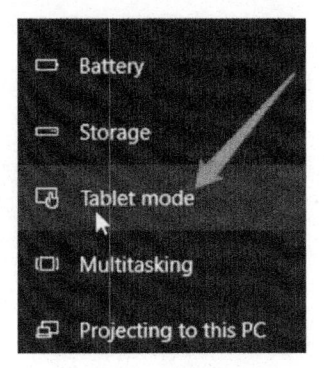

Look at your right-hand side, you will see this illustration below.

"When I sign in" gives you the privilege to select your preferred choice between tablet mode, desktop mode, or your hardware appropriate mode (which is the default settings of your device).

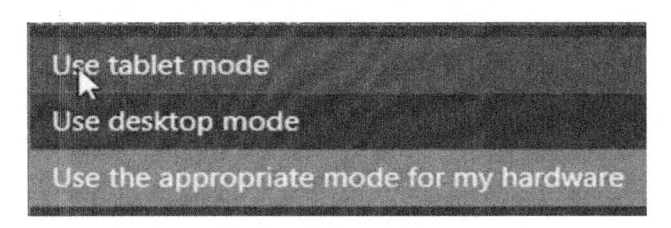

> Use tablet mode
> Use desktop mode
> Use the appropriate mode for my hardware

"When this device automatically switches tablet mode on or off", this allows you to determine what happens to your switching mode between tablet mode and desktop mode. "Don't ask me and don't switch" gives you a fixed mode of your current using mode choice. "Always ask me before switching" gives you access to authorization mode. "Don't ask me and always switch" takes away the privilege of awareness when switching.

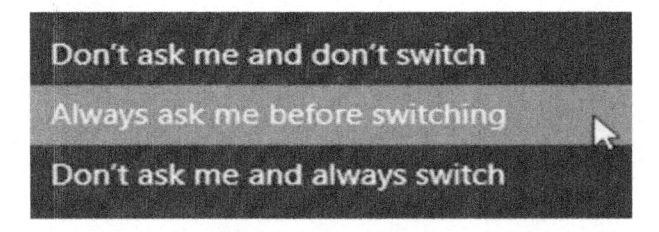

> Don't ask me and don't switch
> Always ask me before switching
> Don't ask me and always switch

And also, you can hide **application icons** on the taskbar in tablet mode, and also hide the taskbar in ***tablet*** mode

> Hide app icons on the taskbar in tablet mode
> On
>
> Automatically hide the taskbar in tablet mode
> On

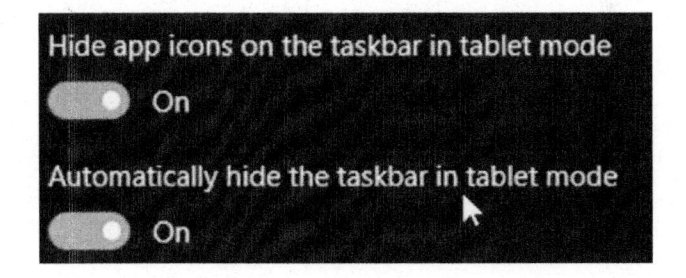

The Power Key

The Power key enables your system to do three things;

i. **Sleep:** This happens in two ways; firstly, when your computer has been inactive for long without using it, by default, it turns into sleep mode just like a human being staying long without doing anything which does result in taking a nap. And secondly, you can manually place your system on sleep mode yourself by clicking on the Start menu; by your left-hand side you will see your power button, click it and you will see the sleep option; once you select "sleep", by default it goes to resting-state as illustrated above.
NOTE: Sleep mode enables your PC to stay on but uses low power. Apps also stay open; so when the PC wakes up, you are instantly backed to where you left.

ii. **Shut down:** Shut down is not the same as a dead state, because using shut down for a human being perhaps means the person has been killed; but for a computer, it means a different thing entirely. Shutting down your system brings every running application into elimination and removing every pressure from your RAM, processor, and hard drive. Shut down closes all apps and turns off the PC.

iii. **Restart:** Restarting can also be called restoring. This is majorly used when the operating system is slow. Restarting makes the system work afresh without any complication. Restart closes all applications, turns off the PC, and then turns it on again.

All Apps

"All Apps" is where all your applications reside; once clicked on, you will be shown all installed applications on your PC.

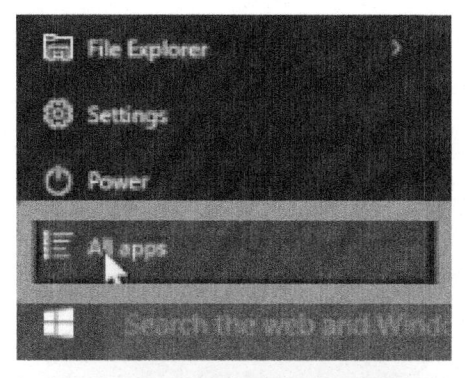

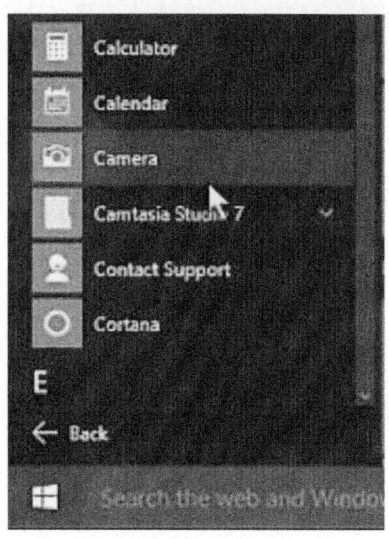

PC User Account Name

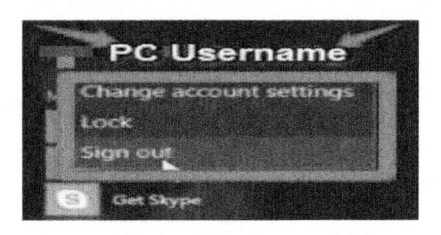

Windows 10 is designed in such a way that every of its user has their PC name. Clicking on "username" gives you three options; Change account settings, lock, and sign out.

- **Change account settings:** It is mainly for users' amendment such as changing of password, creating additional users, and lots more.
- **Lock:** It is very expedient to always lock your PC for security reasons due to unauthorized access.
- **Sign Out:** Sign out gives users the privilege of signing out from the PC.

Changing Your Background Displayed Colour

Windows 10 has made life easier and fun with its flexibility features. Go to "settings", select "personalization".

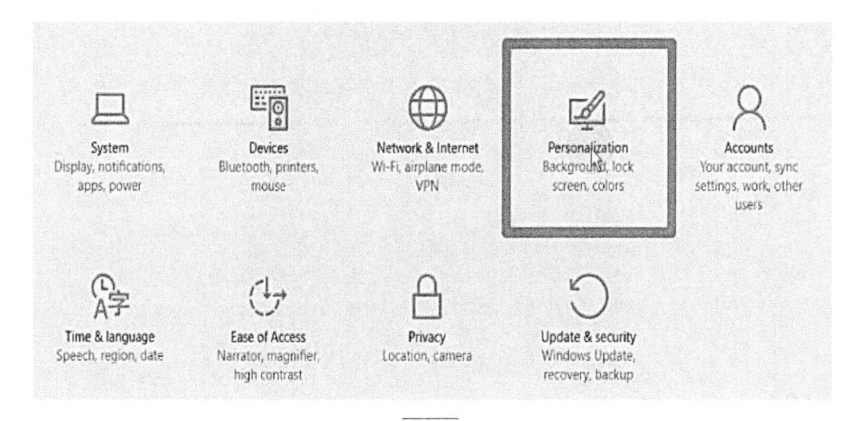

Select "Colors" on the right-hand side; you can choose a color different from your default blue color.

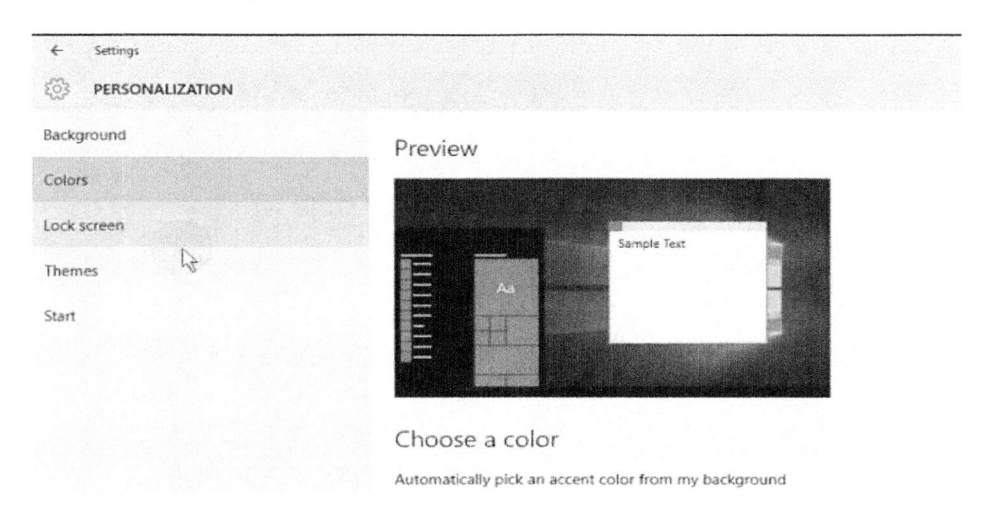

Once you select another color, it will immediately change into the new effect as illustrated below. There are many other colors of your choice to be selected.

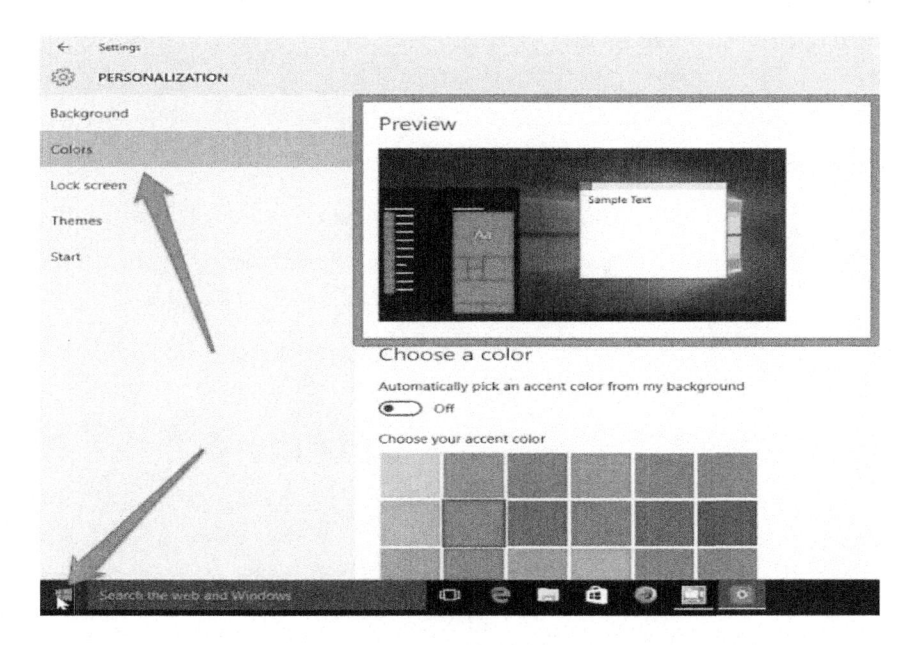

This is the effect of red color instead of blue.

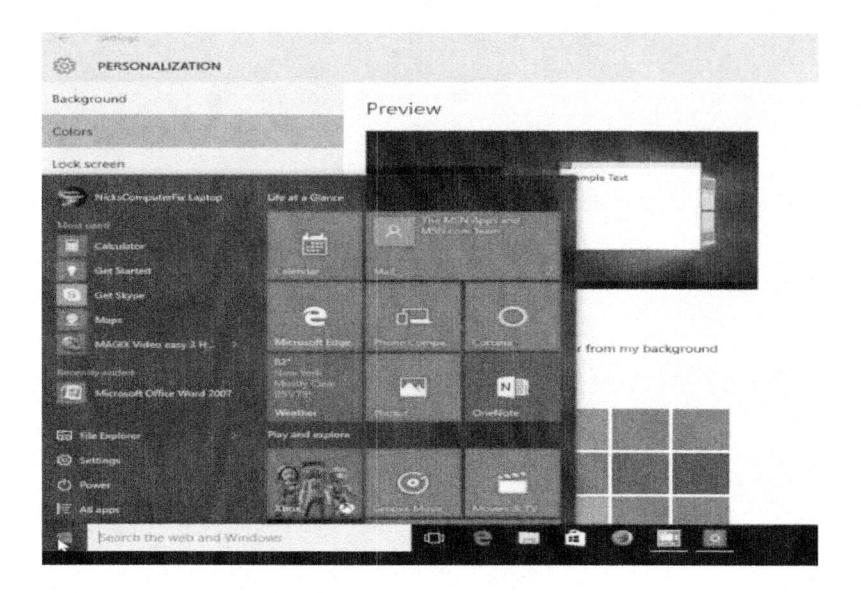

Still under "Settings"; in "Personalization", click on "Start" and four (4) options will be shown; turning it on will result in seeing them on "Start Menu", likewise turning it off might also result in not reflecting on "Start Menu".

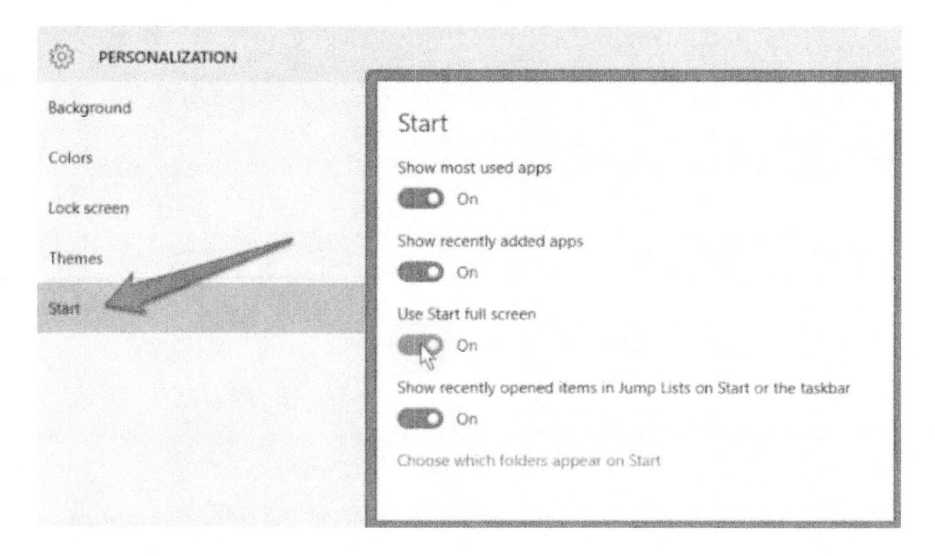

How to Adjust the Screen Resolution

On your window desktop, right-click on the desktop interface, a dialog box will appear; click on "Display settings".

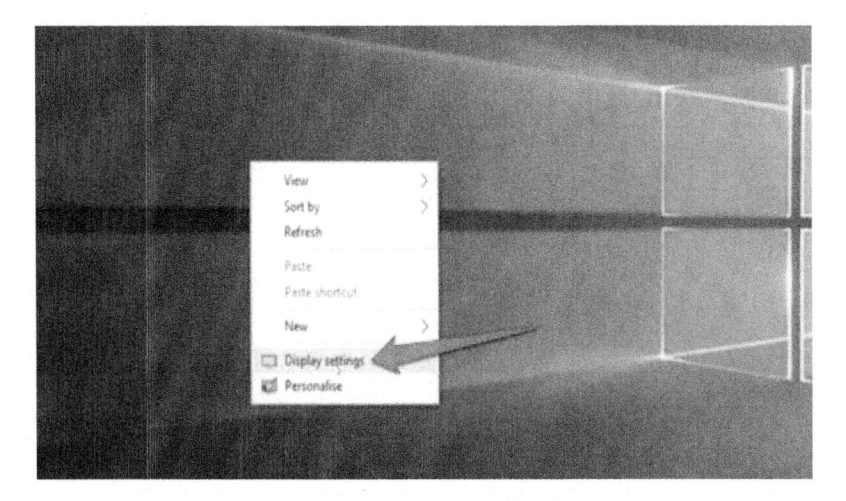

On your left-hand side, you will see "Display"; make sure you click on it, then at your right, scroll down and double click on "Advanced display settings".

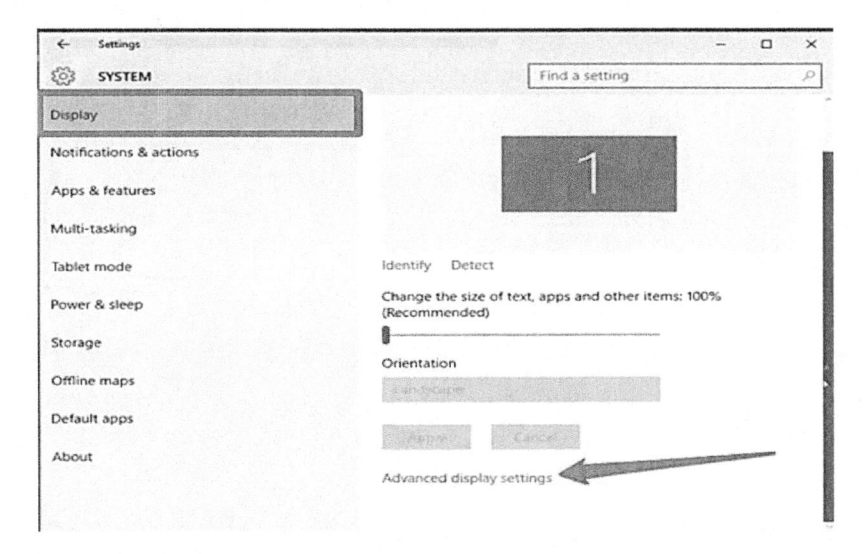

Click on the box below Resolution to adjust your display screen to your preferred choice.

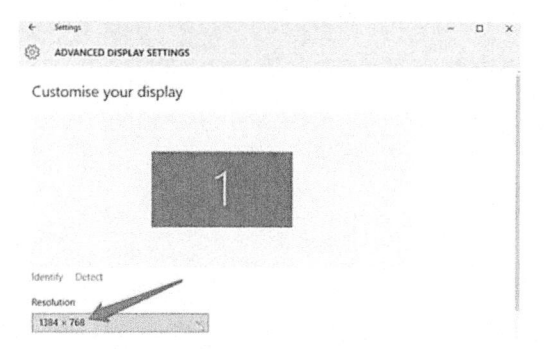

Let's assume we want to adjust your screen resolution to 1024 x 768, click and search for 1024 x 768; once selected, click "Apply".

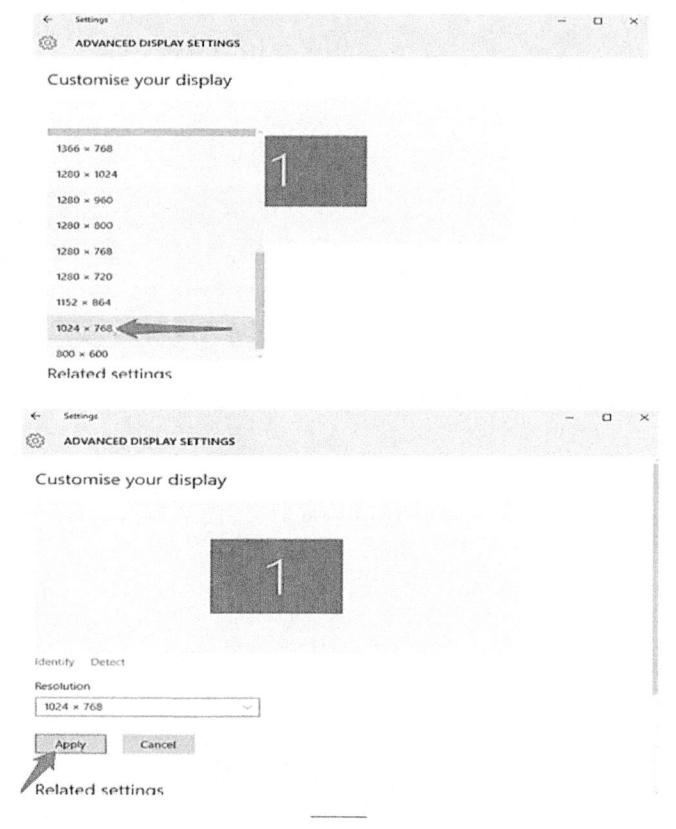

110

You will be informed to "keep changes" or "revert", click "keep changes" and it will automatically have effect; and if you don't click on any, by default, it will revert after 15 seconds. Go ahead and check your desktop interface effect.

Difference between Settings and Control Panel

The settings inbuilt application is a more simplified easy-to-use version that emanated from the old Windows control panel that served a similar purpose. Microsoft is gradually moving many settings as many as possible to the new interface so that there will be a single user experience across desktops, laptops, tablets, and phones. Both settings and control panel can be used interwoven. Soon, the control panel will be fully replaced with settings.

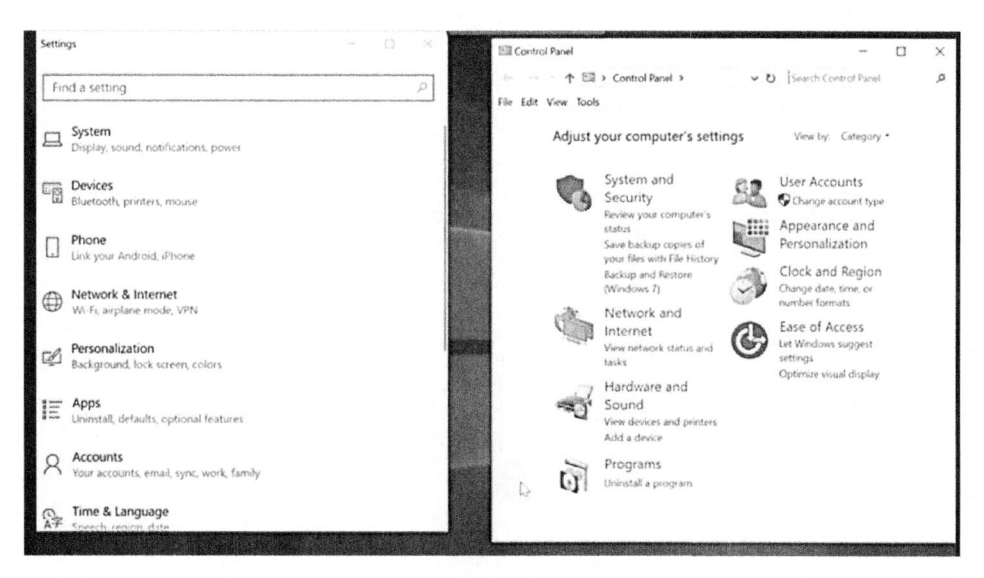

111

Settings and control panel are the control rooms for effect, changes, style, execution, connection, creating a password, new users' interface, etc.

Note: Settings and Control panel are interlinked in functionality. For this guide, we are going to be using systems as our illustration for exploring it.

CHAPTER SIX

HOW TO ADD A SHORTCUT INTO YOUR DESKTOP ENVIRONMENT

There are many ways to this, one of them is searching for what you want to add to your desktop environment or interface by typing it in the search box. For example, adding Chrome browser you type "chrome browser" in your search box as illustrated below; right click on the chrome icon that is highlighted in blue

Click on *"open file location"*, it will take you into the chrome icon shortcut folder.

Next, right-click on Google Chrome, and another dialog box will open, select *"Send to"* another dialog box will pop up, select *"Desktop (Create shortcut)".* It will appear automatically on your desktop screen.

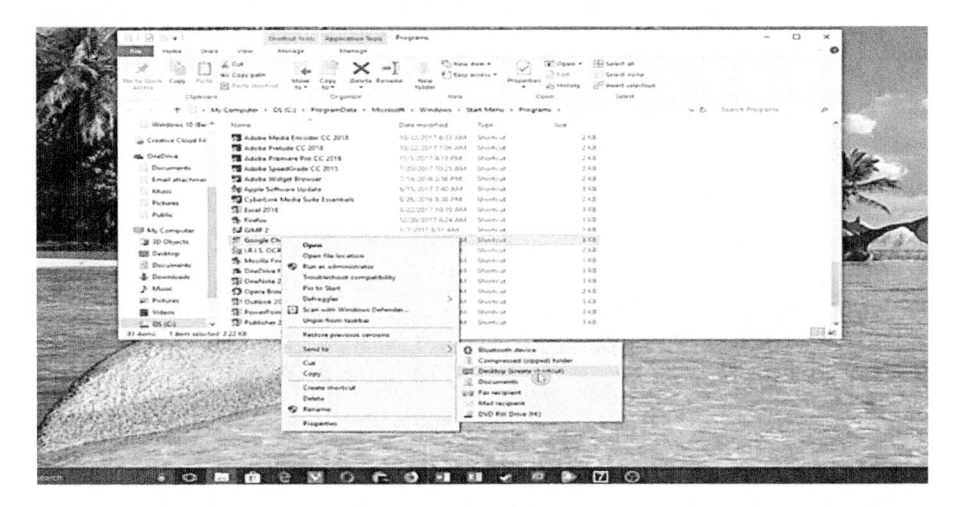

The second way is by clicking on your "Start menu", search for the application then click and drag it into the desktop environment.

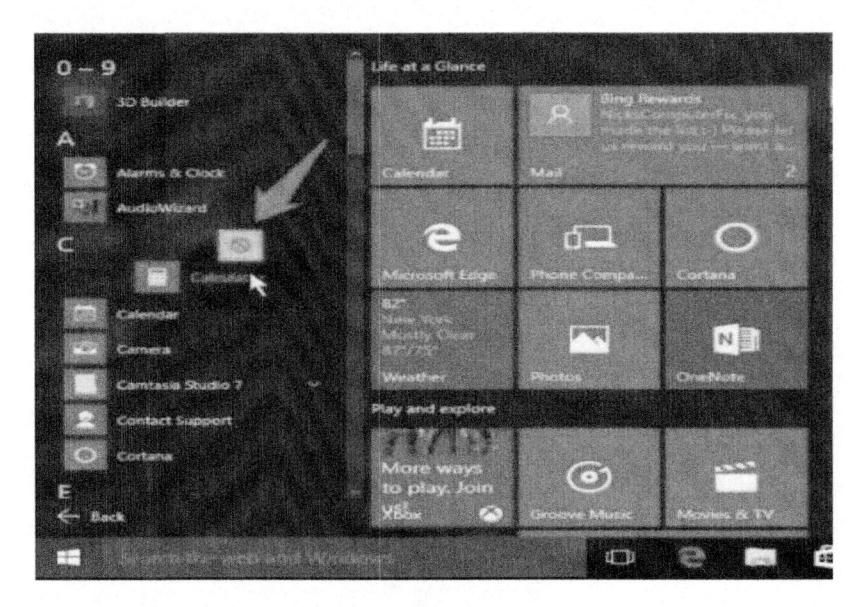

It will reflect on the desktop without affecting its source in the "Start menu".

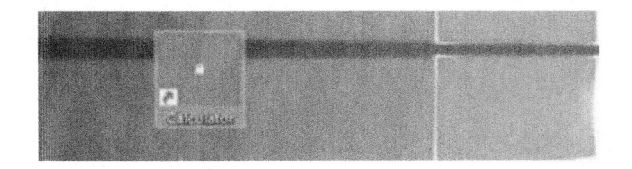

Rechecking the Start menu to confirm that only a duplicated copy was moved, not the actual app, the same process can be applied to the taskbar.

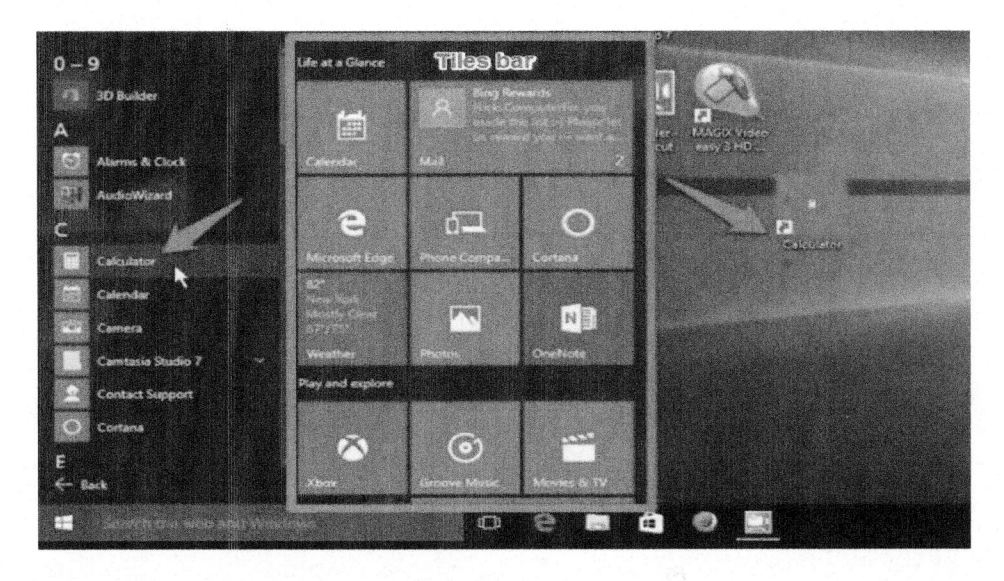

Windows 10 Shortcut Keys

The focal point for Windows is to make things simplified and flexible for easy usage and less stress. Shortcuts are structured to make windows users faster and quicker in their usage. It is very important to know that Windows has many built-in functions of shortcuts for making life easier. Below are many more keys that can be used to improve efficiency and time usage.

115

Note: Some of these keys work for Windows operating system and installed applications such as Word, Excel, PowerPoint, and so on.

Ctrl + A	Highlight all items
Ctrl + B	Bold text (mainly for Microsoft applications).
Ctrl + C	Copy selected items.
Ctrl + D	Font size, style, color, and lots more.
Ctrl + E	Center Alignment (mainly for Microsoft applications) Also used to search file explorer.
Ctrl + F	To Find (mainly for Microsoft applications).
Ctrl + G	To locate the page. line, section, table, and so on. (mainly for Microsoft applications)
Ctrl + H	Find and replace boxes (mainly for Microsoft applications).

Ctrl + I	Italic (Sloping) text (mainly for Microsoft applications).
Ctrl + J	Justify text (mainly for Microsoft applications).
Ctrl + K	Insert hyperlink (mainly for Microsoft applications).
Ctrl + L	Left alignment (mainly for Microsoft applications).
Ctrl + M	Spacing paragraph (mainly for Microsoft applications).
Ctrl + N	Opening a new document (mainly for Microsoft applications).
Ctrl + O	Open recent work (mainly for Microsoft applications).
Ctrl + P	Print (mainly for Microsoft applications).
Ctrl + Q	Line Spacing (mainly for Microsoft applications).

Ctrl + R	Right Alignment in Microsoft applications.
	Reload the page in the browser.
Ctrl + S	Save a document (mainly for Microsoft applications).
Ctrl + U	Underline selected text (mainly for Microsoft applications).
Ctrl + V	Paste (mainly for Microsoft application).
Ctrl + W	Close active document (mainly for Microsoft applications).
Ctrl + X	Cut selected items (mainly for Microsoft applications).
Ctrl + Y	Redo (mainly for Microsoft applications).
Ctrl + Z	Undo (mainly for Microsoft applications).
Ctrl + Drag	Copy file.

Ctrl + Shift + Drag	Create shortcut (also right-click, drag).
Ctrl + Esc	It Opens the Start menu.
Ctrl + Alt + Del	Lock/Switch User/ Change / open Windows task manager.
Ctrl + Alt + Tab	Switching application.
Ctrl + F6	Cycle program.
Ctrl + F4 or Alt F4	It closes the currently displayed application.
Ctrl + Shift + N	Create a new folder.
Ctrl + N	New file explorer windows.
WINKEY + A	Windows Action Center.
WINKEY + D	Display Desktop Interface.
WINKEY + M	Minimize all windows interface.

WINKEY +	Zooming in and out.
WINKEY + E	Open Microsoft Explorer Folder.
WINKEY + Tab	Cycle through open programs on the taskbar.
WINKEY + F	Display the Windows Search & Find features.
WINKEY + G	For game bar
WINKEY + L	Lock the computer.
WINKEY + F1	Display the Microsoft Windows help or support.
WINKEY + PrtScrn	Take a screenshot.
WINKEY + Pause	For checking computer information.
WINKEY + U	Open utility manager.
WINKEY + P	Connecting Projector.

WINKEY + Q, WINKEY + S	For search.
WINKEY + R	Open the auto-run Window dialog box.
WINKEY + W	Windows Ink Workspace.
WINKEY + X	Windows Mobility Center for a special shortcut.
WINKEY + Tab	To Navigate multiple programs.
WINKEY or Ctrl + Esc	Search your computer.
WINKEY + Ctrl + Arrow key	Switch virtual desktop.
WINKEY + Arrow key	Control open windows.
Alt + Enter	For checking of items' properties by selecting the items majorly used for checking item space.
Alt + Tab	Switch between open applications.
Alt + F4	Close active program.

F1	Universal help command (for all programs).
F2	Rename the selected object.
F5	Refresh Windows interface.
F6	Shifts focus on Windows Explorer.
F10	Activates menu bar options.
Shift + Delete	Permanent delete bypassing Recycle Bin.
Shift + Drag	Move file.
Backspace	Deleting backward.

How to Resize Your Desktop Application

Right-click on the desktop interface (make sure your mouse sensor is not placed on any application), select the view option and select your preference; large, medium, or small.

CHAPTER SEVEN

UNDERSTANDING USER ACCOUNTS

User Accounts

A user account is a unique identity created for a person in a computer or computing system. User accounts can also be created for machine entities such as service accounts for running programs, system accounts for storing system files and processes, root and administrator accounts for system administration.

Types of User Accounts

It is important to note that there are two (2) kinds of user accounts which are:

i. **Local account:** Local account runs without an internet connection. It has controlled access to one single, physical computer. Your local account credentials are stored locally on the PC hard drive, and the PC checks its files to authenticate your login. A local account allows you some level of access to an individual computer but your PC login details can't work on another PC since it is a local account only stored on your PC.

ii. **Microsoft account:** Microsoft account works with an internet connection and its features of accessibility are limitless. Microsoft account comes with synchronization which makes your mobile device to be linked up with your PC. Microsoft account is the new name for what used to be called "Windows Live ID". Your Microsoft account is the combination of an email address and a password that you use to log in to services like OneDrive, Cortana, Outlook.com,

Xbox LIVE, Windows, Phone, and other Microsoft features give you access without you signing in repetitively. With the Microsoft account, all your personal information is stored and secured for reuse on the Microsoft cloud just like Gmail which also gives you access to saved website passwords by itself without you having to remember thousands of passwords of different accounts. You can log in to any PC with your Microsoft account.

User Account Settings

Go to "Start Menu", click on "Settings" or search for "Settings".

Under "Settings", click on "Accounts".

By default, your current user will be shown to you.

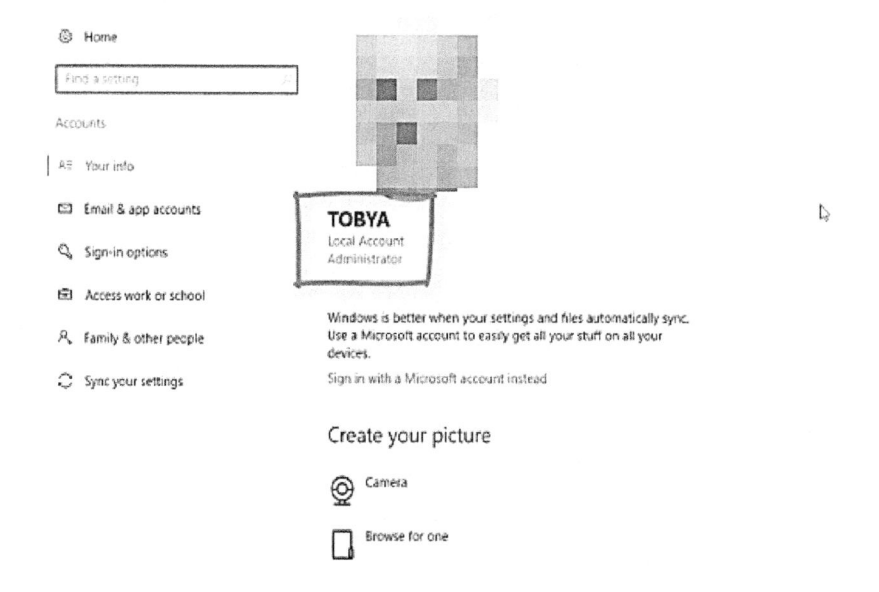

Below is where you can sign in with a Microsoft account; it gives you access to switch from a local account into a Microsoft account. You can also create your picture that will be on your account.

If you don't have an account, go to the left-hand and click on "Email & app account".

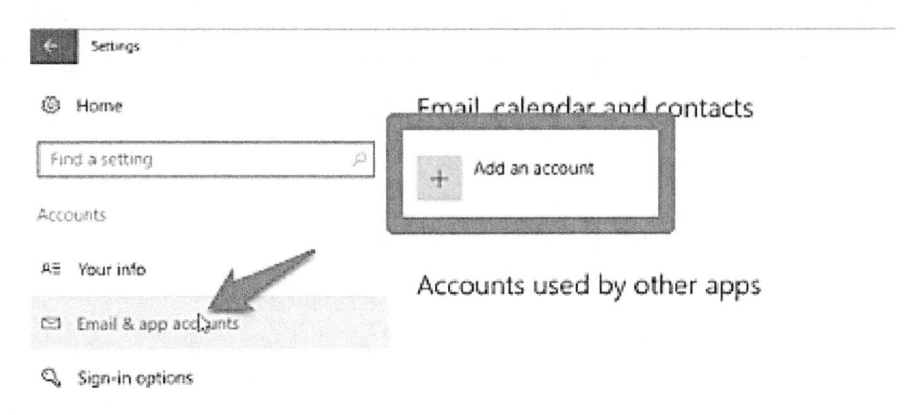

Sign-in Options

Sign-in options give users the privilege to adjust a lot of things; one of them is "Require sign-in", which is when Windows should require you to sign in again.

You either choose *"Never"* or *"When PC wakes up from sleep"*

The **"Never"** option enables its user to log in without requesting a password, while the "*When PC wake up from sleep*" option enables its user to re-login with a password.

Require sign-in

Never — Windows require you to sign in again?

When PC wakes up from sleep

Types of Windows Security

It is also important to note that windows have many options for login in such as password, pin, picture password, and other options based on the user's preference.

Windows Hello
Sign in to Windows, apps and services by teaching Windows to recognise you.
Windows Hello isn't available on this device.
See how it works and find compatible devices.

Password
Change your account password
Change

PIN
Create a PIN to use in place of passwords. You'll be asked for this PIN when you sign in to Windows, apps and services.
Add

Picture password
Sign in to Windows using a favourite photo
Add

Sync means synchronizing all available features. As a Microsoft user, whenever you login into another PC, every feature and information will be duplicated according to the permission you give Microsoft. For security reasons, access to passwords may not be granted until you verify. In the picture below, access to the password was not granted until it was verified.

How to switch from Microsoft Account to Local Account

Let's say you are on a Microsoft account, the option that will be presented to you will be to "Sign in with a local account".

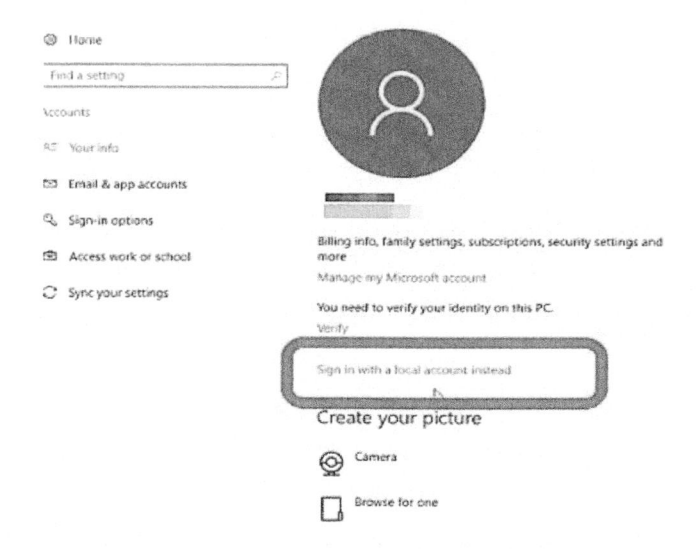

Once you click on "Sign in with a local account", it will switch your Microsoft account into a local account and request for your Microsoft account to verify your request by typing your Microsoft password to switch or convert into a local account.

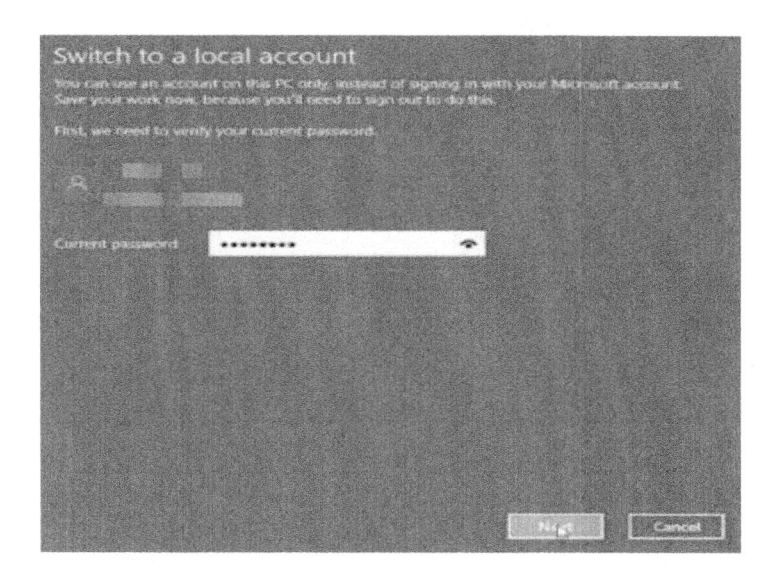

Here is where your converted (switched) local account information will be requested, either to fill in your username or still maintain your previous Microsoft account name. If you maintain your previous account name, it won't work again for Microsoft account since it has been converted into a local account. Fill it and click on Next.

Note that information associated with your Microsoft account still exists, but applications might ask you to sign in before accessing that information; then you can click on the **"sign out and finish"** button.

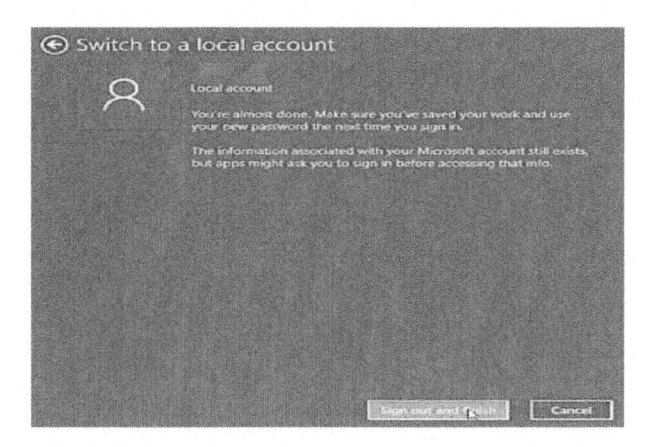

How to switch from Local Account to Microsoft Account

In the first illustration, I explained how to switch a Microsoft account into a local account; the same procedure is also applicable to switching from a local account into a Microsoft account. Let's assume you are on a local account, the option that will be presented to you will be to "Sign in with a Microsoft account".

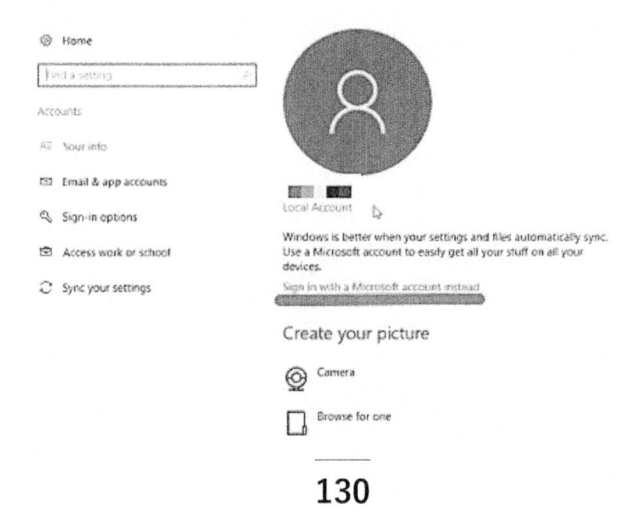

If the local user once had a Microsoft account, login with the email & password; if the user does not have one, you can click on "No account? Create one" as illustrated below

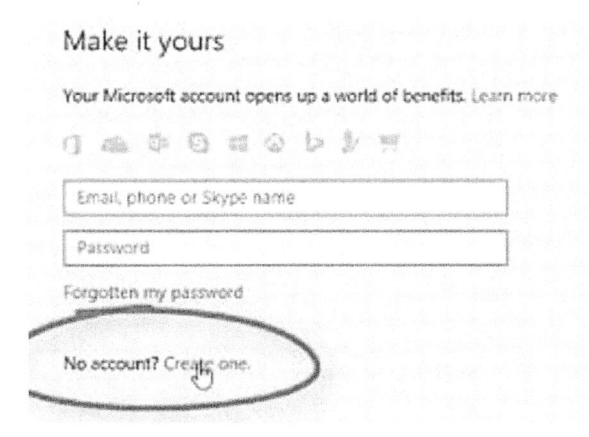

Put in your previous Microsoft account details (the one I once converted into a local account), then sign in.

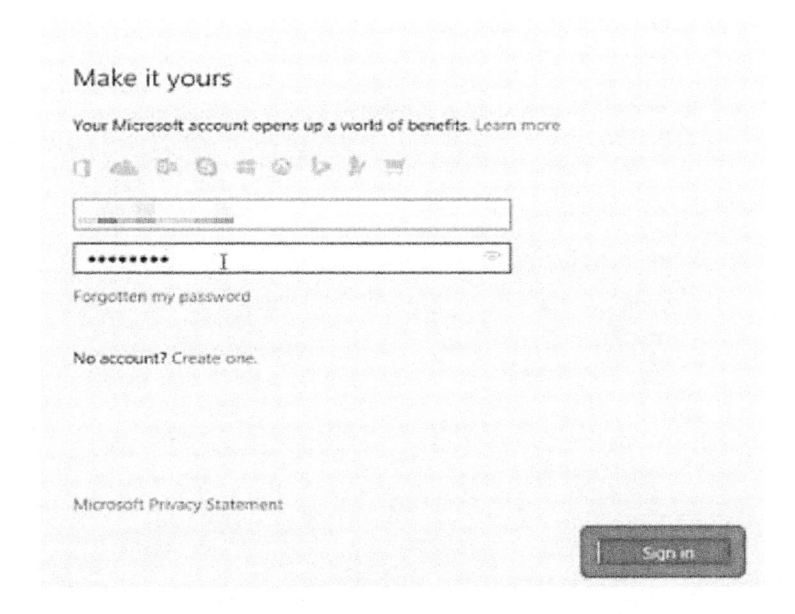

Insert your current local password.

> Sign in to this device using your Microsoft account
>
> From now on, you'll unlock this device using either the password for your Microsoft account or, if you've set one up, your PIN. That way, you can get help from Cortana and find your device if you lose it, and your settings will sync automatically.
>
> To make sure it's really you, we'll need your current Windows password one last time. Next time you sign in to Windows, you'll use your Microsoft account password.
>
> If you don't have a Windows password, just leave the box blank and select Next.
>
> Current Windows password
>
> ●●●●●●●●
>
> Next

Kindly verify your Microsoft account.

> Use Windows Hello
>
> Or enter your PIN to finish setting up your Microsoft account on this device.
>
> Windows Security ×
>
> **Making sure it's you**
>
> We need to verify your identity for toby.a@live.co.uk.
>
> ●●|
>
> I forgot my PIN
>
> Cancel

It will fully switch back to Microsoft account.

132

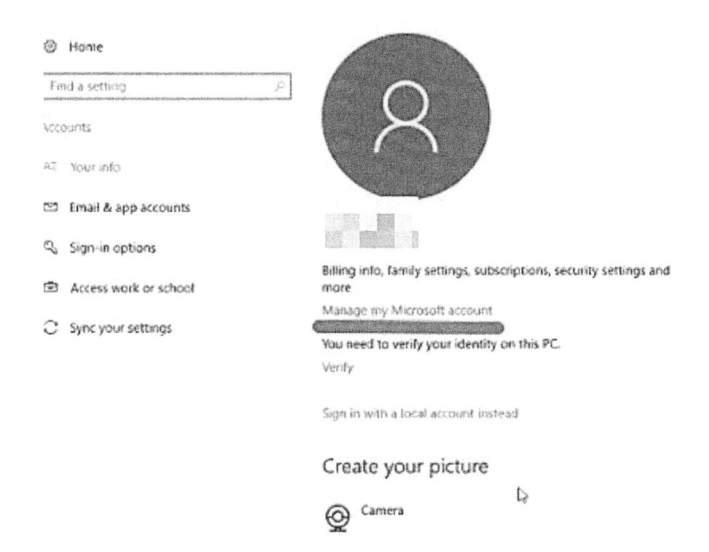

How to Create a New User

Adding a new user can only be done by an Administrator account. Under "Settings", by your left-hand side, click on "Family & other people"; by your right-hand side, you will see "Add someone else to this PC".

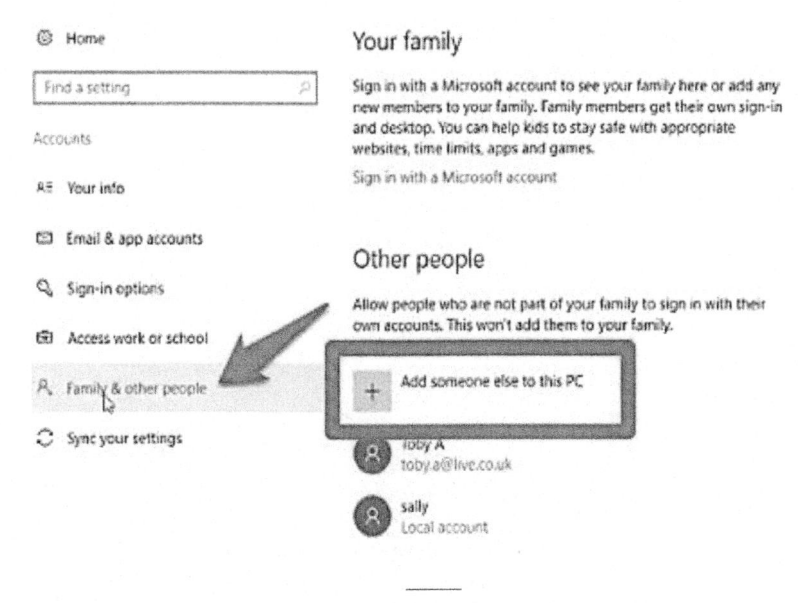

133

Here is where you will be brought to once you click on "Add someone else to this PC", which is titled "How will this person sign in?" You can enter the email address or phone number of the person you want to add if they use Microsoft Windows; if not, click on **"I don't have this person's sign-in information"** as illustrated by the arrow below; then "Next".

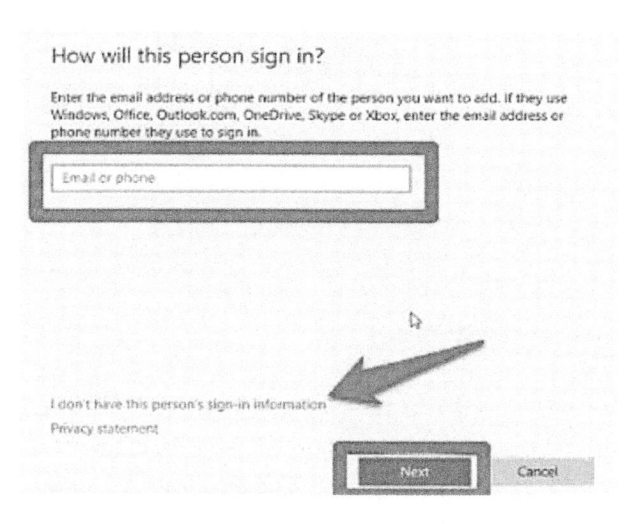

By default, Microsoft Windows 10 will suggest to you to create a new Microsoft email for your new account; you can decide to create one. Click on "Add a user without a Microsoft account", and then click "Next".

134

After clicking "next", it will display a page showing "Create an account for this PC". Don't forget this is a local account; make sure your password is easy to remember. You can use "hint password" which enables you to remember your password. For example, if my hint password is "DDMMYYYY" which represents day, month & year. That is to say, my password will be on the numerical figure of a particular date. Once done, click "Next".

Note: If you want to choose a password, choose something simple for you to remember but difficult for others to guess.

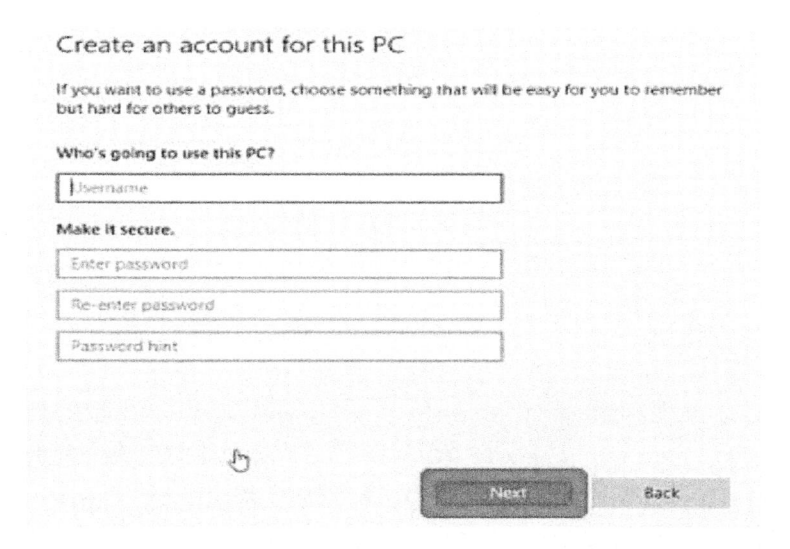

By default, it will be added to your Windows operating system as the local account that was chosen.

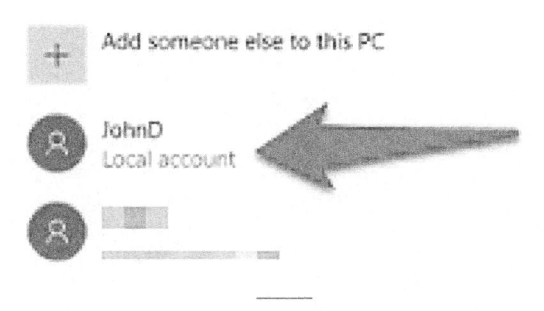

How to Remove a User

To remove a user account, always note that you must be an administrator (that is, your account must be an "administrator account") to have the full access/permission to authorize it.

Go to "Settings", click on "Account"; by the left-hand side, select "Family & other people".

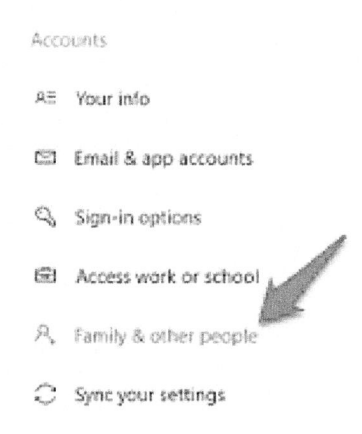

Check your right-hand side; below, you will see the added account on your PC, click on the one you want to remove; two options will be shown to you either to "Change account type" or "Remove", click on "Remove".

Once you click on remove, a dialog box will be shown to you instructing you on the consequence of your action. If you agree, proceed and click *"Delete account and data",* then, you have successfully removed the user.

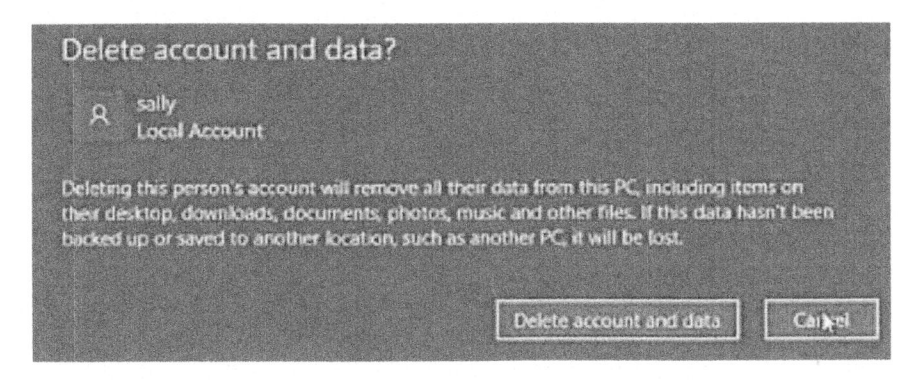

Changing an Account Type

Go to "Settings" under settings look at your left-hand side and double click on family & other people.

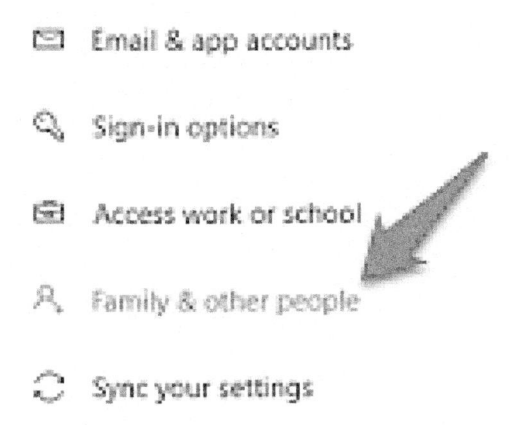

By your right-hand side after clicking on family & other people, you will see all users on your PC; click on the one you want to change and you will be given an option to *"Change account type".*

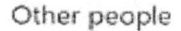

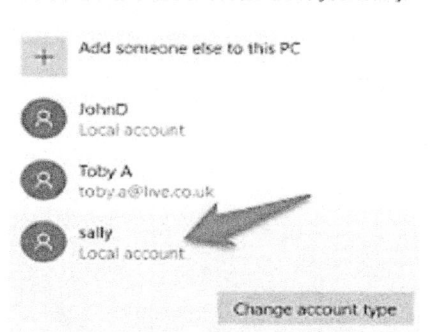

There are two kinds of account type

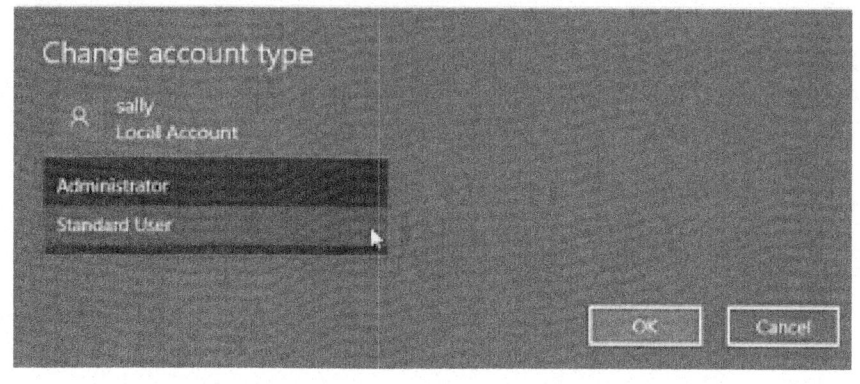

- **Administrator account:** An administrator account is a user with additional permissions. An administrator can add, edit, delete and assign users on the PC. As a rightful owner of your PC, it is highly recommended to be the one running the Administrator account.
- **Standard Account:** Standard account is similar to an administrator account; but in access and permission, a standard account is limited. Only the administrator can decide how and what should be assigned to a standard account.

Managing User Accounts and Parental Controls

Managing User account and parental control is essential for securing one's account and also guiding the children due to the voluminous information on the internet and the power of a PC. You can use Parental Control to help manage how your children use the computer. For example, you can set limits on the hours that your children can use the computer, the types of games they can play, and the programs they can run.

When Parental Control blocks access to a game or program, a notification is displayed that the program has been blocked. Your child can click a link in the notification to request permission for access to that game or program. You can allow access by entering your account information.

To set up Parental Controls for your child, you'll need your administrator user account. Before you get started, make sure each child that you want to set up Parental Control for has a standard user account. Parental Controls can be applied only to standard user accounts as explained above.

Step 1

Go to "Start Menu", click on "Settings"

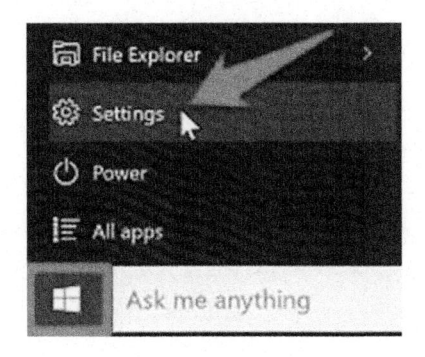

Step 2

Under "Settings", click on "Account"

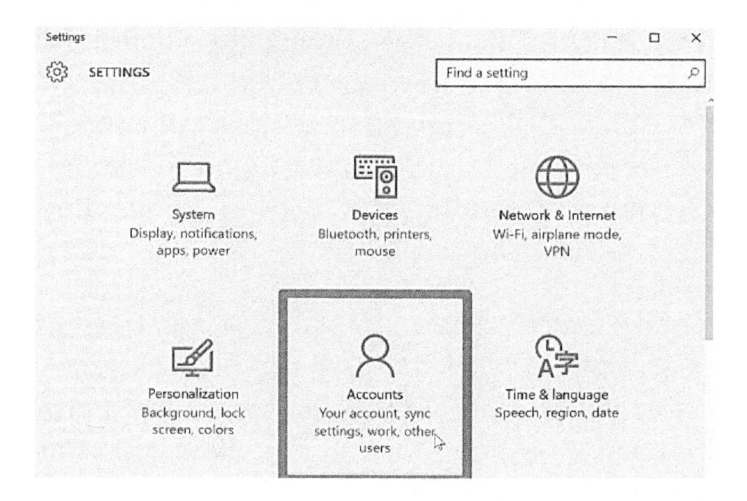

Step 3

Scroll to "Family & other users"; by your right-hand side, you will see "Add a family member", click on it.

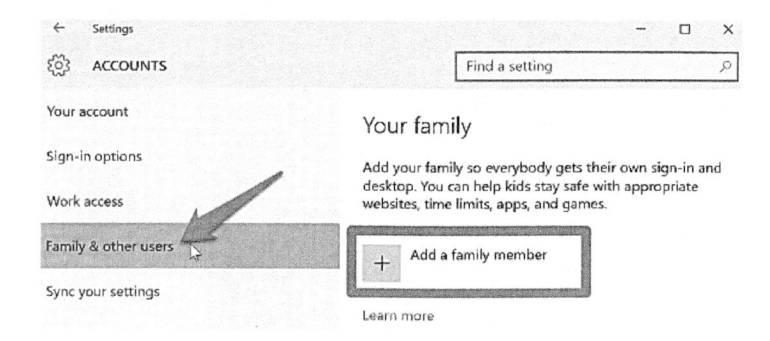

Step 4

A dialog box will pop-up asking to ***"Add a child or an Adult",*** select your preferred choice. If the parental control account has an email, you can insert it and click on "Next".

Note: Parental control is only available to Microsoft account and not available to a Local account.

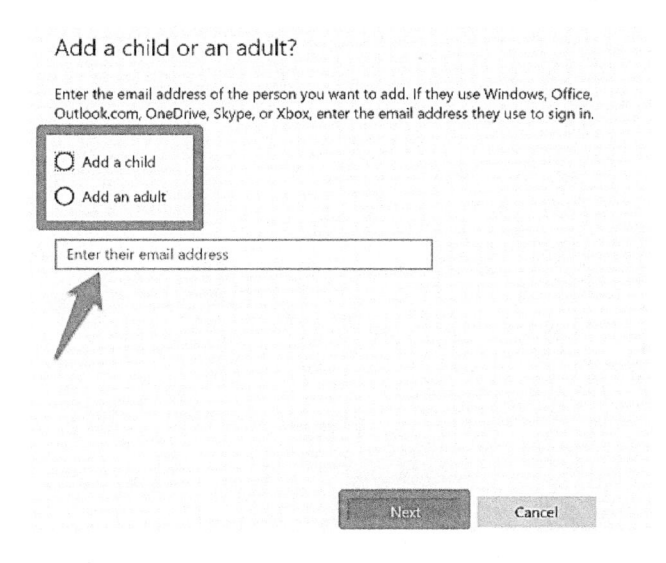

Stage 5

You will be asked to confirm your request to add the new user email, click on "Confirm" to proceed.

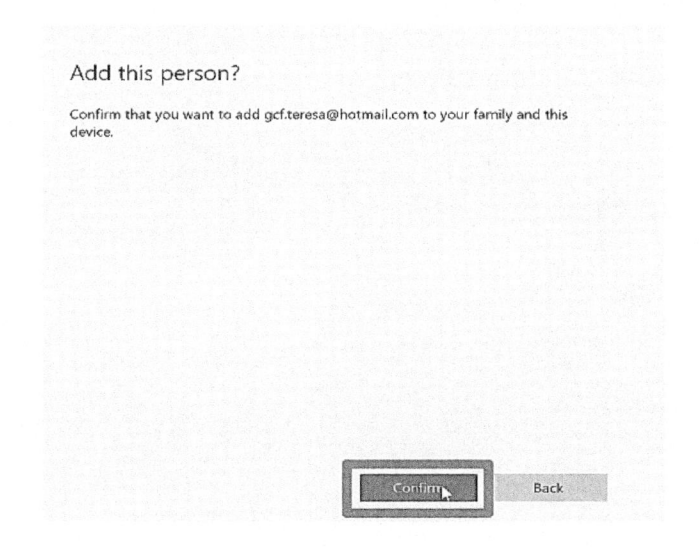

Stage 6

The newly added child user must confirm your request through his/her email before the "Pending" sign will be removed and fully active for use. You can also click on "Manage family settings online" to see your control panel.

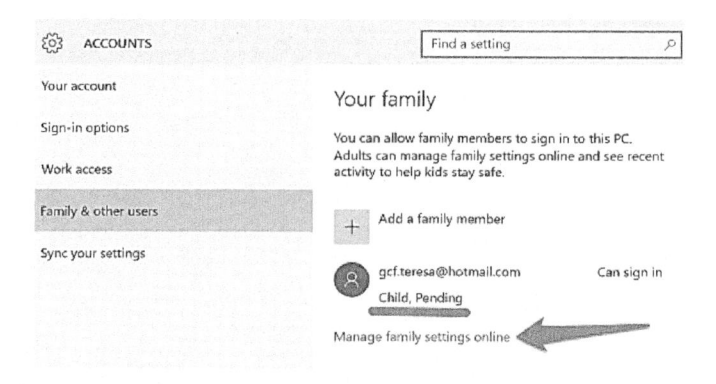

Stage 7

"Manage family settings online" will take you online to see your control panel dashboard where you can fully monitor the activities of your children and other monitored accounts.

Recent activity can be turned on for reports and Email weekly updates.

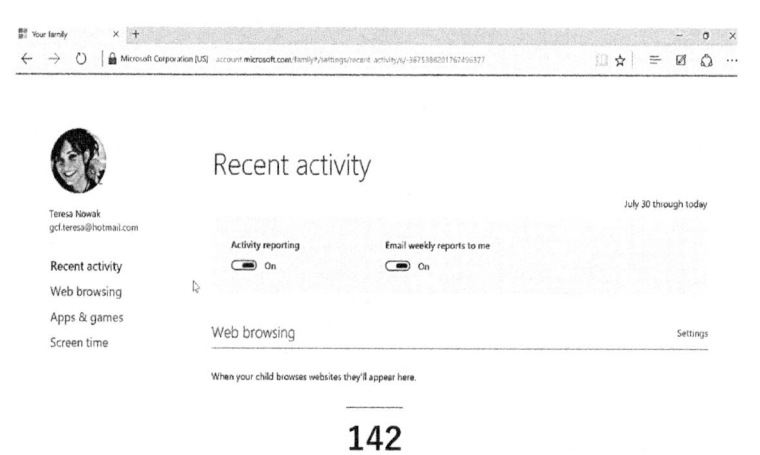

Stage 8

Web browsing helps to set a restriction on inappropriate websites. By turning it on, it blocks inappropriate sites for your children.

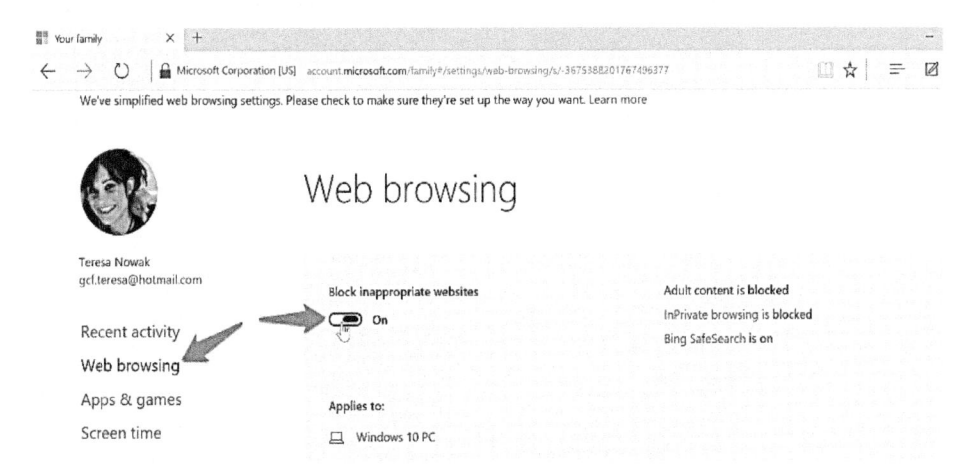

Stage 9

Apps & games must be turned on for a better experience. It enables you to monitor the children's apps and games by deciding what should be accessed and what should not be accessed.

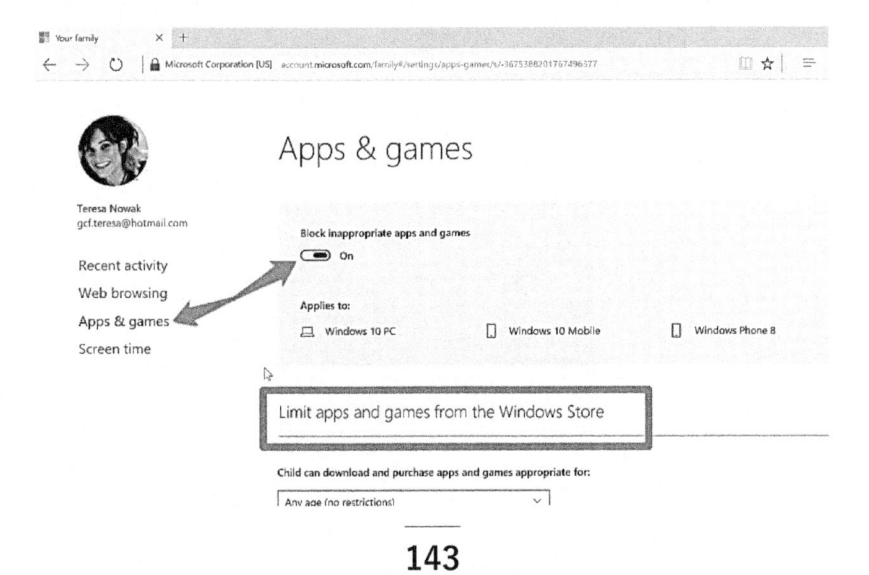

Step 10

Screen time must also be turned on to give the possibility to monitor when the children should log in daily, and also, the duration per day can be assigned on every device the child can log in through.

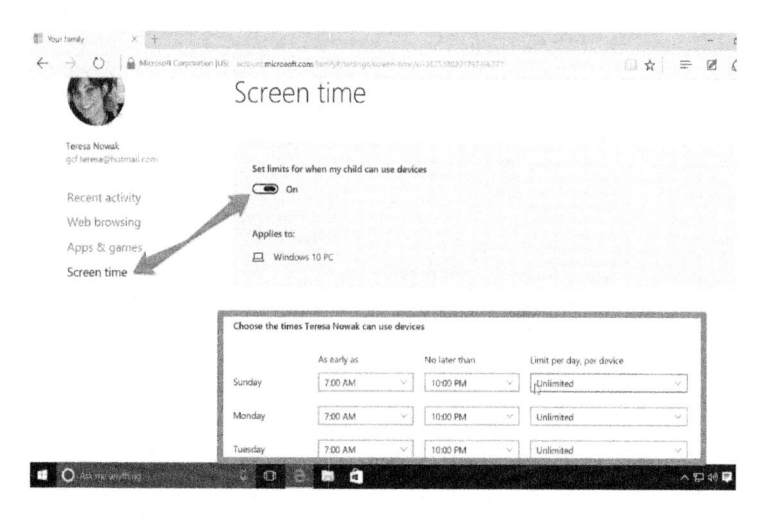

It is important to note that by default, your computer has one administrator account; it is the one you first created the time you set up Windows 10 account which is your account by default. Subsequently, you can make any user an administrator if need be.

How to Sign Out or Switch Users

Go to "Start menu".

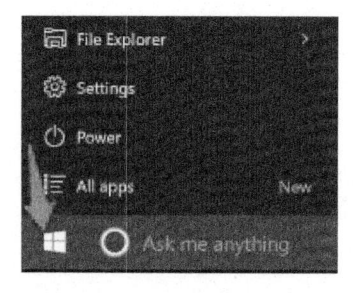

Above click on the current user's name and **Sign out** or click on another account to switch user.

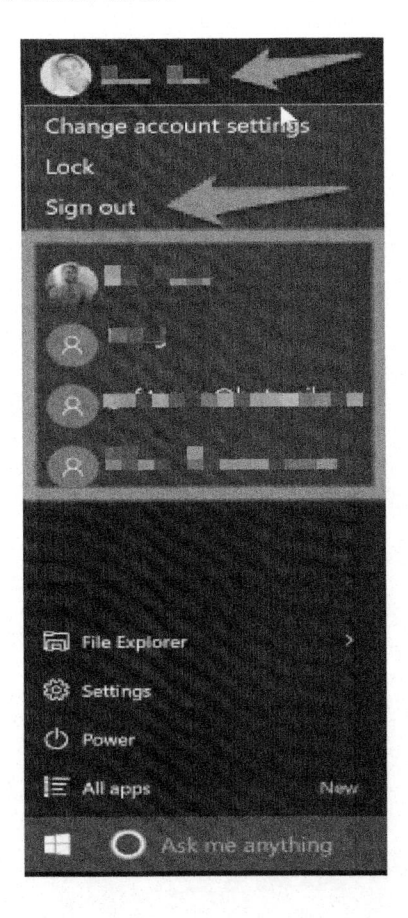

CHAPTER EIGHT

EXPLORING SETTINGS FEATURES

Settings Features

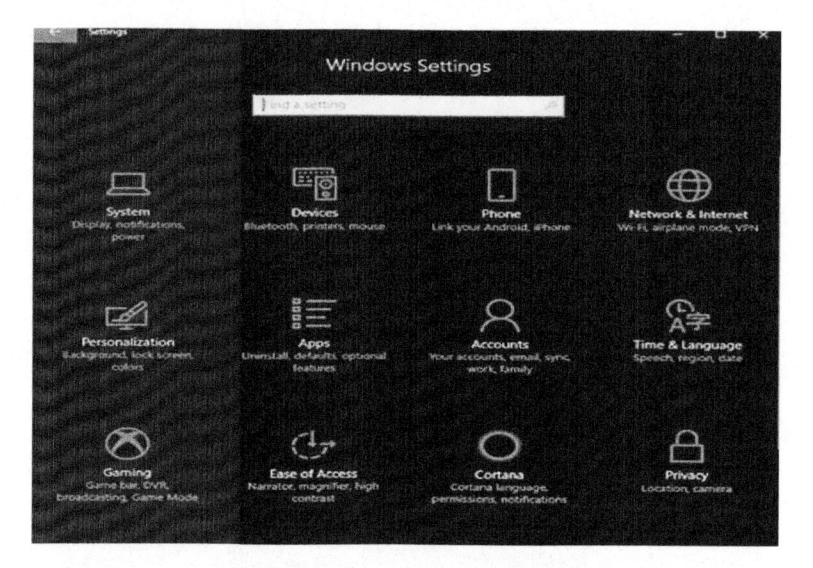

Display settings

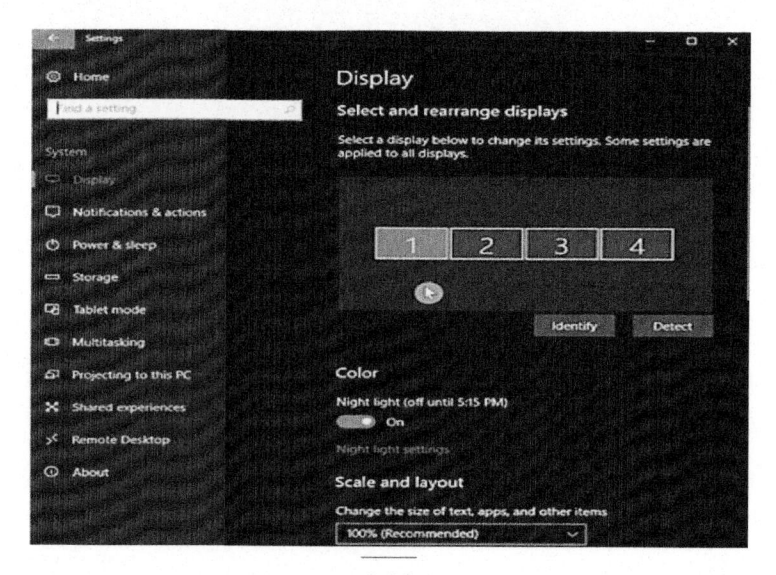

"Display" enables its users to select above to change its settings.

Color – grants privilege to switching of lightening from white to black as illustrated above.

- **Night light** – gives access to night light adjustment which can be turned on and off or amended based on individual preference. The night light is majorly to control the exposure to light.
- **Scale & Layout** – this feature gives access to changing the text size and other items.

Notification

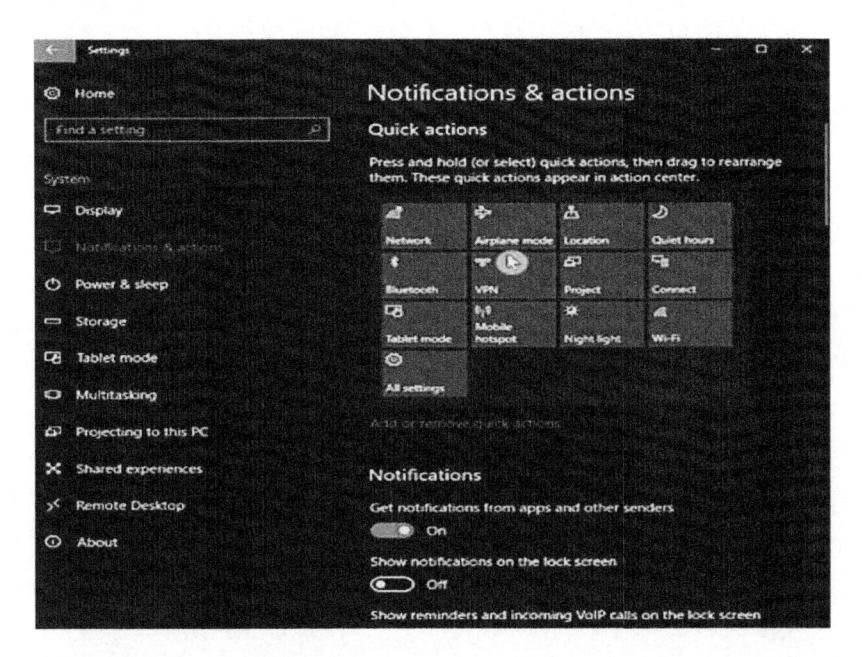

With notification, you can add or remove quick action. Quick action appears in "Action Center". "Action Center" is the one in charge of notification(s) popping up such as Windows update, alarm, autoplay, and other prompting notification(s) from applications.

Power & Sleep

This is where you set your power settings, select additional power, decide when your PC goes to sleep mode while charging and when the screen turns off. Power settings represent the battery life; select what plan best works for you.

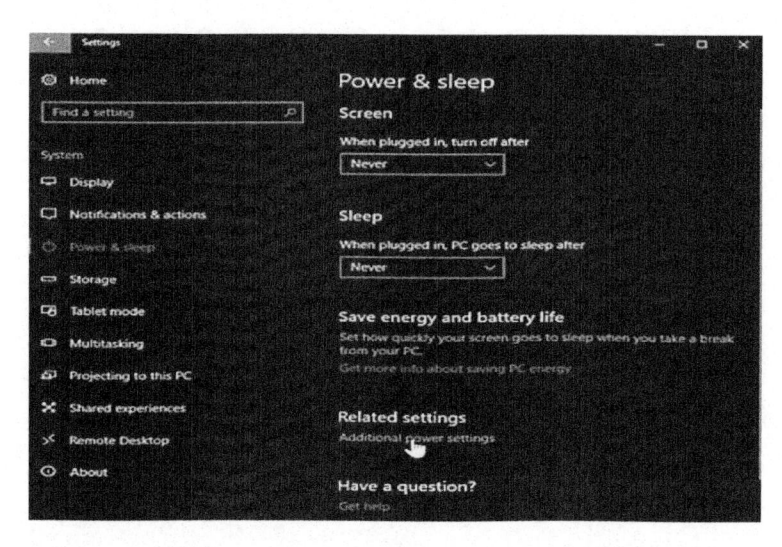

Storage

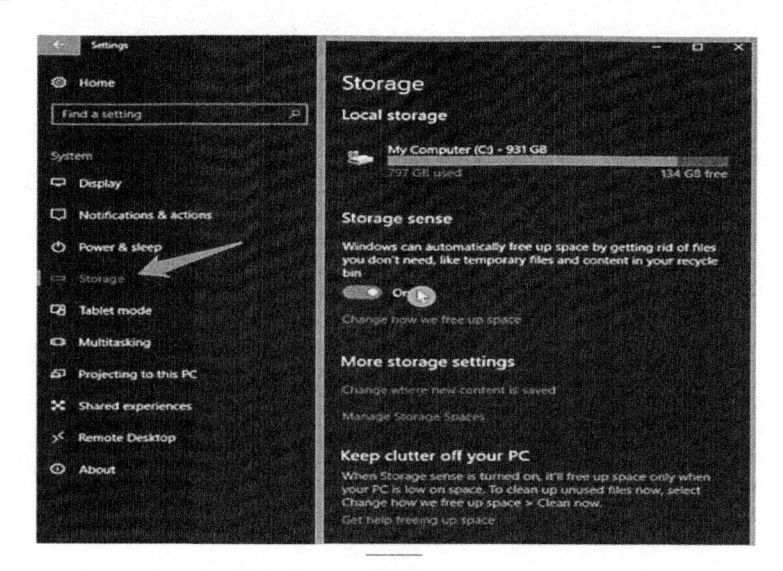

Storage settings help Windows to automatically free up space by getting rid of files you don't need, like temporary files and contents in your recycle bin. Storage settings also enable you to decide where new content should be saved and manage storage space. When storage sense is turned on, it will only free up space when your PC has low storage.

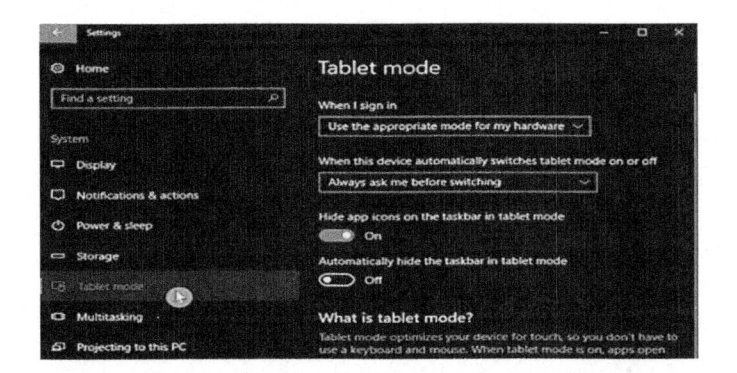

Tablet Mode

Tablet mode boosts your device for touch, so you don't have to use a keyboard and mouse. When tablet mode is on, apps open full-screen; taskbar and desktop icons are reduced. Tablet mode also enables its user to hide taskbar and apps icon and other features' settings.

Multitasking

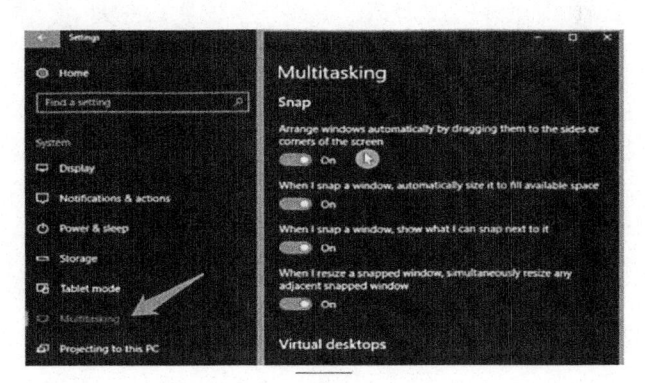

Multitasking helps in switching apps, snapping objects to fit into the available size, and capturing things around. Multitasking also enables its users to see all opened windows.

Projecting to this PC

This is majorly designed by Microsoft to solve the issue of conference presentation and screen duplication for the audience to see what a presenter or an anchor is communicating virtually by connecting a single system with a projector.

Share Experiences

Windows 10 makes it much easier for information to be shared.

Remote Desktop

Remote Desktop is specifically designed to make use of other systems with the help of a single interconnected system.

Bluetooth & Other Devices' Settings

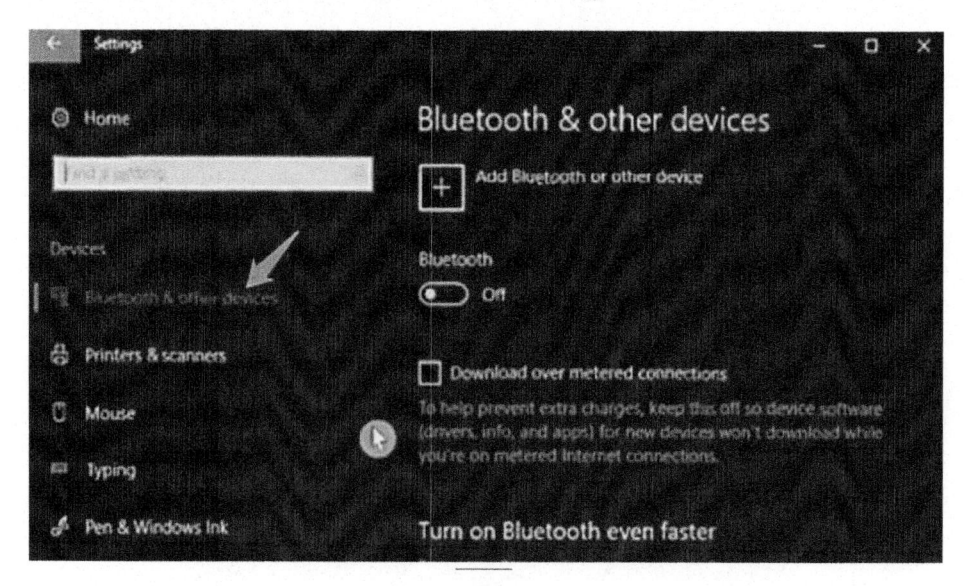

With the help of Microsoft Windows 10, Bluetooth possibility has been achieved on all Windows 10 software which makes external Bluetooth not needed. With Bluetooth, you can connect with another device without the need for a USB port or other means of connection such as a wireless keyboard, wireless audio player, and so on.

Printer & Scanner

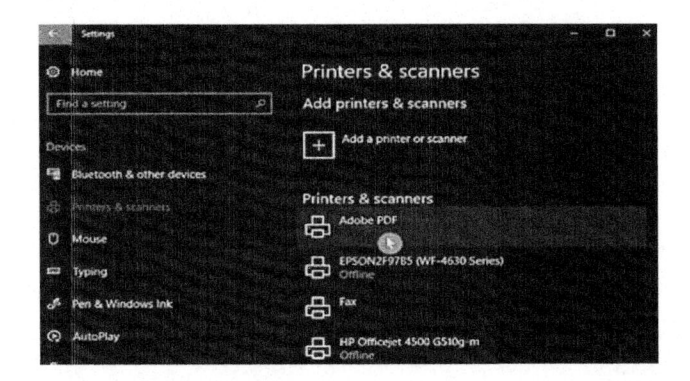

Printer & Scanner are external devices used to convert softcopy into hardcopy and also hardcopy into softcopy. The printer & Scanner can be connected to your PC in two ways; USB port and Wireless connection. This setting helps to control the Printer & Scanner activities on your PC.

Mouse

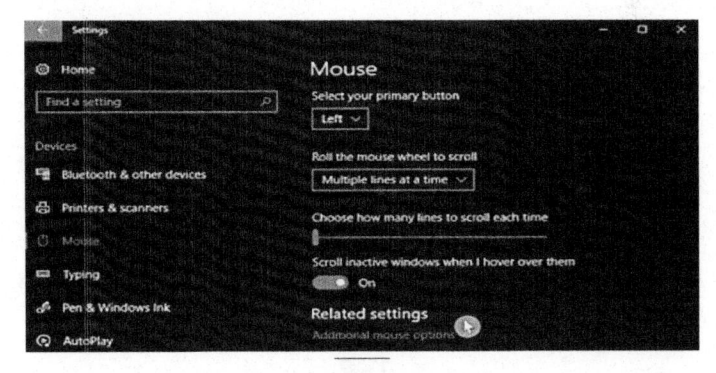

Mouse settings gives more access to how your mouse should operate on your PC such as primary button, scroll inactive while on hovering, changing of mouse sensor, and other advanced settings depending on its users' preference.

Typing

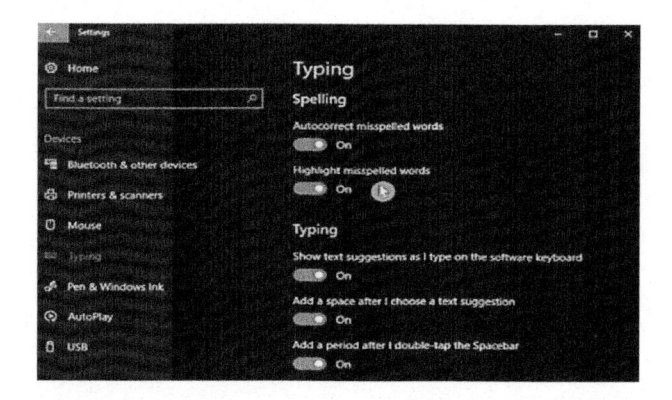

Typing settings enable its users to set choice preferences such as autocorrect misspelled words, highlight misspelled words, showing of text suggestion, adding of space after a text, and so on.

Pen & Windows Ink

Pen & Windows Ink settings are software suites designed for getting kinds of stuff done with pen in Windows 10 that contain applications and features oriented towards pen computing. The suite includes Sketchpad and Sticky Notes, Screen sketch applications. Its settings help to modify Windows Ink into its user's specialized needs.

AutoPlay

AutoPlay is a built-in feature to notify whenever activities are trying to seek permission for execution, most especially in a disc environment.

USB

USB Port setting enables you to get notified if issues are connecting to the USB device, only if you turn it on by ticking it.

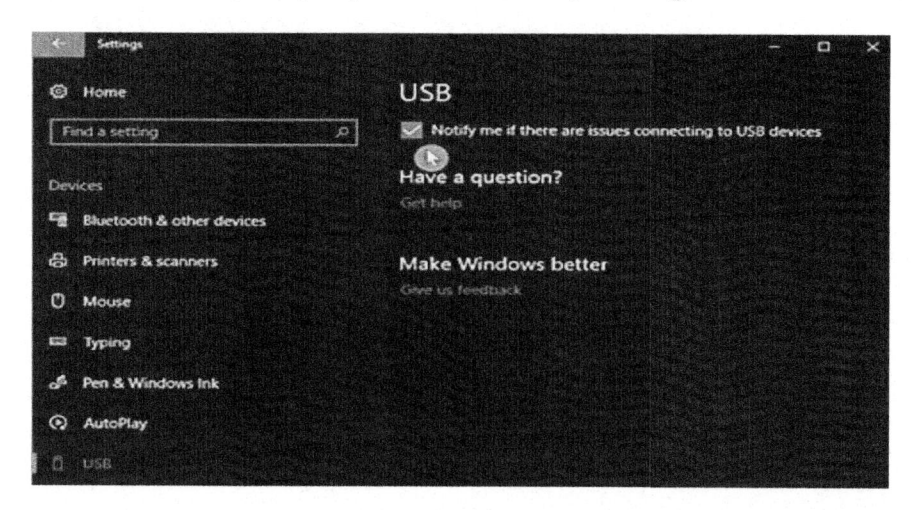

Phone

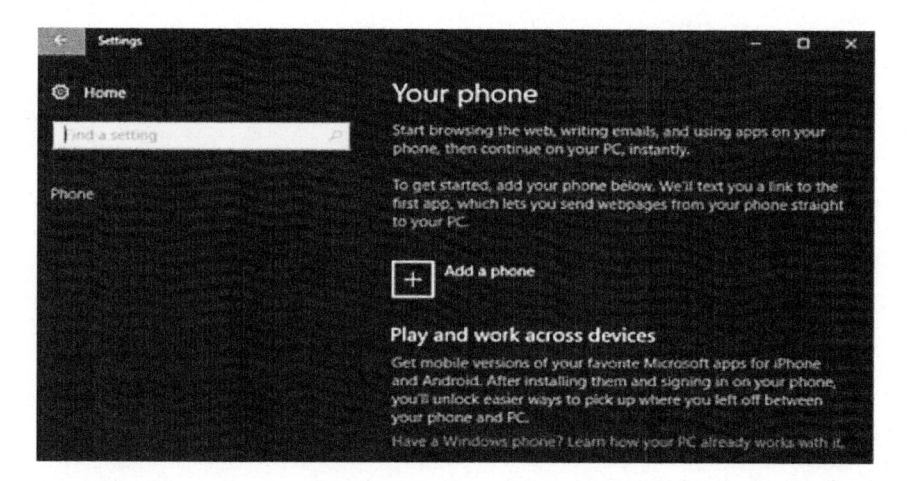

This is another amazing feature in Windows 10 that gives its users access to add phone devices that synchronize every activity on your PC into your phone and the other way round also for continuation from where you left off on your phone and PC.

Network & Internet

Network & Internet settings give access for modification of multiple options.

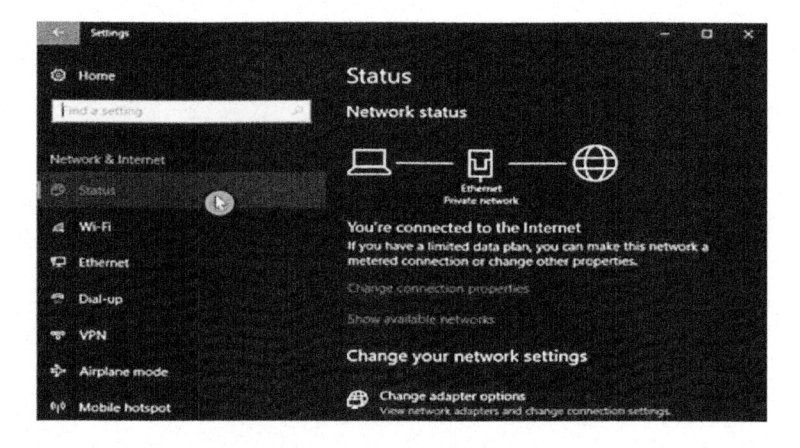

Status

It gives an overview of network connection, changes adapter options, sharing options, homegroup, and network troubleshooting.

WIFI

WIFI is a short name for Wireless fidelity; it is used for searching available internet access; its major aim is to give room for connectivity to be able to transmit data.

Ethernet

Ethernet is a way of connecting some computers to create a local area network (LAN). It has been the most generally used technique of linking computers together in LANs since the 1990s. The purpose for which it was designed is for multiple computers to have access to it and send data at any time.

Dial-Up

Dial-Up is another means of connecting your PC with the internet to surf the web; it is the opposite of Ethernet because Dial-Up never gives room for sharing. An example is a modem.

VPN

VPN is a short name for Virtual Private Network. It allows you to create a secured connection to another network over the Internet. VPNs can be used to become anonymous, access restricted country websites, shield your browsing activity from the public watch, and also making its users untraceable. It is good but dangerous when used for an illegal act.

Airplane mode

Airplane mode gives access to disable the cellular wireless so you can't receive or send voice calls or text messages over cellular.

Mobile hotspot

A mobile hotspot is all about data transmission to available WIFI. With a mobile hotspot, other devices can easily be joined together.

Data usage

This is another great feature in Windows 10 which gives access for controlling data usage and other advanced settings.

Proxy

Proxy settings allow a middle-man to come between your web browser and another computer, called a server. A Proxy serves as a gateway between a local network and a large-scale network. The proxy server stores data and send it to your computer without going through the main server.

Personalization

Personalization is where you can make changes to the overall look of Windows 10.

Background

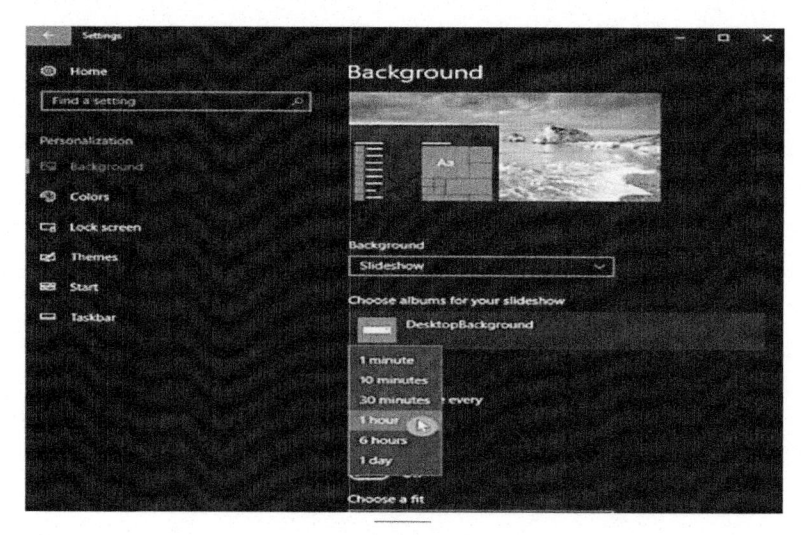

Background under personalization comes with a lot of features to be customized into users' preferences such as picture, solid color, slideshow, selection of albums for desktop background slideshow, changing of pictures on a certain time frame, and so on.

Colors

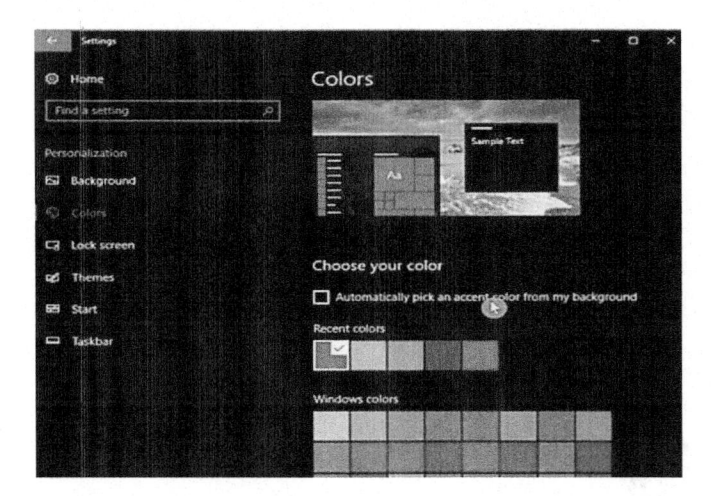

Colors under personalization give access to multicolor for user's preference. It also gives room for transparency effects, options for default apps mode color and contrast settings.

Lock screen

Still, under personalization, the lock screen enables its users to select a background image for lock screen mode such as Windows spotlight, picture, and slideshow.

Theme

Another interesting thing about personalization is that it also gives room for theme selection and downloading of themes from the Microsoft store which can be modified.

Taskbar

The taskbar is used for modification of space and selection of preferred options.

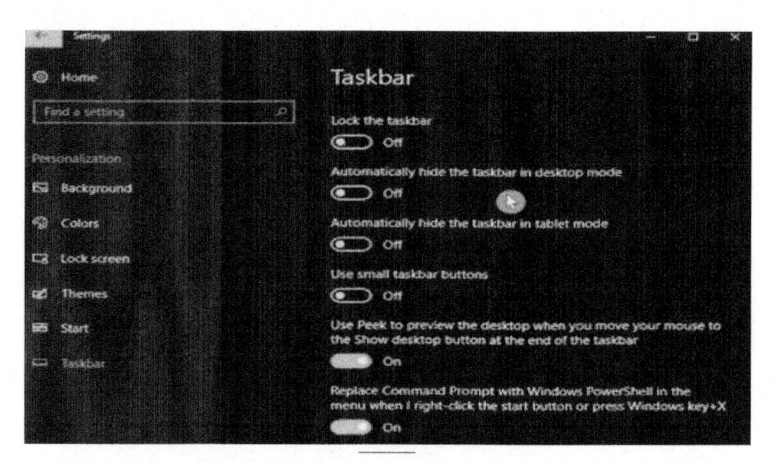

Apps & features

One of the uniqueness of Windows 10 is the freedom of choice; with apps settings, you can decide where your application can be downloaded from, but it is advisable to download any and everything under Microsoft store for the sake of your privacy. Many third-party applications outside of Microsoft gain unauthorized access into your privacy which might lead to fraudulent acts. Under Apps, you can see all installed applications on your PC which also gives access to uninstall any unwanted programs.

Default apps

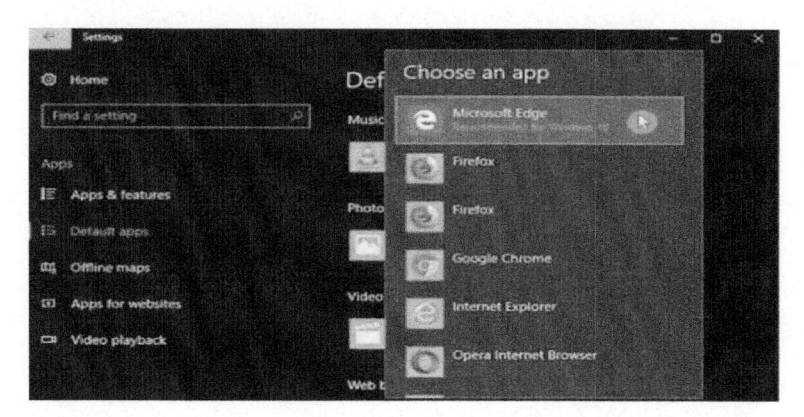

By choosing default apps, it automatically opens up different applications according to its specialization (protocol) such as web browser, maps, music, video, email, and so on. By default, Microsoft products always default in all features such as Microsoft Edge.

Accounts Settings

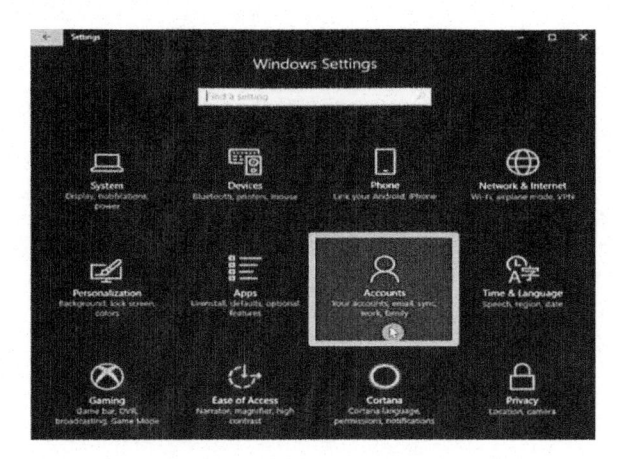

"Accounts" is an environment that gives its user the privilege of adding multiple accounts into a single system and also access control for children's usage.

Time & Language

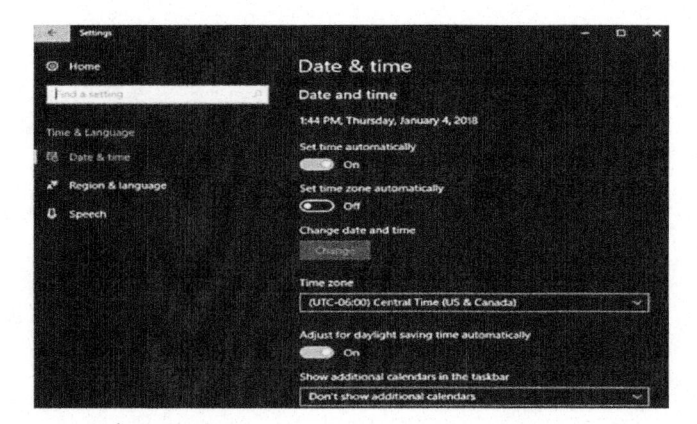

Date & Time

Date & time settings assist the user to adjust the date & time if not correct. Note that your selected region determines the correctness of your time while the date is general in all countries. These settings also enable its user to determine how the calendar should look like, DD-MM-YYYY, MM-DD-YYYY or YYYY-DD-MM, Y represents year, M represents month while D represents day.

Region & language

Region & language works hand in hand with date & time; your region must be selected correctly for a better experience with Windows 10 operating system. Language also matters; what you choose is how Windows will relate to you. The general language for all is English.

Speech
Speech is the one in charge of voice settings such as text to speech, speed of speech, speech recognition, and changing of voice.

Gaming

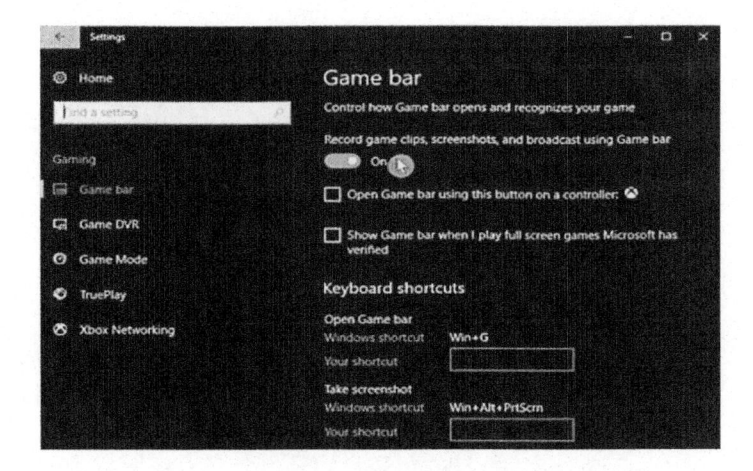

Game bar settings help to control how game bar opens and recognize your game, record game clips, screenshot, broadcast using the game bar, and also a keyboard shortcut for access to games.

Ease of Access

It is where you will like to go. If you are having difficulty with your hearing, seeing or, working with your keyboard or mouse, just select one of the categories on the left side that you think will help you out and adjust the settings

Cortana

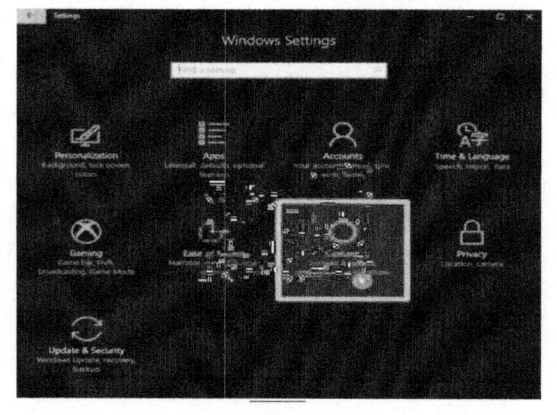

Cortana is a personal assistant that processes your request and responds immediately; mainly, it is structured to get things done by scheduling, reminding, finding facts and, lots more. With Cortana, you can accomplish anything; all that is required is to speak. For a better experience, connect your PC to the internet.

Privacy Settings

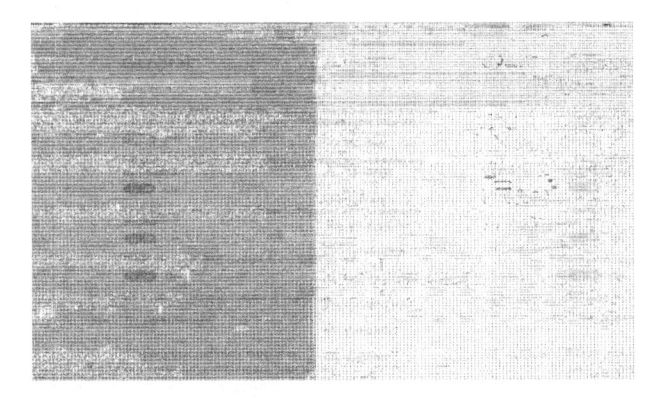

The Privacy setting is designed to select what should give you notifications and what you don't want to pop up such as adverts, tracking of applications, suggested content, managing your information that is stored in the cloud, access authorization, call history, account info and a lot more options.

Update & Security

Update & Security are mainly for windows update and protection against malicious software, files and, unknown extensions.

Windows Update

As mentioned above, it is also used to reschedule update hours whenever its user has other things to do and doesn't want to automatically turn off the PC. You can also determine when to restart your PC by selecting **Restart options** and set it the way you prefer.

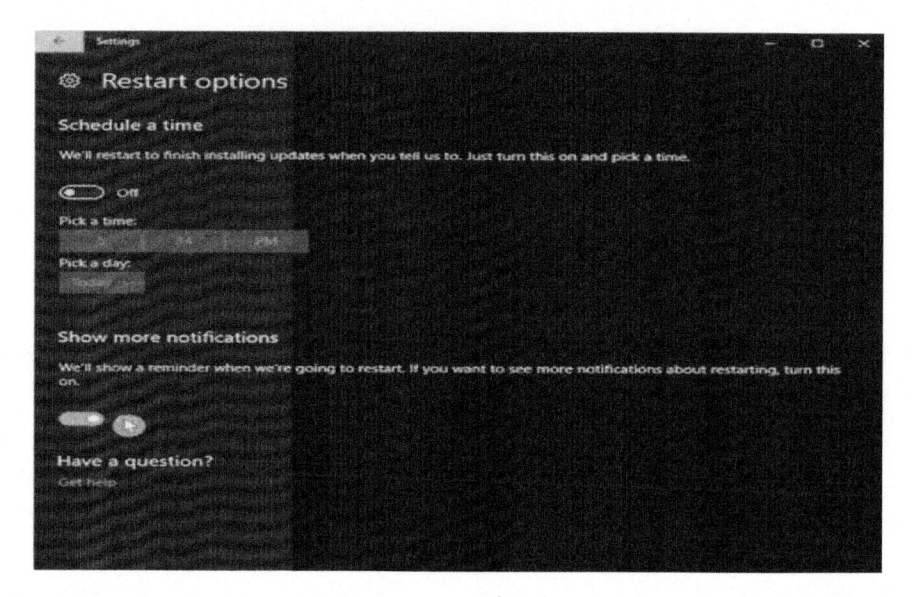

CHAPTER NINE

ENHANCING YOUR PC PERFORMANCE

How to Speed Up Your Windows 10

There are many options towards speeding up your PC for better performance which are:

i. **Ultimate Performance**

Your Windows 10 PC has a speed setting that is responsible for your PC performance.

Step 1

Go to your PC start menu, click on **settings** or, type "Settings" on the search bar.

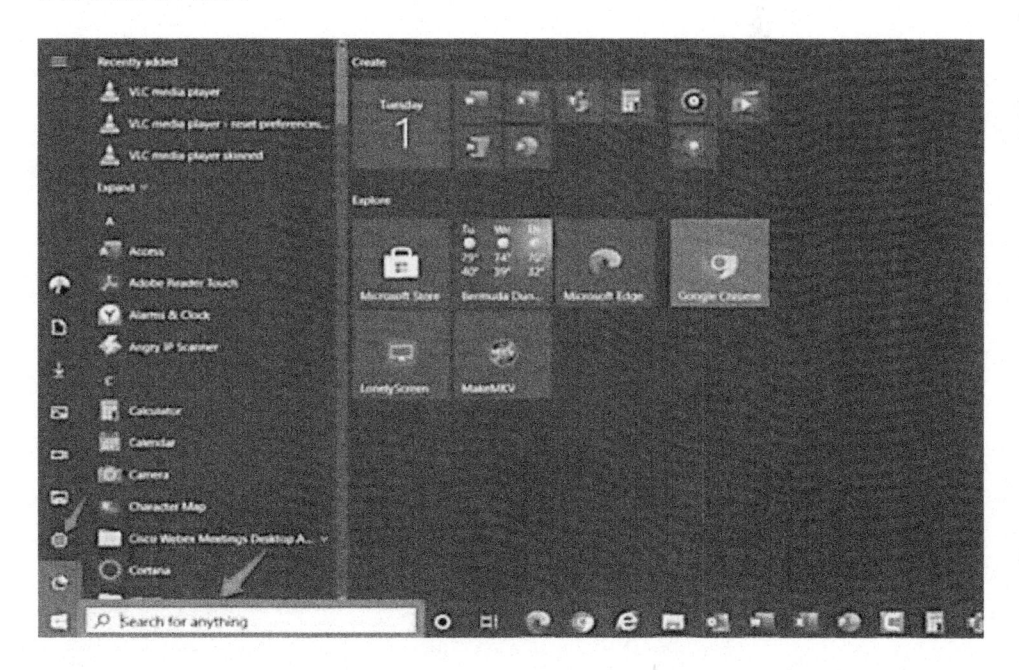

Step 2

Select "System".

Step 3

Select "Power & sleep"; over to the right, click on "Additional power settings"

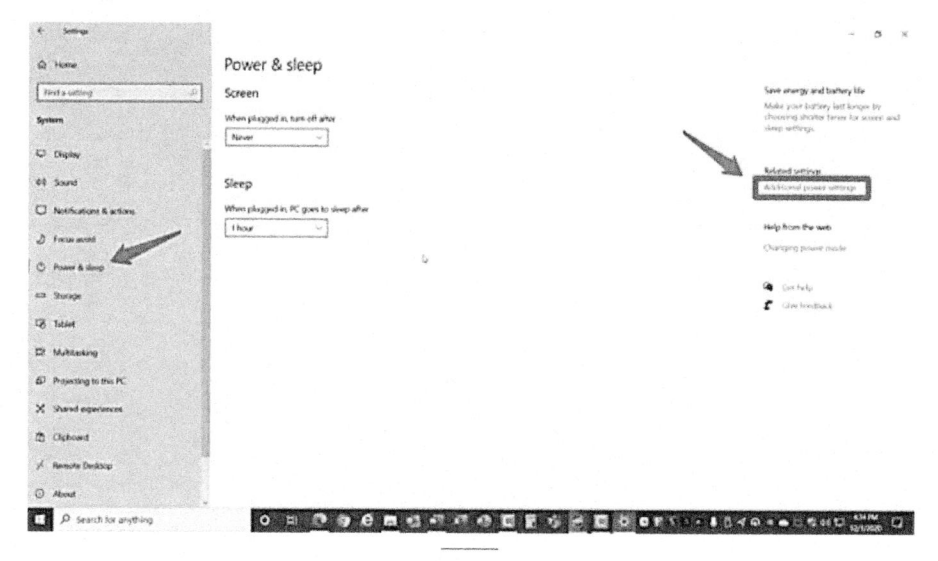

Step 4

A dialog box of "Power Options" will pop up, you will be given a list of additional power saving options to improve the speed or the power saving consumption. Select *"Ultimate Performance"* if available in the list, otherwise select *"High Performance".* That will maximize the speed of your computer at the expense of the power consumption (battery).

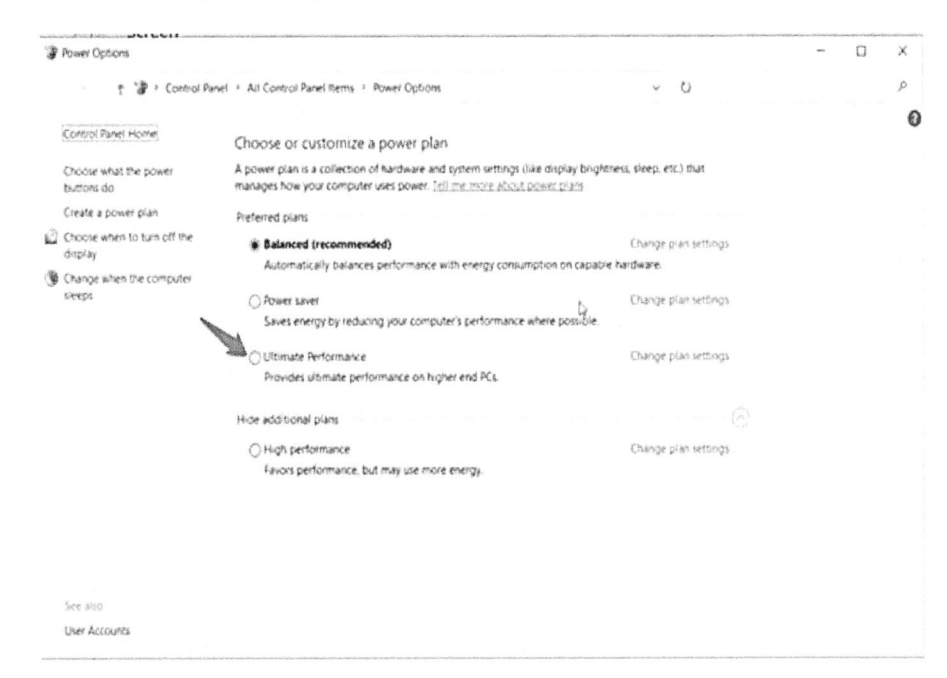

ii. **Advanced System Settings**

In case the *"Ultimate Performance"* is not giving you up to what you want, you can proceed in the *"Advanced System Settings"* by following the steps below:

Step 1

Click on your "Start menu".

167

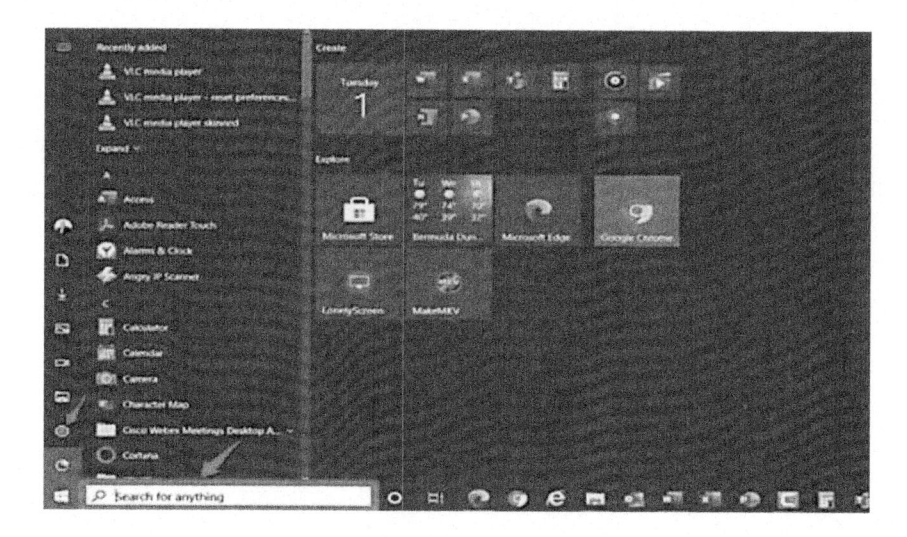

Step 2

Click on "Settings" and select "System".

Step 3

Select "About"; on the right-hand side, choose "Advanced system settings".

168

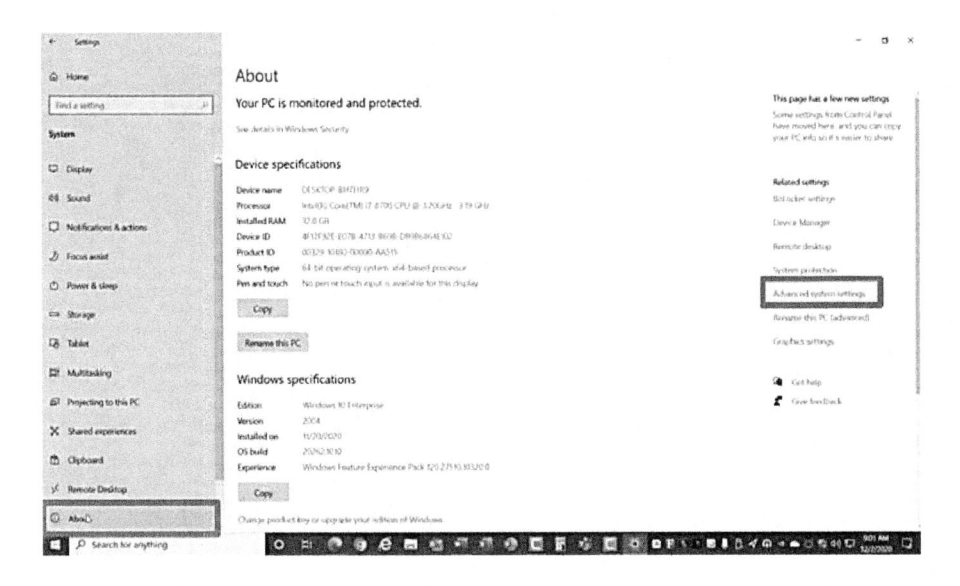

Step 4

Under "Advanced system settings", click on "settings".

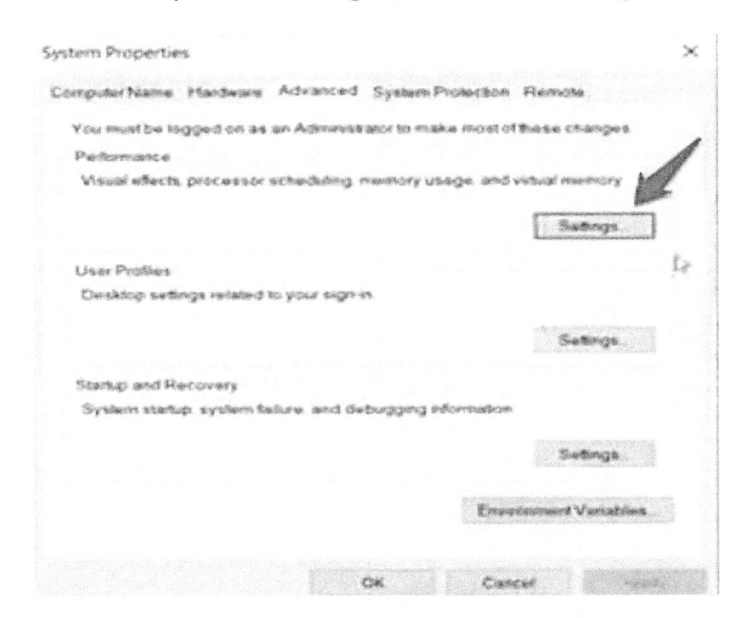

This results in 3 options under **Visual Effects:**

169

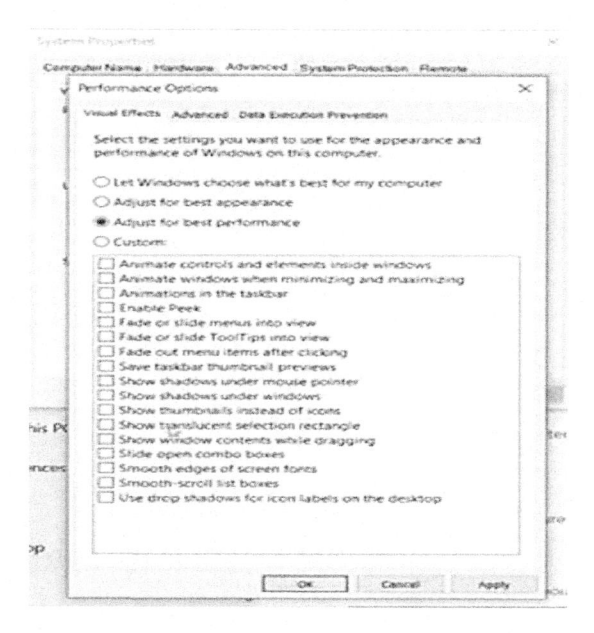

- "Let Windows choose what's best for my computer"
- "Adjust for best appearance"
- "Adjust for best performance"

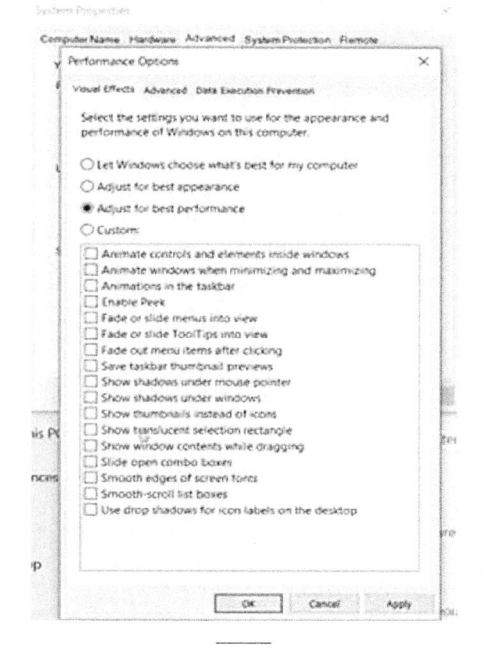

You can choose the last option *"Adjust for best performance"* and I recommend that you also tick *"Smooth edges of screen fonts"* and *"Show thumbnail instead of icons"*, this will automatically change it from Adjust for best performance to *"Custom"*.

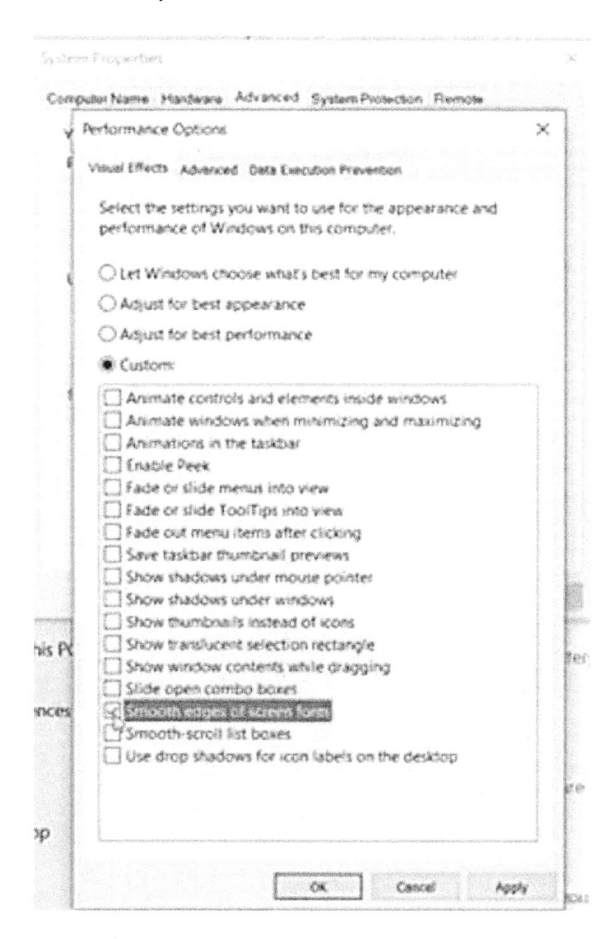

Step 5

Click on *"Advanced"* under the "Advanced" tab, make sure "Adjust for best performance" is set as *"Programs"* rather than *"Background services"* that will keep your foreground applications running, and then click "OK".

171

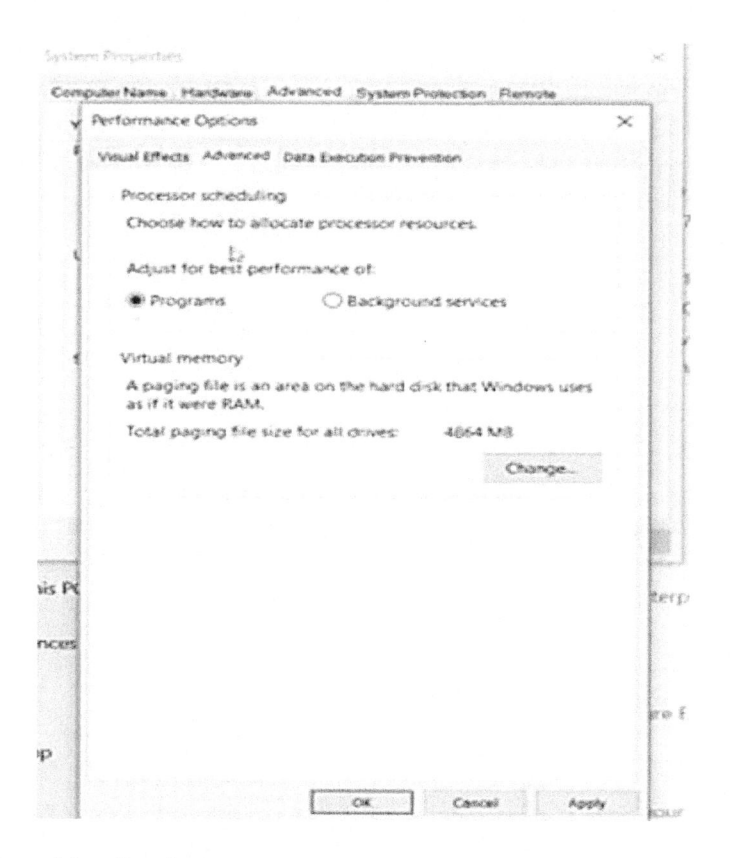

iii. Graphics Performance

Graphics performance deals with your graphics display interface for better performance, how to enhance your graphics performance; below are some steps:

Step 1

Go to your PC *"Settings"*.

Step 2

Click on *"Display"* on the left, scroll down on the right side to the bottom and, select (click) *"Graphics settings"*.

Step 3

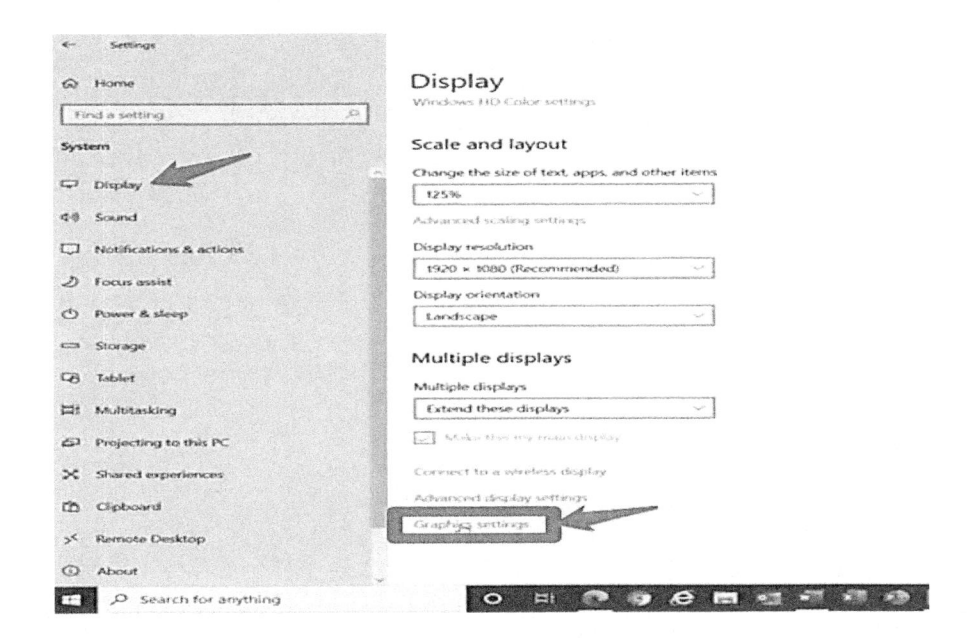

In Graphics settings, select (click) **"Change default graphics settings".**

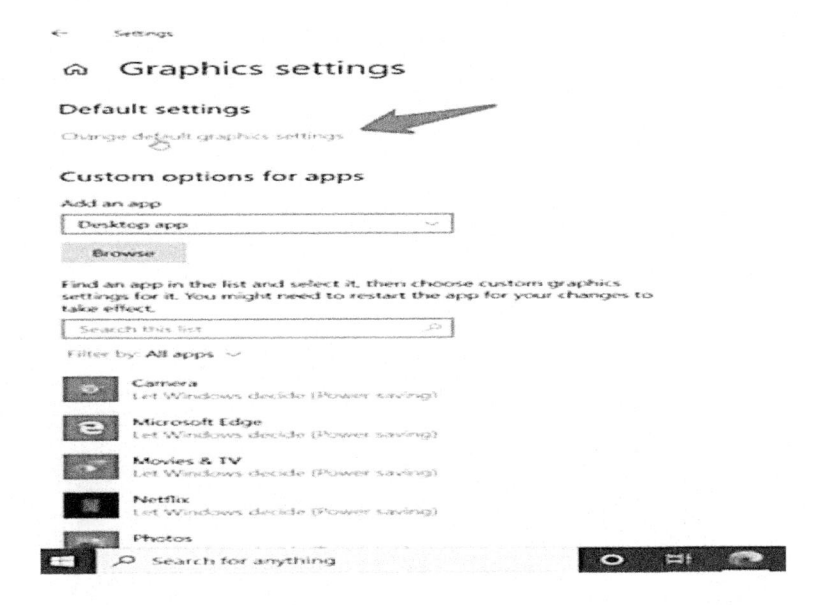

173

Step 4

Under Default graphics settings, turn the tick box on, which in turn will take advantage of the GPU acceleration of your graphics adaptor.

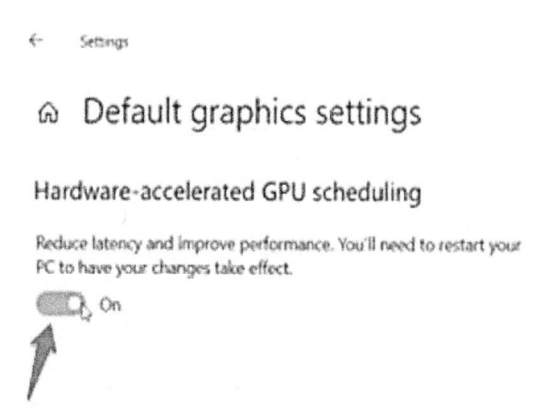

Step 5

Go back to Step 3 (Change default graphics settings), this time, don't click on it, just scroll down, click on one of the applications and, select "options" as illustrated below:

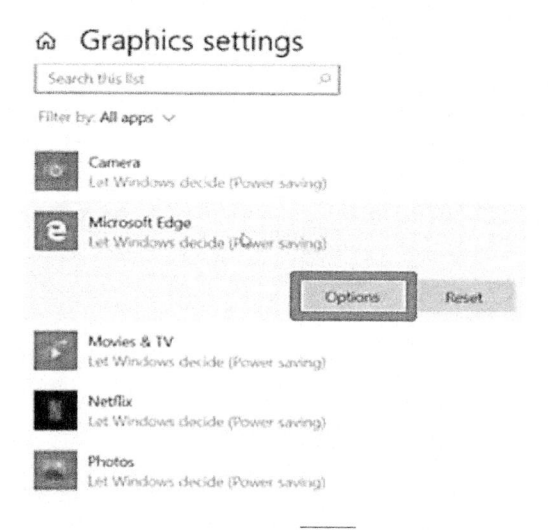

Step 6

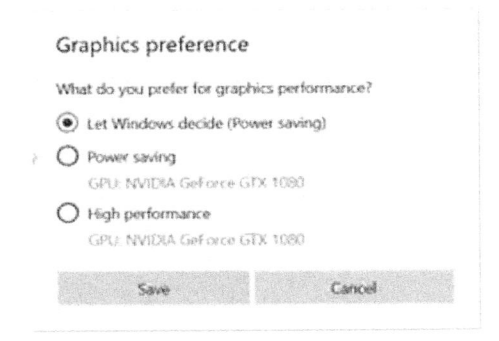

A dialog box will pop up immediately you click on "options" as illustrated above. The new displayed box will show **"Graphics preference"** select **"High performance"** which gives you the privilege to manually select installed applications for better graphics performance, then **"Save"**.

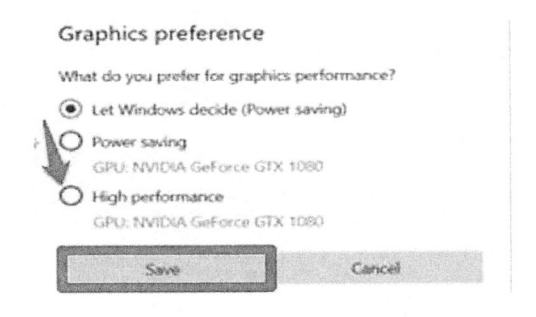

Step 7

You can also add other applications not listed into *"All Apps"* by clicking on *"Browse"* and locate the application and click on *"Add"*.

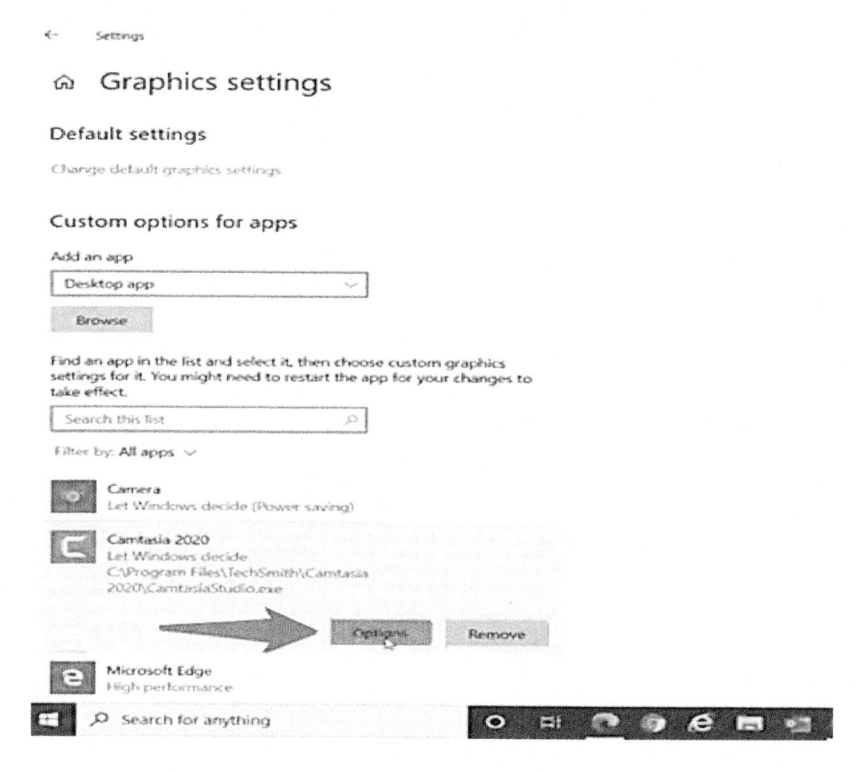

Once it has been added, apply Step 5 & Step 6 by repeating the same process.

These processes will ensure you are using the fastest graphics adaptor on your computer.

iv. **System Configuration**

   Step 1

   Go to *"Start menu",* search for *"Windows Administrative Tools"* in the search box

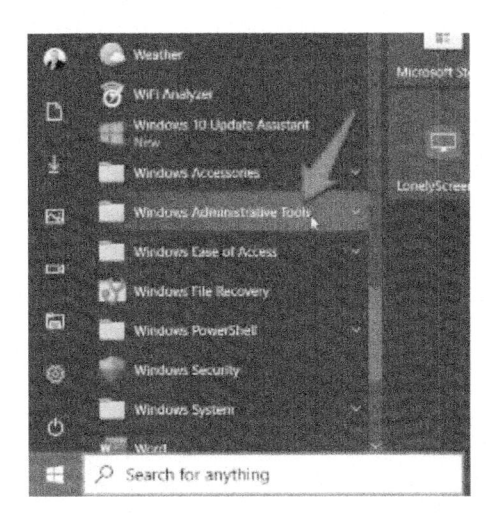

Step 2

Under ***"Windows Administrative Tools",*** search for ***"System Configuration"*** and open it.

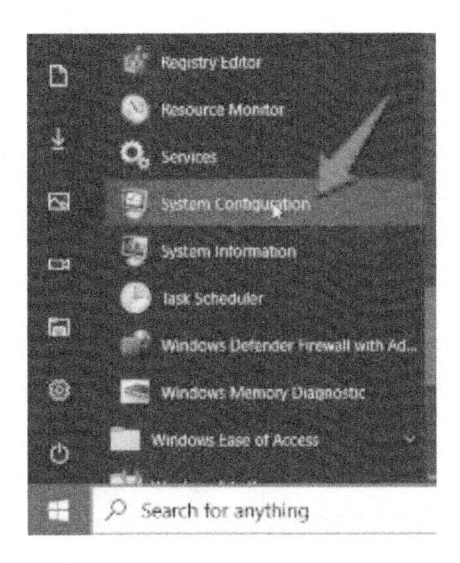

Step 3

In ***"System Configuration",*** select "boot" and tick "No GUI boot", which gives your system fast optimization in booting.

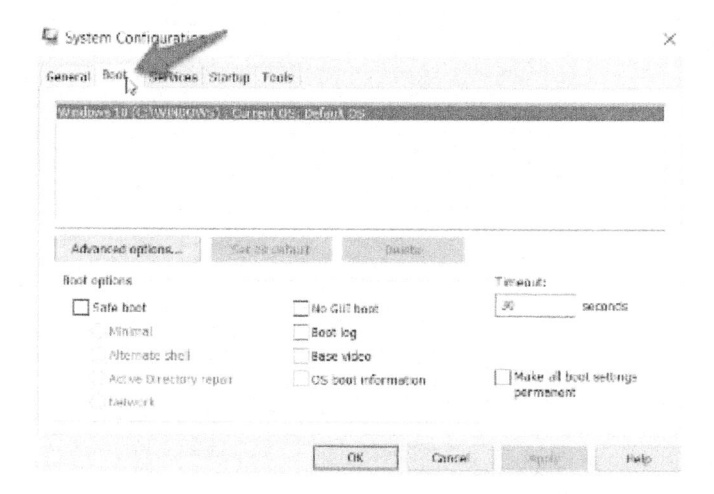

Step 4

Also, click on *"Advanced options"*.

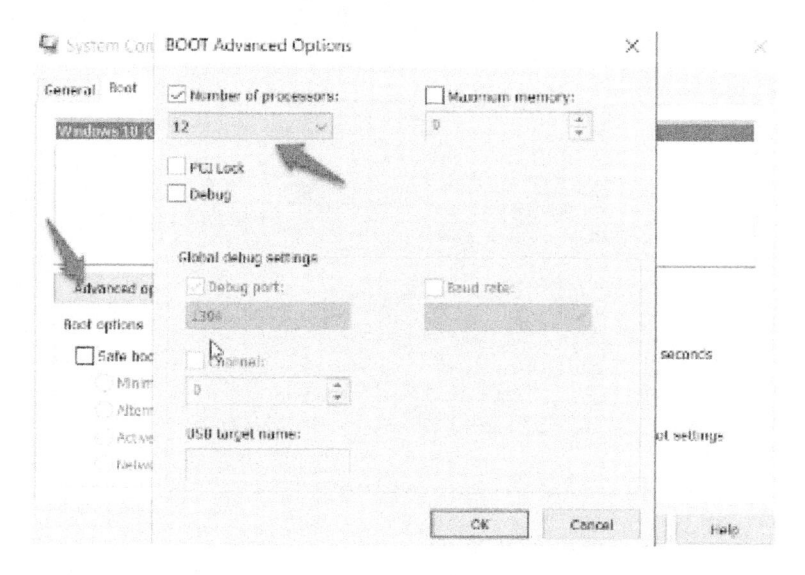

Step 5

Make sure your *"Number of processors"* is turned off and select the highest number of processors available; once done, press the "ok" key.

Step 6

Now, click on the "services" tab at the top as illustrated below.

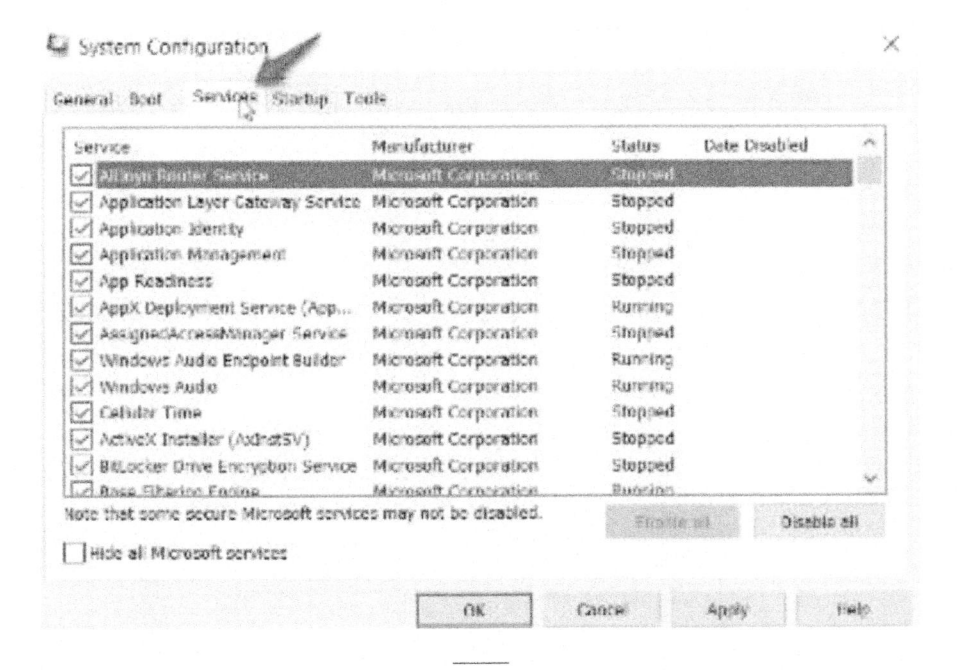

Step 7

Hide all the Microsoft services by ticking the box as illustrated below, then look through the list if any services are running that you know you don't need; once you notice any, you can turn them off so that they won't be part of your system when you turn on your computer.

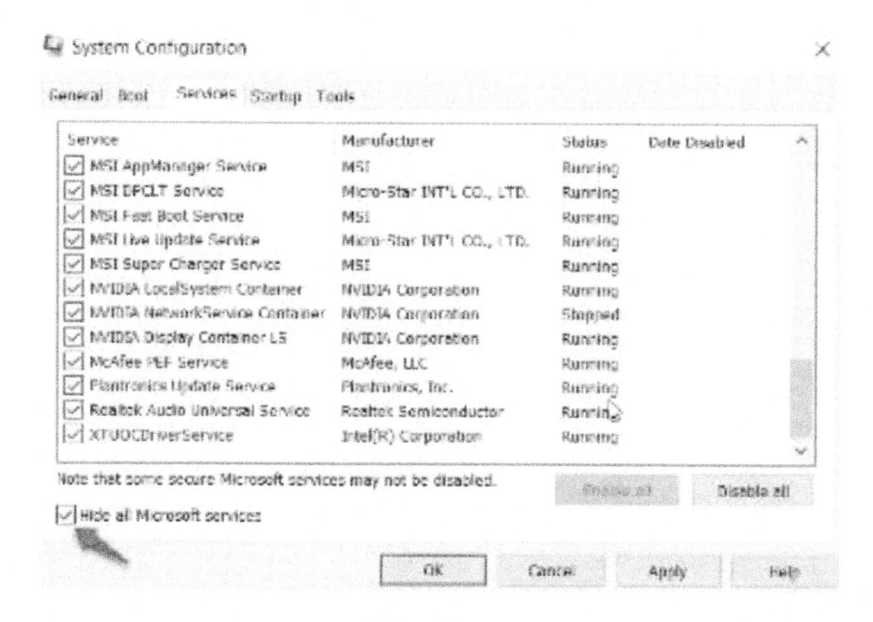

Step 8

When you are done, press "OK" which will prompt you to restart your computer. Restart now if you want to execute those changes.

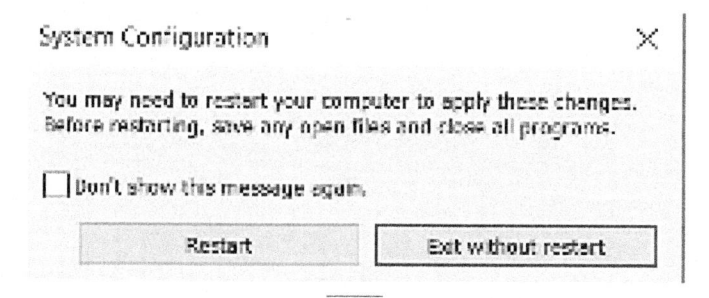

v. **Privacy Settings**

There are some features under "Privacy settings" that can slow down your operating system. Turn them off following the steps below:

> *Stage 1*
>
> Go to privacy under ***"Settings"***

Stage 2

Turn off "advertising ID", "accessing my language", "windows track app", and "suggested content for better performance".

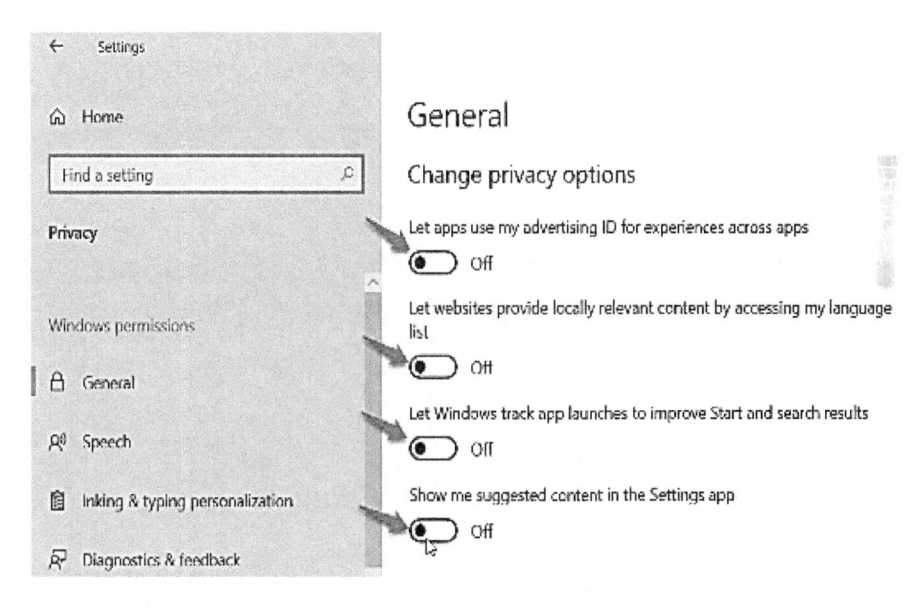

Stage 3

Click on ***"Diagnostics & feedback",*** turn it off and, also turn off ***"Tailored experiences";*** this eliminates the collection of diagnostics data which can slow your PC.

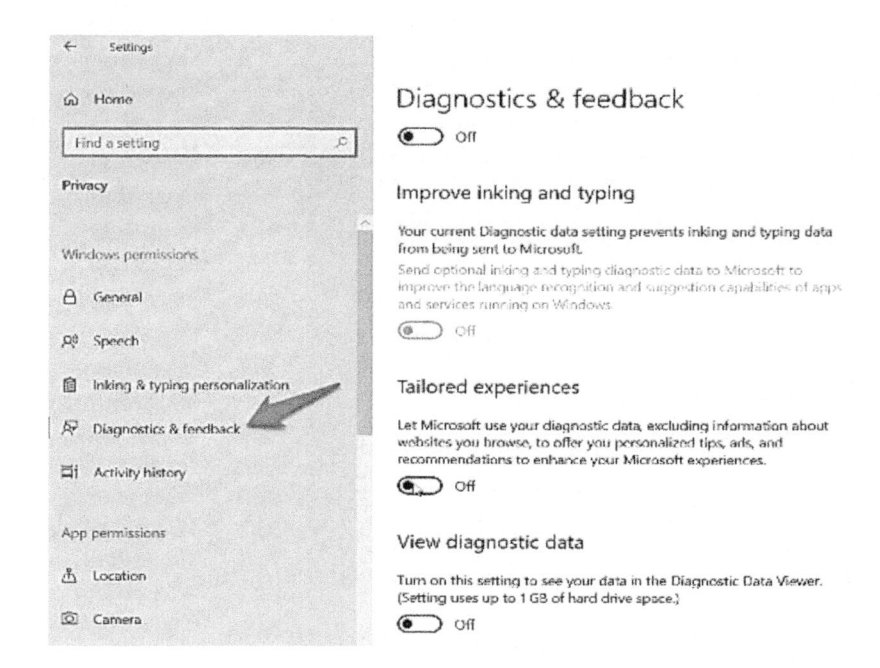

vi.   Disk Cleanup

It is very important to know the effect of disc cleaning on your PC; it helps to eliminate unwanted files downloaded by default while browsing through the internet and other files stored by installed applications such as temp files, prefetch files and, others. Disk cleanup enhances the computer's performance.

Stage 1

Go to the Start menu, search for *"Disk Cleanup"*

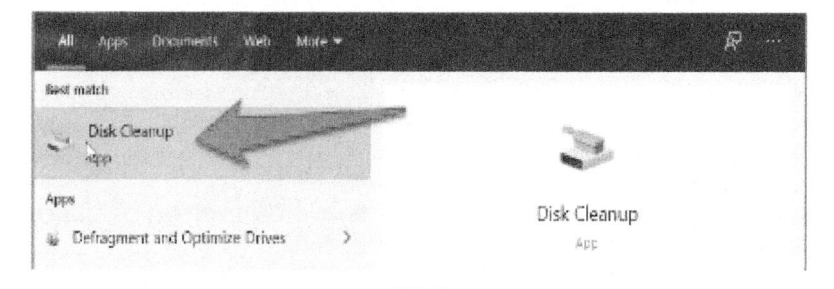

Stage 2

A default dialog box will pop up, click "ok" (Make sure it shows the part of your hard drive) Windows (C:)

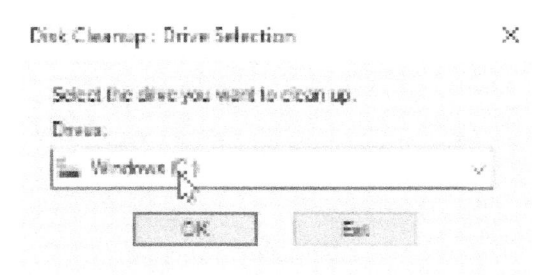

Stage 3

You will see another dialog box indicating the amount of space been used; select *"Clean up system files"* and choose your default hard drive which is "Windows (C:)"

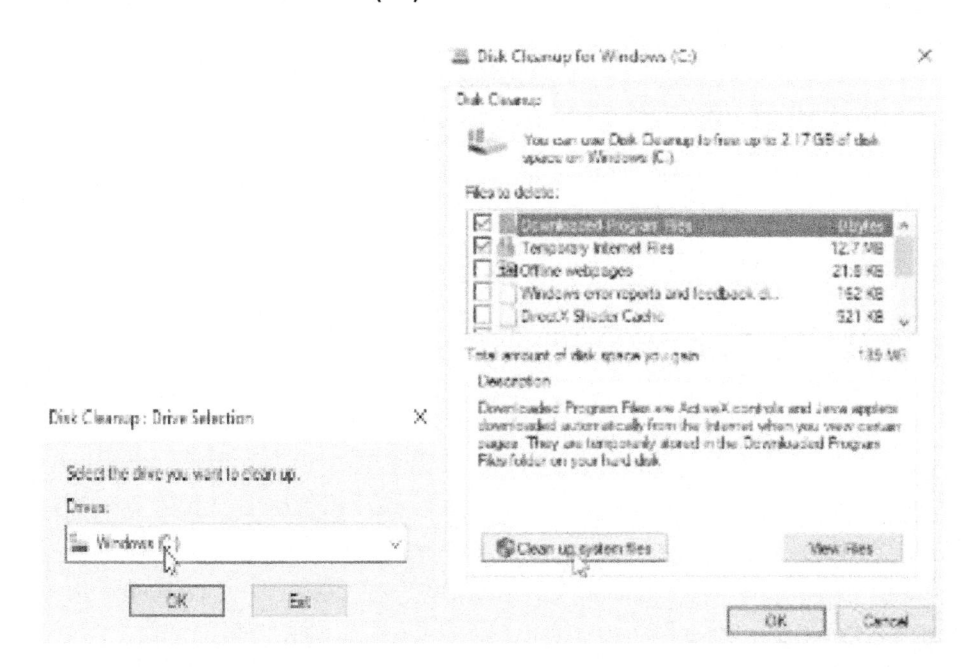

183

Stage 4

The process of cleaning up will commence immediately. Once it is done, tick "unwanted files" and press "OK "to permanently delete them and free up space on your PC.

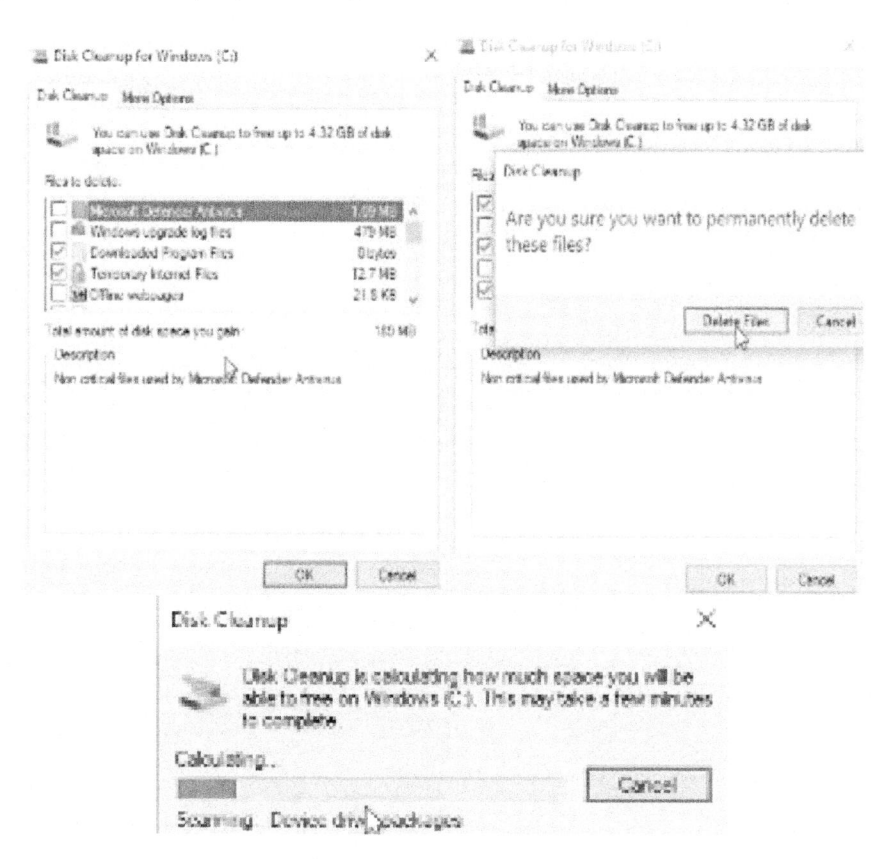

vii. Remove Desktop Shortcuts

If you have a screen like this with a million icons on it, this will slow down the performance of your computer every time windows switches between applications or different windows which have to reload all these icons. If you want to increase your PC performance, remove them or move them into another folder on your desktop to avoid all of these loadings whenever you're switching windows.

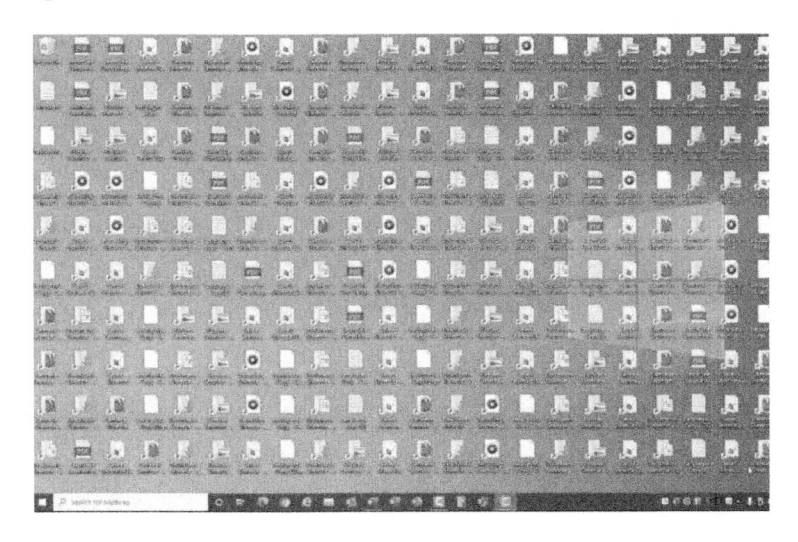

viii.   **Delivery Optimization**

For more speed on your operating system, go to *"settings"*, choose *"Update & Security"*.

Stage 1

Click on "Update & Security", and select *"Delivery Optimization"*; on the right-hand side, turn off the *"Allow downloads from other PCs"*.

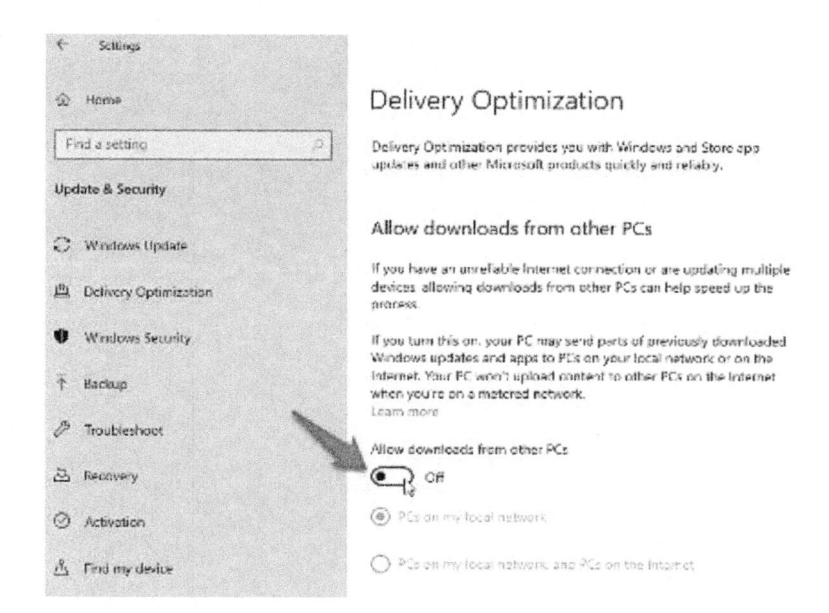

Stage 2

Go to *"Advanced options"* to also turn off advanced settings or turn it on and reduce its consumption rate.

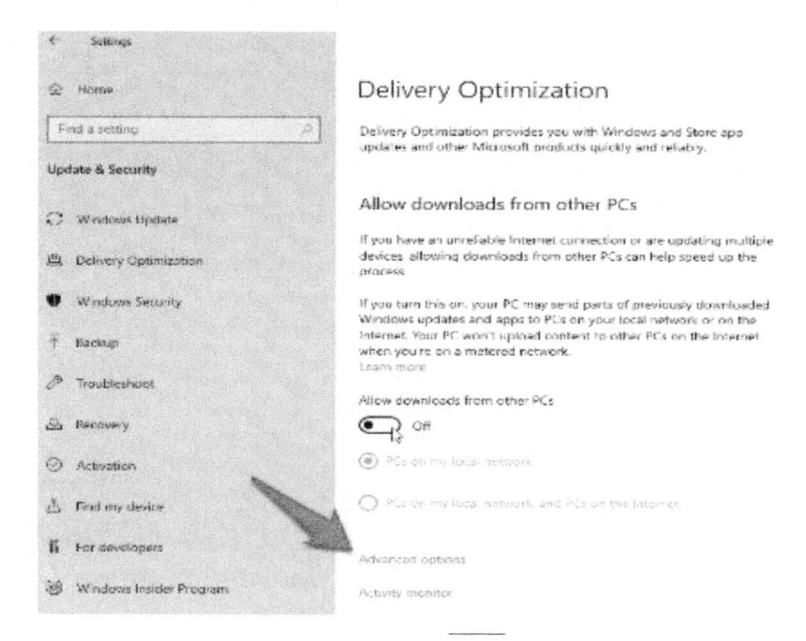

← Settings

⌂ Advanced options

◉ Absolute bandwidth

☐ Limit how much bandwidth is used for downloading updates in the background

   [1] Mbps

☐ Limit how much bandwidth is used for downloading updates in the foreground

   [5] Mbps

◯ Percentage of measured bandwidth (measured against the update source)

☐ Limit how much bandwidth is used for downloading updates in the background

   ——————●—————— 45%

☐ Limit how much bandwidth is used for downloading updates in the foreground

   ————————●———— 90%

Upload settings

☑ Limit how much bandwidth is used for uploading updates to other PCs on the Internet

●——————————————— 5%

☑ Monthly upload limit

●——————————————— 5 GB

Note: when this limit is reached, your device will stop uploading to other PCs on the Internet.

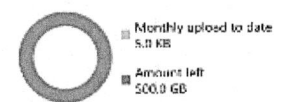

  Monthly upload to date
  5.0 KB

  Amount left
  500.0 GB

187

CHAPTER TEN

TROUBLESHOOTING WINDOWS 10

How to Treat Windows Unexpected Issues

Windows reset enables Windows users to return to their normal state of operation. Windows reset enhances the operating system to an early state condition.

Method 1

Go to "settings", click on "Update & Security".

Select "Recovery", and by the right-hand side, choose "Reset this PC" which gives you the privilege to restore every misbehavior on your PC, click on "Get started" as indicated below.

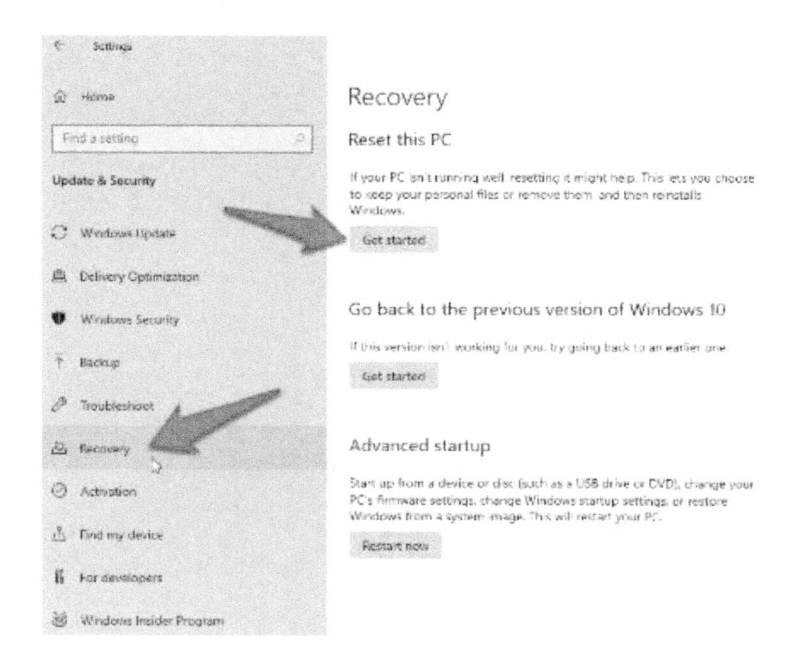

Once you are through with the stage 2 process, you will be brought here. You'll be given two options to choose from, "Keep my files" which removes apps, and settings, but keeps your files, and "Remove everything" which removes all your files, apps, and settings". It is highly recommended to choose "Keep my files" because applications can be easily downloaded back, but your files' data might not be recovered back, except if you do not need them.

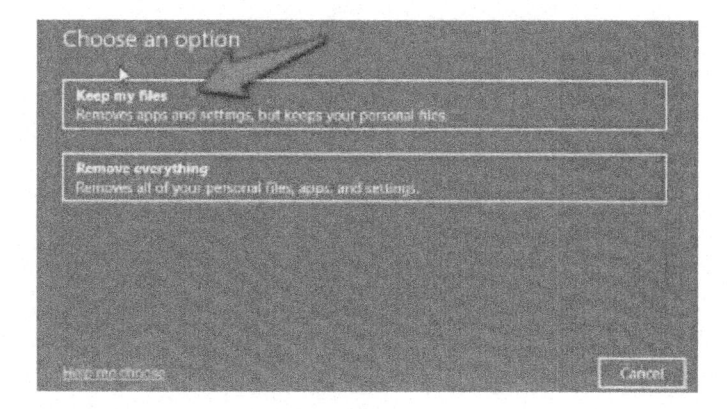

189

Method 2

You can also use another similar method to reset your PC. Resetting of PC is similar to smartphone factory settings, just that in PC, your information remains intact. Windows is designed in such a way that in itself, you can restore your operating system into an earlier state which is majorly known as "system restore point". To achieve this, go to your *"start menu"* and type *"system restore".*

The search bar will automatically search it out.

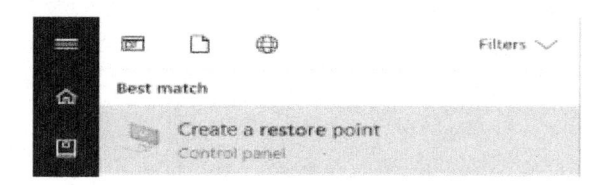

If you left-click on "Create a restore point", a dialog box will pop up.

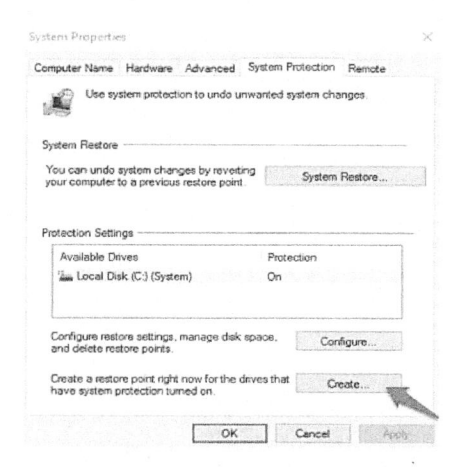

You will see your active Disk turned on for protection, click on **"Create"**.

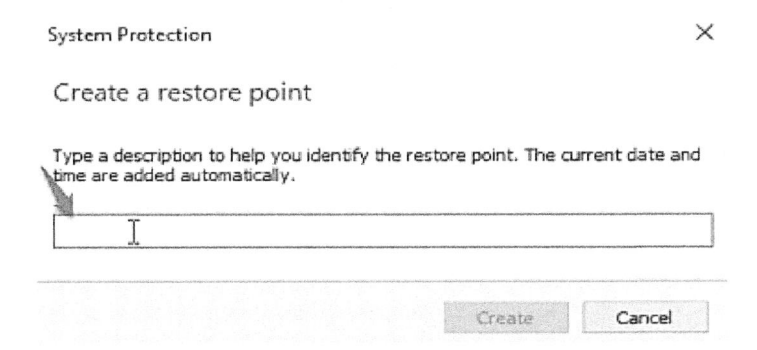

Write the name of your restore point and click on the "Create button", which will create and save the system restore point.

You can also "Configure" restore settings and also manage disk space. Click on **"Configure"**.

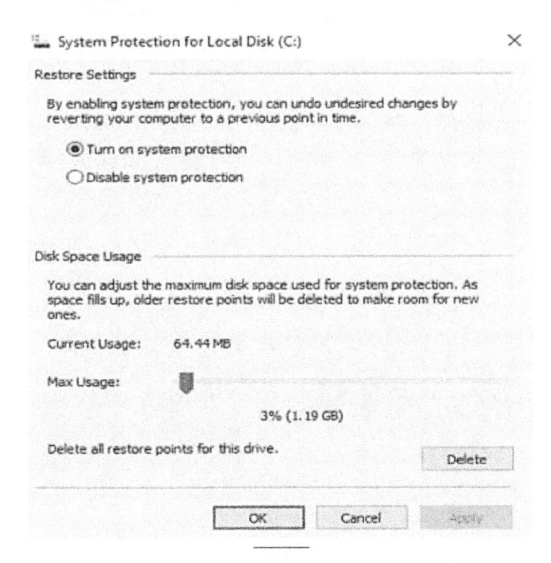

Make sure your System Protection is always turned on, which gives the privilege to always restore the system to an easier state. You can also assign capacity storage for your restored point; this space must not be more than your total hard disk.

To Undo System Settings and Files to an Earlier State

Click on *"System Restore"* under "Create a restore point" as illustrated below:

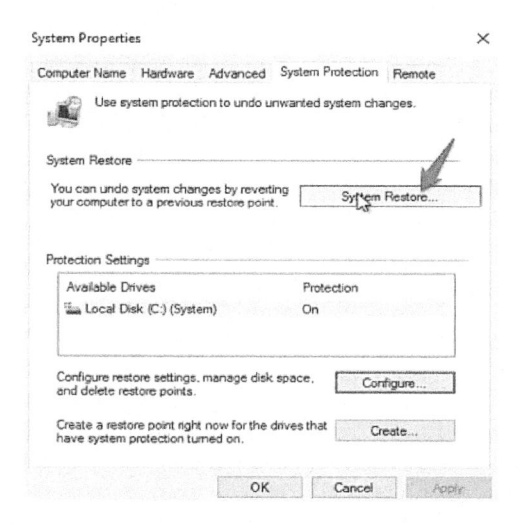

A dialog box will be shown to you which will process your system restore point for you to decide which restore point will be best for you.

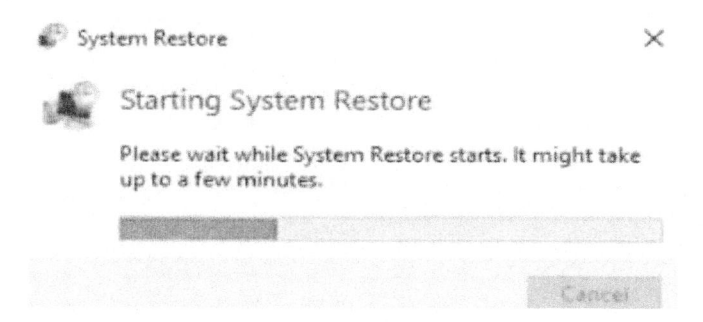

192

With the "System Restore", your system can gain more stability and enhancement of performance; click on "Next" to proceed.

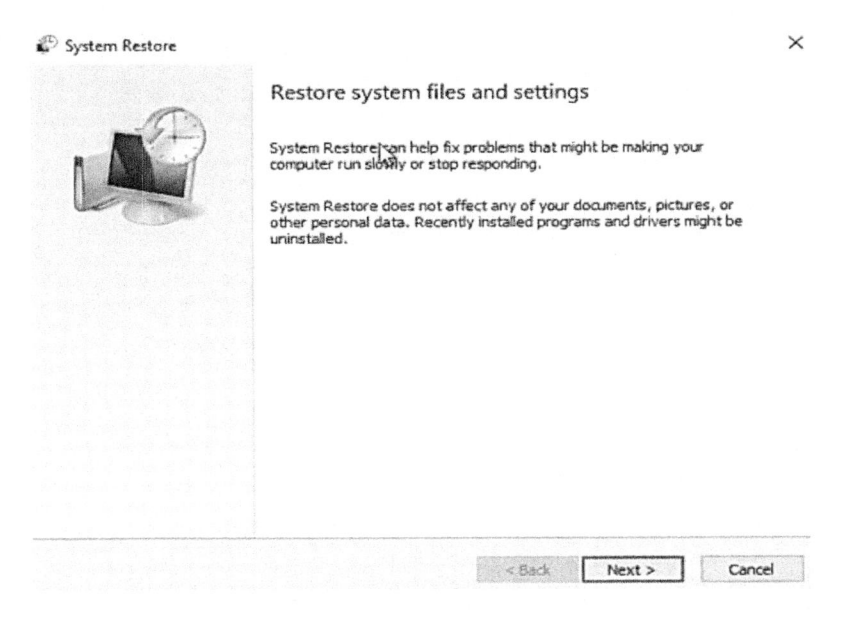

You will be brought here to choose your preferred restore point, by using date or description to identify it.

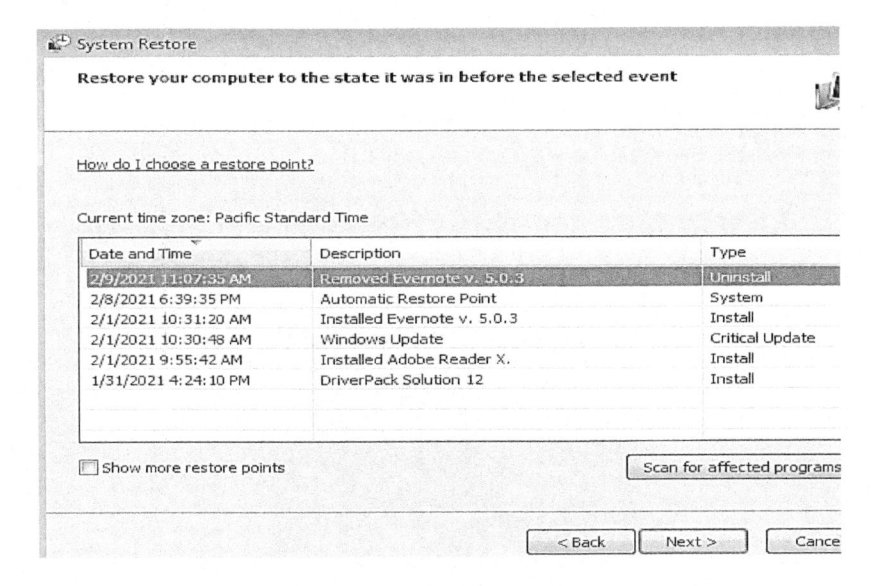

193

The next stage will tell you to confirm your action, kindly click on "finish".

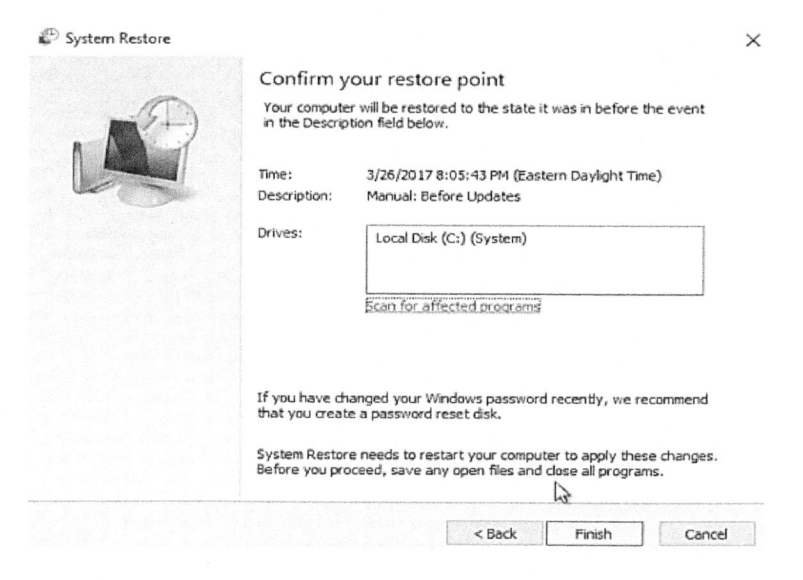

Method 3

You can also make use of this method to handle any malfunctioning surfacing in your PC if methods 1 & 2 are not solving it. Kindly follow these steps.

Go to "Start menu", right-click on the "power button"; three (3) options will be shown to you; sleep, shut down and restart.

Hold on the **Shift key** from your keyboard, don't remove your hand from your shift key button then click on ***"Restart".***

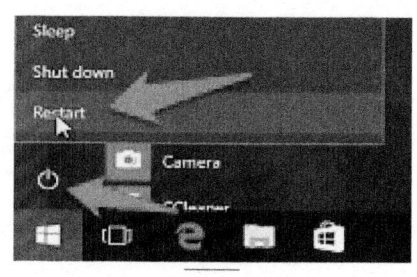

This will launch the troubleshooting utility (still hold on shift key from your keyboard) until "troubleshooting options" appear.

Once you can see *"Choose an option"* (still holding on the shift key button on your keyboard), then you can now click on **"Troubleshoot"**.

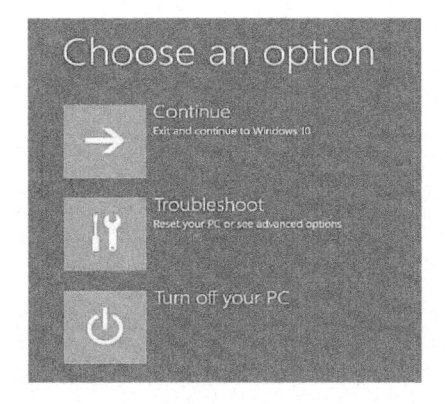

By clicking on troubleshoot, you will be brought here, then select *"Advanced options"*

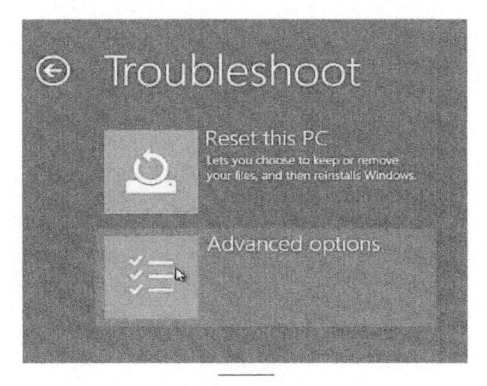

Click on the *"System Restore"* option which will lead to your PC restoration point.

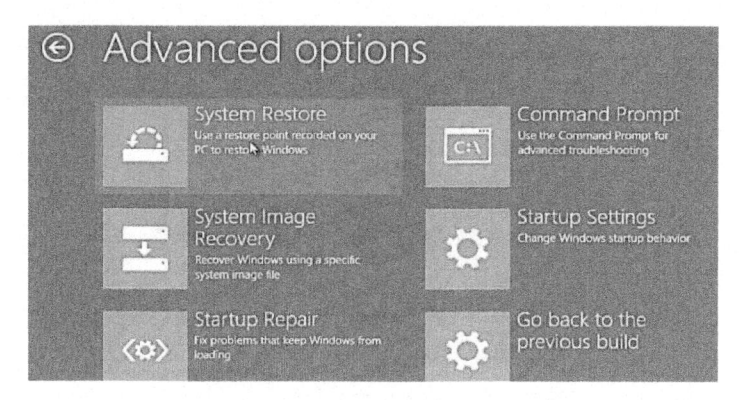

Next windows will load the "system restore".

To complete system restoration, you must log in to your PC; if your account is not showing kindly click on the "don't see your account" option below. Note that only an administrator can perform this process, a standard user can't undo anything without the administrator's permission.

Next, type in your password to proceed with your restoration.

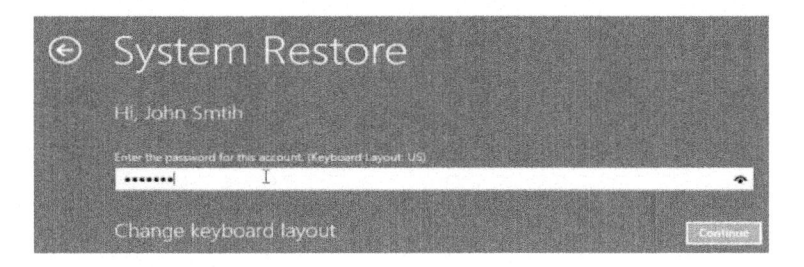

Initializing of your system restoration.

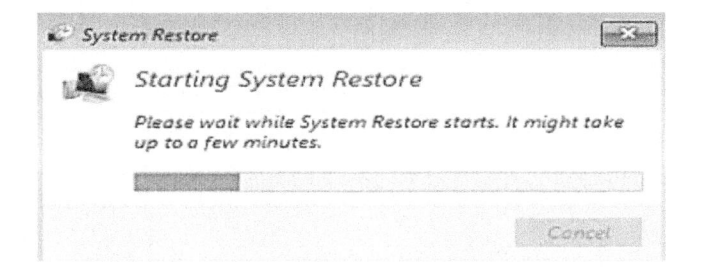

Here, you will be told about system restoration purpose, *system restore can help fix problems that might be making your computer run slowly or stop responding. System restore does not affect any of your documents, pictures or, other personal data. Only recently installed programs and drives might be uninstalled.* kindly click on "Next".

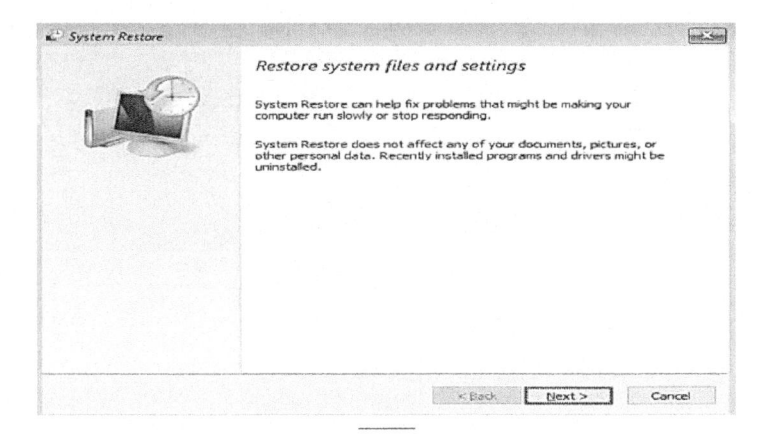

197

Kindly click on *"Show more restore points"* to decide which point to backdate your PC.

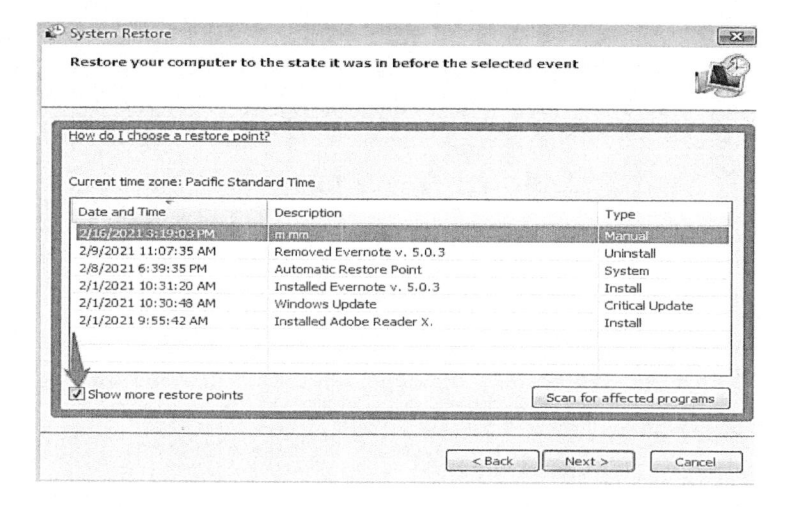

The next stage will tell you to confirm your restore point before clicking on "Finish" to finalize it.

Note: if you have changed your Windows password recently, it is recommended that you create a password reset disk.

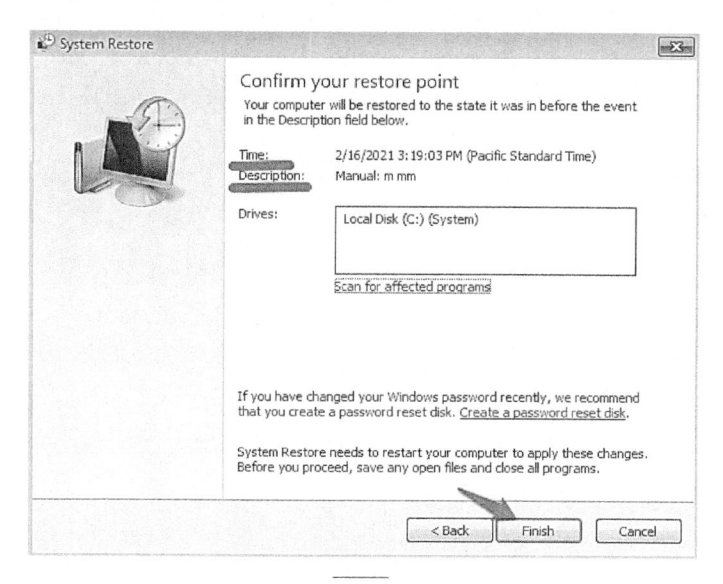

A dialog box will pop up instructing you that once you proceed by clicking "Yes", it can't be reversed.

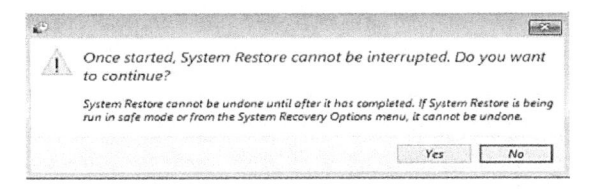

System restoration finalizing.

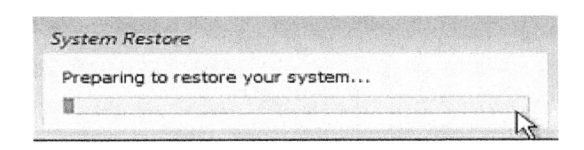

Initializing.

Restoring files in progress.

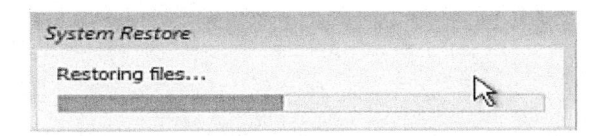

Finalizing file restoration might take much time depending on your PC.

Finished.

Restoration completed, click on "restart" to restart your PC, for full restoration effect.

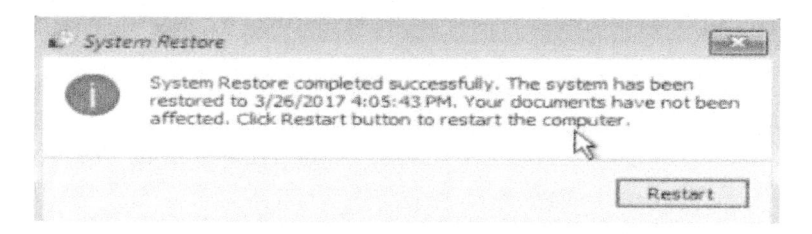

Once you restart your PC, login with your password

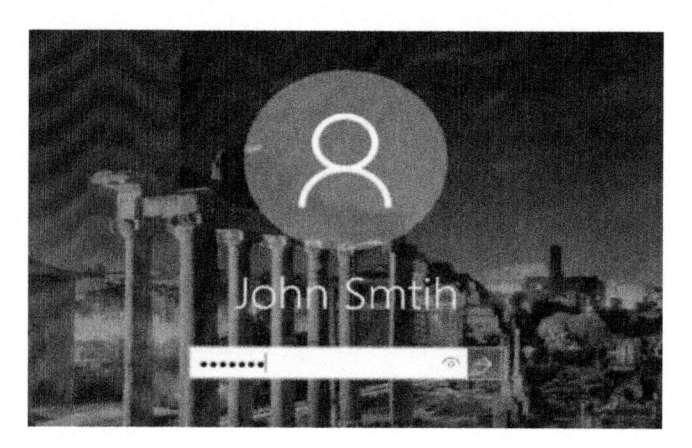

A notification box will display for the completion of your system restoration.

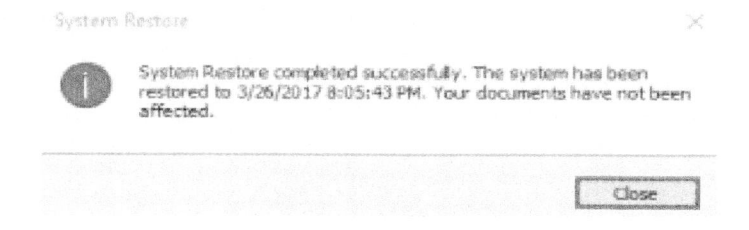

Frequently Asked Questions about System Restore Point

i. How does System Restore work?

"System Restore" uses restore points to return your system files and settings to an earlier point in time without affecting personal files. Restore points are created automatically every week and just before significant system events, such as the installation of a program or device driver. You can also create a restore point manually.

ii. What is System Restore?

"System Restore" helps you restore your computer's system files to an earlier point in time. It's a way to undo system changes to your computer without affecting your files, such as documents, videos, music, email, and photos.

Sometimes, the installation of a program or a driver can cause an unexpected change to your computer or cause Windows to behave unpredictably. Usually, uninstalling the program or driver corrects the problem. If uninstalling doesn't fix the problem, you can try restoring your computer's system to an earlier date when everything worked correctly.

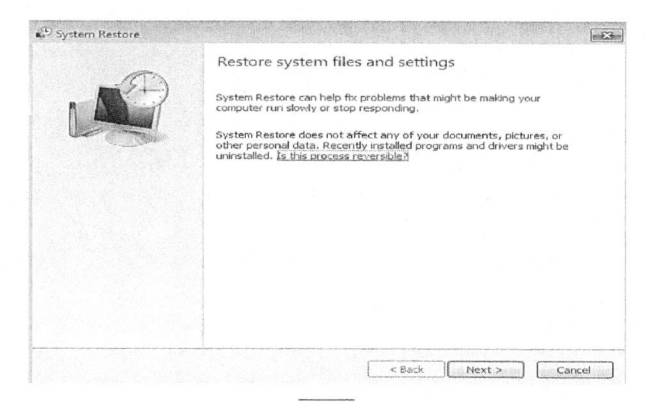

"System Restore" uses a feature called **system protection** to regularly create and save restore points on your computer. These restore points contain information about registry settings and other system information that Windows uses. You can also create restore points manually.

System image backups stored on hard disks can also be used for System Restore, just like the restore points created by system protection. Even though system image backups contain both your system files and personal data, your data files will not be affected by System Restore.

System Restore isn't intended for backing up personal files, so it cannot help you recover a personal file that has been deleted or damaged. You should regularly back up your files and important data using a backup program.

iii. What is system protection?

System protection is a feature that regularly creates and saves information about your computer's system files and settings. System protection also saves previous versions of files that you've modified. It saves these files in "restore points", which are created just before significant system events, such as the installation of a program or device driver. They're also created automatically once every seven days if no other restore points were created in the previous seven days, but you can create restore points manually at any time. System protection is automatically on for the drive that Windows is installed on. System protection can only be turned on for drives that are formatted using the NTFS file system.

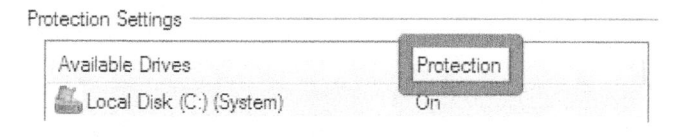

Protection Settings	
Available Drives	Protection
Local Disk (C:) (System)	On

There are two ways that you can take advantage of system protection:

If your computer is running slowly or isn't working properly, you can use System Restore to return your computer's system files and settings to an earlier point in time using a restore point. If you accidentally modify or delete a file or folder, you can restore it to a previous version that's saved as part of a restore point. You can right-click on the folder and select ***"Properties"*** then locate ***"Previous Version"*** and select the modification date available to be restored, this will work if your System protection is turned on. See the example in the below illustration.

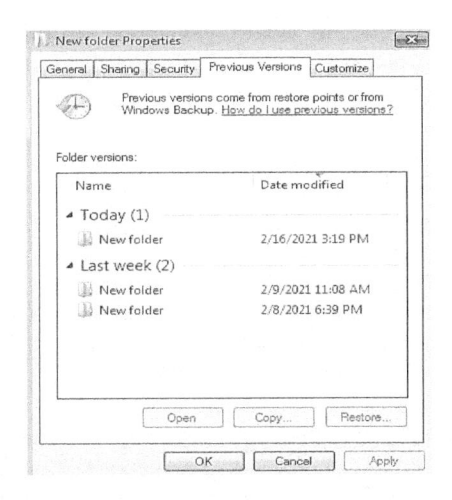

iv.   Can I undo the changes System Restore makes?

Yes. Every time you use System Restore, a restore point is created before proceeding, so you can undo the changes if they don't fix your problem. If you use System Restore when the computer is in safe mode or using the System Recovery Options, you cannot undo the restore operation. However, you can run System Restore again and choose a different restore point if one exists, as illustrated below

203

2/9/2021 11:07:35 AM	Removed Evernote v. 5.0.3	Uninstall
2/8/2021 6:39:35 PM	Automatic Restore Point	System
2/1/2021 10:31:20 AM	Installed Evernote v. 5.0.3	Install
2/1/2021 10:30:48 AM	Windows Update	Critical Update
2/1/2021 9:55:42 AM	Installed Adobe Reader X.	Install

v. What files are changed during a system restore??

System Restore affects Windows system files, programs, and registry settings. It can also make changes to scripts, batch files, and other types of executable files created under any user account on your computer. System Restore does not affect personal files, such as e-mail, documents, or photos, so it cannot help you restore a deleted file. If you have backups of your files, you can restore the files from a backup.

vi. How do I choose a restore point?

System Restore automatically recommends the most recent restore point created before a significant change, such as installing a program. You can also choose from a list of restore points. Try using restore points created just before the date and time you started noticing problems. The descriptions of the restore points that are created automatically correspond with the name of an event/activity, such as "Windows Update" being described as "installing an update". System Restore returns your computer to the state that it was in before choosing the restore point that you chose.

2/9/2021 11:07:35 AM	Removed Evernote v. 5.0.3	Uninstall
2/8/2021 6:39:35 PM	Automatic Restore Point	System
2/1/2021 10:31:20 AM	Installed Evernote v. 5.0.3	Install
2/1/2021 10:30:48 AM	Windows Update	Critical Update
2/1/2021 9:55:42 AM	Installed Adobe Reader X.	Install

vii. **How long are "restore points" saved?**

Restore points are saved until the disk space, "System Restore" reserves is filled up. As new restore points are created, old ones are deleted.

If you turn off system protection (the feature that creates restore points) on a disk, all restore points are deleted from that disk. When you turn system protection on, new restore points are created.

viii. **What if System Restore doesn't fix the problem?**

If System Restore doesn't fix the problem, you can undo the restore operation or try choosing a different restore point. If System Restore doesn't display any restore points to choose from, make sure you have system protection turned on and that you have at least 300 MB free space left on your hard disk if it is 500 MB or larger, or have at least 50 MB of free space if your hard disk is smaller than 300 MB. If System Restore doesn't fix the problem, you can also try an *advanced recovery method*.

2/9/2021 11:07:35 AM	Removed Evernote v. 5.0.3	Uninstall
2/8/2021 6:39:35 PM	Automatic Restore Point	System
2/1/2021 10:31:20 AM	Installed Evernote v. 5.0.3	Install
2/1/2021 10:30:48 AM	Windows Update	Critical Update
2/1/2021 9:55:42 AM	Installed Adobe Reader X.	Install

- **Choosing an advanced recovery method**

The advanced methods available in "Recovery" in Control Panel can return Windows to a usable state if it's badly damaged.

The first method uses a type of backup called "a system image", which you need to have created earlier. The second method reinstalls Windows, either from a recovery image provided by your computer manufacturer or from the original Windows installation files.

To access advanced recovery methods:

To locate "Advanced recovery method", type this in your file explorer Control Panel/All Control Panel Items/Recovery by default you will be taken to this illustrated image

> Restore this computer to an earlier point in time
>
> System Restore can resolve many system problems, and is the best recovery method to try first. For serious problems, use the advanced recovery methods.
>
> System Restore
>
> Undo recent system changes, but leave files such as documents, pictures, and music unchanged. This might remove recently-installed programs and drivers.
>
> [Open System Restore]
>
> [Advanced recovery methods]

Or

- Search for Recovery and then open it.
- Click "Advanced recovery methods".

Warning

Both methods can result in loss of data. Before beginning either method, you'll be prompted to back up your files to an external location such as a USB hard disk. After the recovery completes, you can reinstall your programs using the original installation discs or files, and restore your files.

ix. How Can I Backup My Files Against Loss of Data?

File's backup is in three (3) ways; one is called "online backup", while the other two are referred to as external backup & internal backup.

- **Online Backup**

Online backup is classified into two forms, online backup (cloud) and external hard disk storage backup. Windows 10 makes it easier for all its users to have access to the OneDrive storage feature which comes with 15gigabytes; all that is required is to register with your valid email; every google mail(Gmail) also comes with google drive storage of 15gigabytes, iCloud storage, dropbox, and, other online cloud storage services.

- **External Backup**

While the external hard disk also can be used as a backup, depending on an individual's choice, an organization should use cloud backup or both to avoid unexpected hard disk issues; but, if it is for personal use, a hard disk is okay.

- **Internal Backup**

Internal backup has to do with the same hard disk in a PC, which is majorly used as a "partition" to back up some vital data, your hard disk can be partitioned as much as you wish depending on your hard disk capacity.

Note: Hard disk that carries Windows icon is purposely dedicated for the operating system which if deleted might lead to the operating system shutting down; never make the mistake to categorize all as the same. Default hard disk is named Windows or Local disk.

Devices and drives (5)

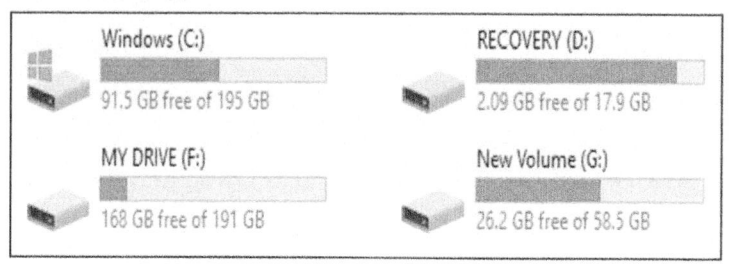

🪟	Windows (C:) 91.5 GB free of 195 GB	💿	RECOVERY (D:) 2.09 GB free of 17.9 GB
💿	MY DRIVE (F:) 168 GB free of 191 GB	💿	New Volume (G:) 26.2 GB free of 58.5 GB

x. What is Partition??

A partition is an area of a hard disk that can be formatted and assigned a drive letter. On a basic disk (the most common type of disk), a volume is a formatted primary partition or logical drive (the terms volume and partition are often used interchangeably). Your system partition is typically labeled with the letter C. Letters A and B are reserved for removable drives or floppy disk drives. Some computers have hard disks that are partitioned as a single partition, while other computers might have an additional partition that contains recovery tools, in case the information on your C partition becomes damaged or unusable.

CHAPTER ELEVEN

WINDOWS SECURITY

Windows Defender

Windows Defender is antispyware software that's included with Windows and runs automatically when it's turned on. Using antispyware software can help protect your computer against spyware and other potentially unwanted software. Spyware can be installed on your computer without your knowledge any time you connect to the Internet, and it can infect your computer when you install some programs using a CD, DVD, or other removable media. Spyware can also be programmed to run at unexpected times, not just when it's installed. To locate Windows Defender, go to "Start menu bar" and type "Windows defender".

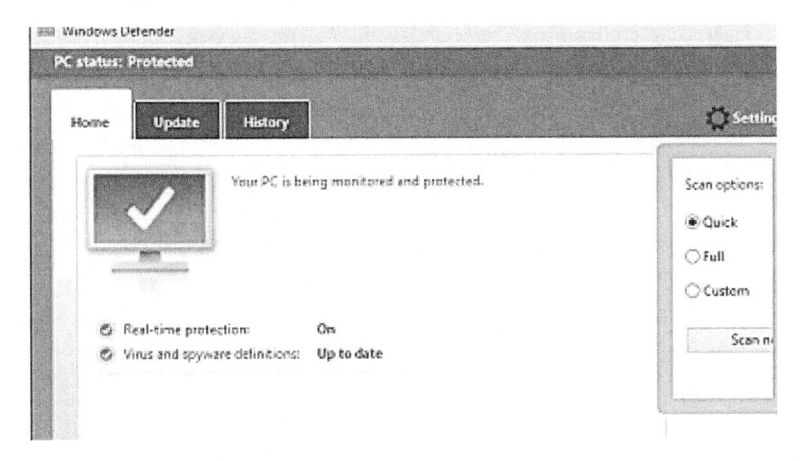

Windows Defender offers two ways to help keep spyware from infecting your computer:

- ***Real-time protection.*** Windows Defender alerts you when spyware attempts to install itself or to run on your computer. It also alerts you when programs attempt to change important Windows settings.

- **Scanning options.** You can use Windows Defender to scan for spyware that might be installed on your computer, schedule scans regularly, and automatically remove anything that's detected during a scan.

When you use Windows Defender, it's important to have up-to-date definitions. Definitions are files that act like an ever-growing encyclopedia of potential software threats. Windows Defender uses definitions to alert you to potential risks if the software detected is spyware or other potentially unwanted software. To help keep your definitions up to date, Windows Defender works with Windows Update to automatically install new definitions as they're released. You can also set Windows Defender to check online for updated definitions before scanning.

It is important to note that Windows 10 comes with a lot of features, one of which is Windows Security; its major purpose is to defend its users from suspicious items on the PC. Scanning on PC can be done in various ways.

Understanding Windows Defender Real-Time Protection

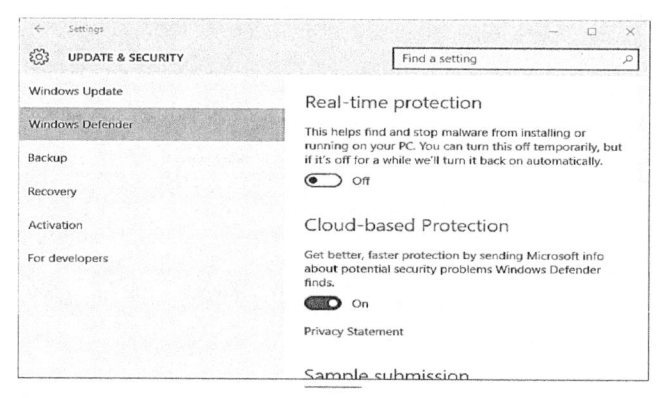

Real-time spyware protection alerts you when spyware and other potentially unwanted software attempts to install itself or run on your computer. Depending on the alert level, you can choose one of these actions to apply to the software:

- **Quarantine.** Moves the software to another location on your computer, and then prevents it from running until you choose to restore it or remove it from your computer.
- **Remove.** Permanently deletes the software from your computer.
- **Allow.** Adds the software to the Windows Defender allowed list and allows it to run on your computer. Windows Defender will stop alerting you to risks that the allowed software might pose to your privacy or your computer. Add software to the allowed list only if you trust the software and the software publisher.

You can choose the software and settings that you want Windows Defender to monitor, but I recommend that you use all of the real-time protection options, called **agents**. The following table explains each agent and why it's important.

Real-time protection agent	Purpose
Downloaded files and attachments	Monitors files and programs that are designed to work with web browsers. These files can be downloaded, installed, or run by the browser itself. Spyware and other potentially unwanted software can be included with these files and installed without your knowledge.

Programs that run on your computer	Monitors when programs start and any operations they perform while running. Spyware and other potentially unwanted software can use vulnerabilities in programs that you have installed to run malicious or unwanted software without your knowledge. For example, spyware can run in the background when you start a program that you frequently use. Windows Defender monitors your programs and alerts you if suspicious activity is detected.

What is Spyware?

Spyware is software that can advertise (such as pop-up ads), collect information about you, or change settings about you on your PC generally without obtaining your consent.

How to use Quick scan, Full scan, and Custom Scan

Windows scanning comes with a lot of flexibility which gives room for multiple options, such as quick scan, full scan, and custom scan. Below at the right-hand side is an illustration of Quick scan, Full scan, and Custom scan.

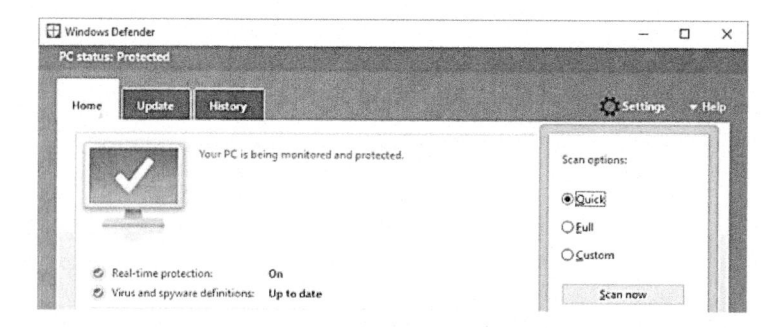

Types of Scanning

- ***Quick Scan:*** A quick scan checks the regular folders and the commonly used files. Quick scan is one of Windows Defender features that gives room for rapid scanning, majorly used to scan specific areas such as memory, tasks and startup items, running programs, and boot sectors. "Quick scan" may not discover some viruses, but it can still notify you about a virus if your computer is infected. It doesn't consume a lot of time; Quick scanning is daily recommended.
- ***Full Scan:*** Full Scan is the most recommended but time-consuming scanning depending on your hard drive capacity which thoroughly searches all segments such as files, folders, cookies, memory, programs, and other segments on your computer. Full scanning is recommended weekly
- ***Custom Scan:*** Custom Scan deals with users' preference, you are the determinant of what to be scanned by selecting your items.
- ***Windows Defender Offline Scan:*** It is a scan that will be done when you restart your PC, until your PC restarts, Windows might be finding it difficult to remove it. In a very tough and difficult situation, an offline scan is recommended for your PC.

◉ Quick scan
Checks folders in your system where threats are commonly found.

○ Full scan
Checks all files and running programs on your hard disk. This scan could take longer than one hour.

○ Custom scan
Choose which files and locations you want to check

○ Windows Defender Offline scan
Some malicious software can be particularly difficult to remove from your device. Windows Defender Offline can help find and remove them using up-to-date threat definitions. This will restart your device and will take about 15 minutes.

Scan now

There is also a *manual scanning* which is carried out without the need to open Windows defender, just select any item to be scanned, right-click and select "Scan with Windows Defender"

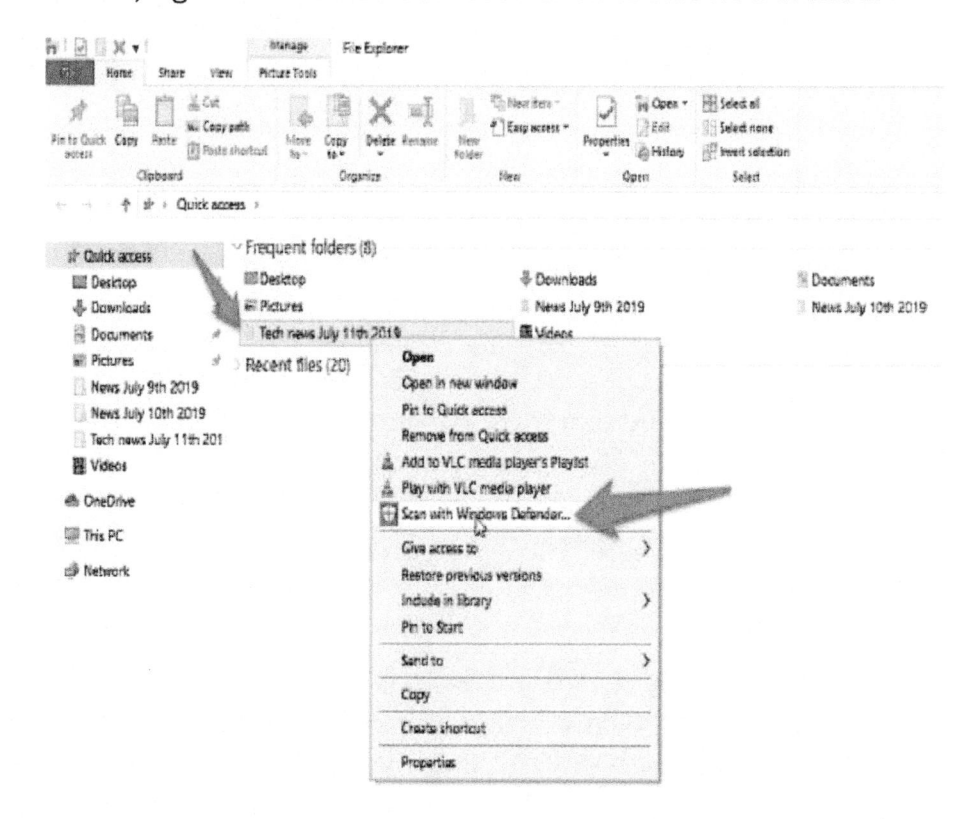

What is Firewall?

A firewall is a software or hardware that checks information coming from the Internet or a network, and then either blocks it or allows it to pass through to your computer, depending on your firewall settings. Even if you think there's nothing on your computer that would interest anyone, a worm could completely disable your computer, or someone could use your computer to help spread worms or viruses to other computers without your knowledge.

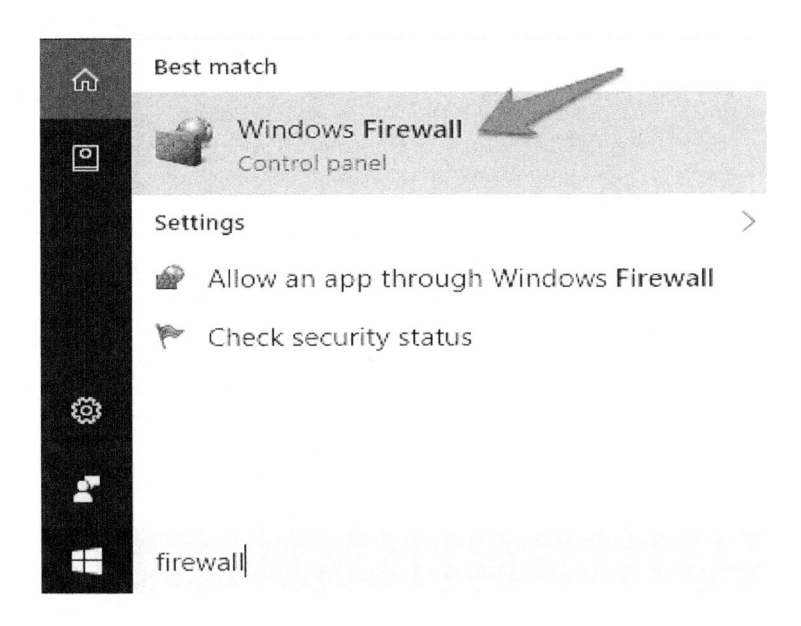

How to Locate Your Firewall

- Go to "windows settings"

- Click on "Network & Internet"

- Under Network & Internet scroll down the page and you will see *"Windows Firewall"*

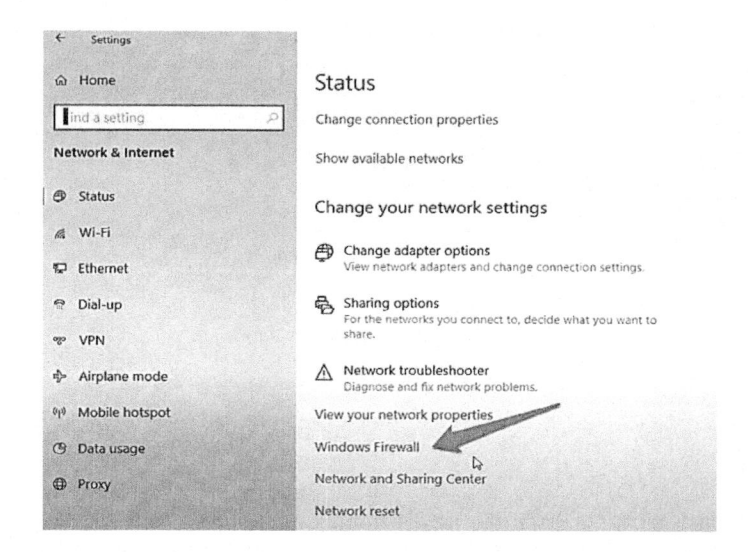

- You will see your Firewall status, which is categorized into three:

    - Domain network
    - Private network
    - Public network

- Make sure everything is turned on for security purposes.

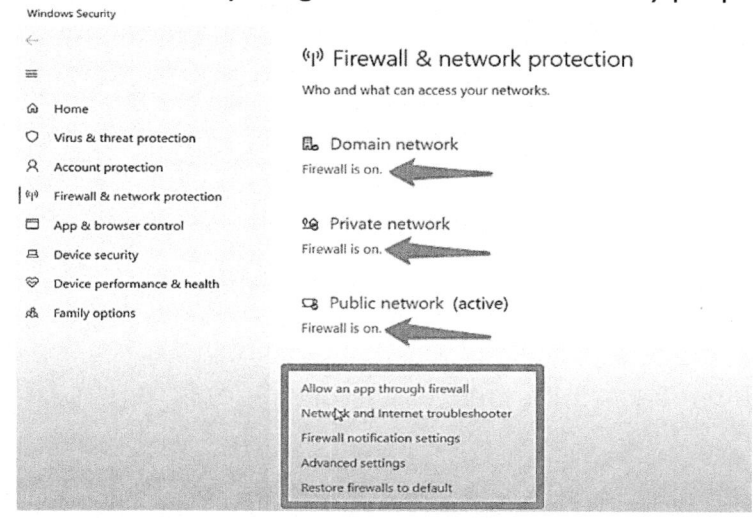

What does "allowing a program to communicate through the firewall" mean?

Allowing a program to communicate through the firewall, sometimes called **unblocking**, is when you allow a particular program to send information through the firewall. You can also allow a program to communicate through the firewall by opening one or more ports.

How to Block a Program With Windows Firewall

- Search for "Windows Firewall", double click on it.

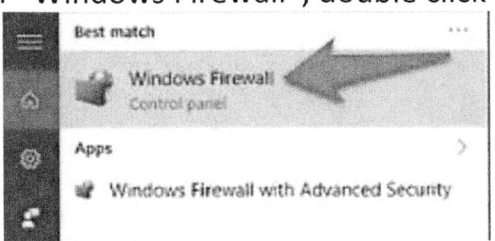

- On the left-hand side, click on "Advanced settings".

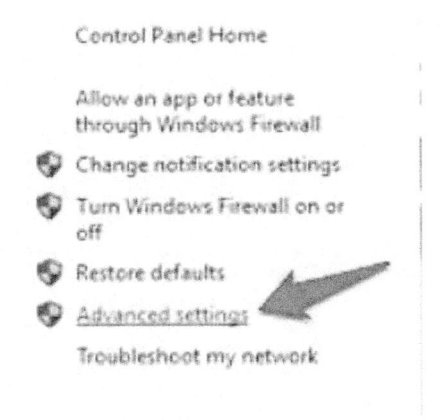

- On the left-hand side, you will see **inbound rules** and **outbound rules**; assuming you want to block inbound rules select "inbound rules".

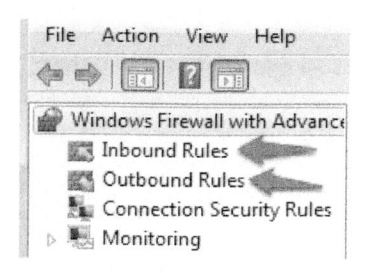

- Check your left-hand side, you will see "new rules", click on it.

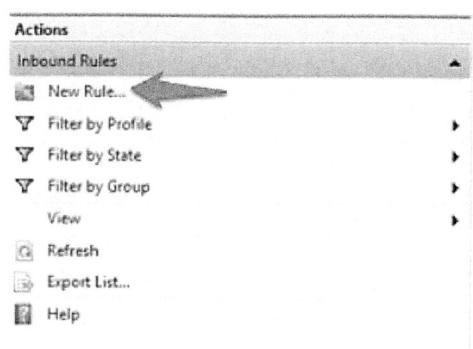

- Select "program", then press "Next"

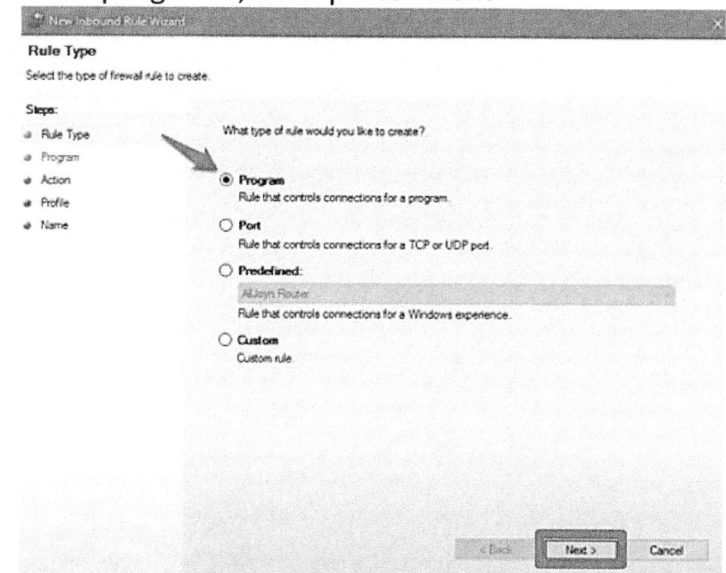

- Select the specific program path by clicking on "Browse".

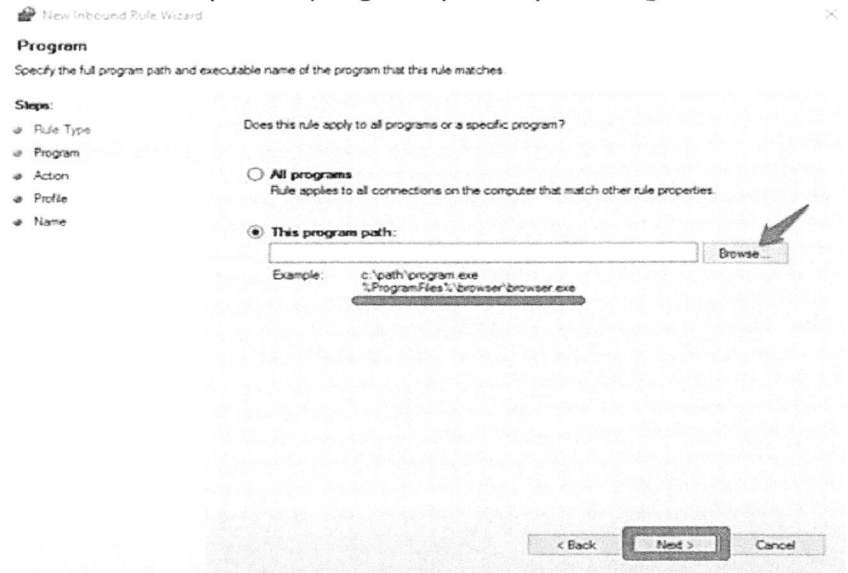

- Or right-click on the shortcut icon from your desktop and select *"Properties"*.

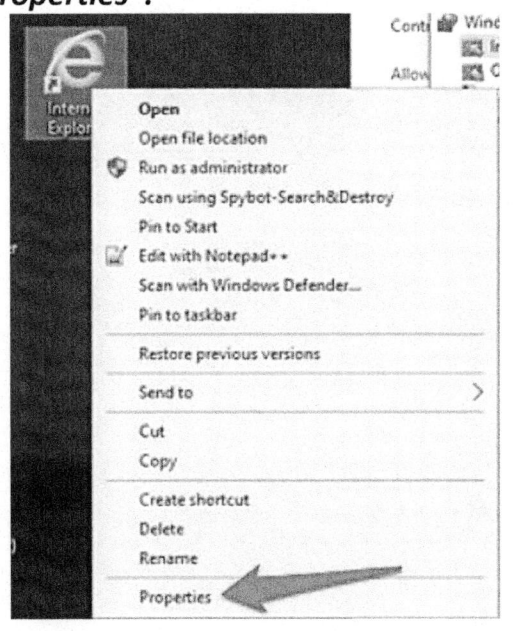

- Now come down and look for *"Target"*, copy the location as illustrated below.

- And then paste it inside the empty box or you "Browse" it out. Then click "Next".

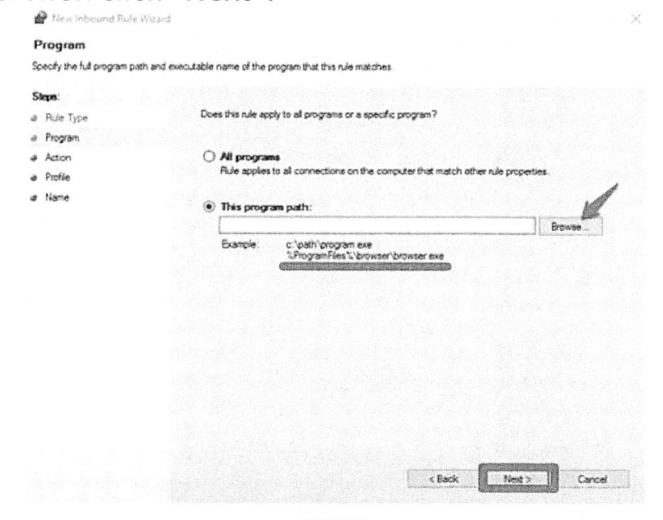

- Now, we are going to decide on what to do, either allow it or block it.

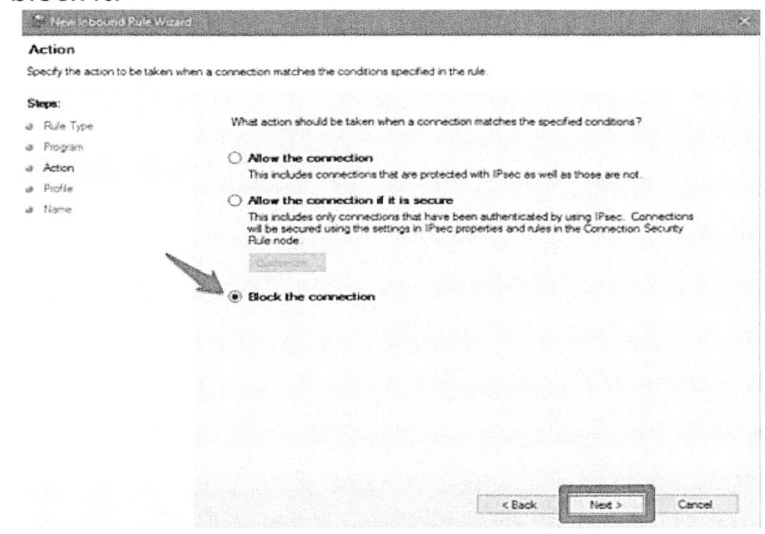

- Blocking the program comes with three (3) options to be ticked Domain, Private, and Public; assuming you ticked all, click "Next".

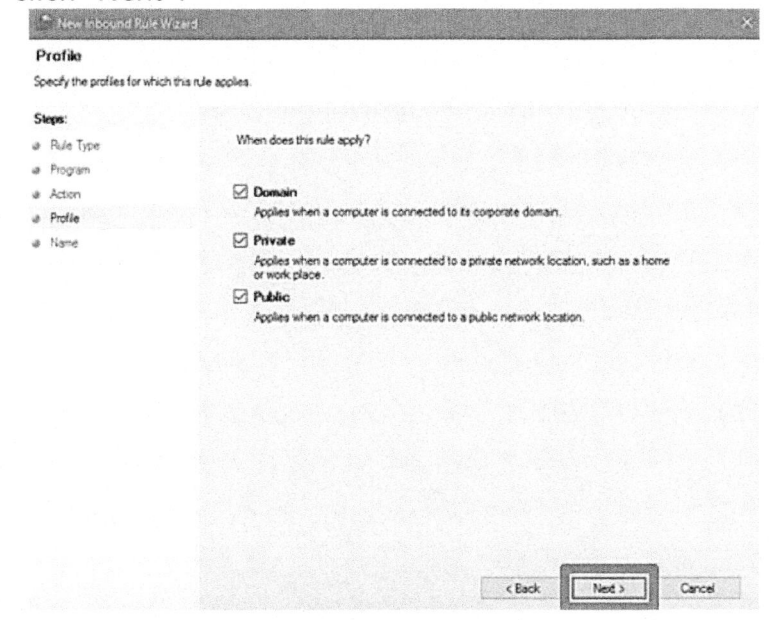

- Finally, name the blocked program in an identifiable way, then click "Finish".

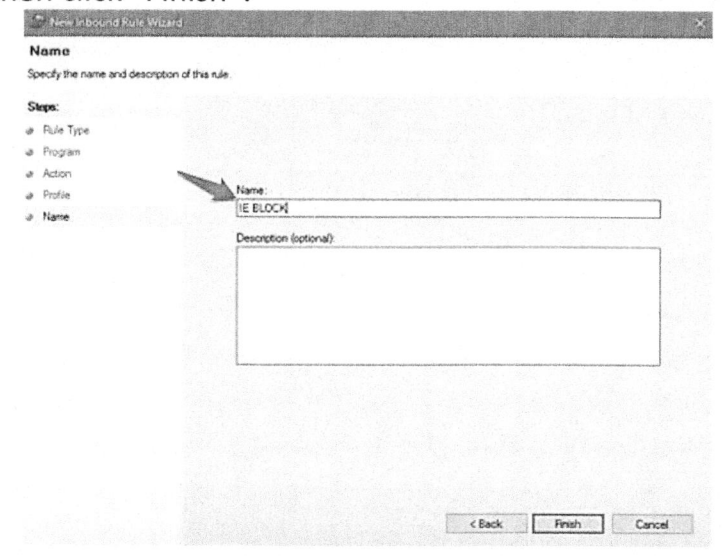

- Repeat the same process for "Outbound rules". The selected program will be automatically blocked from sending a request or receiving a request on the internet.

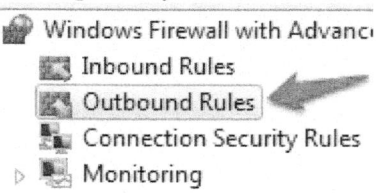

- Outcome result on Explorer which is the program used to test run the above blocking.

CHAPTER TWELVE

CONNECTIVITY

How to Connect Your Windows 10 PC to the Internet

The internet is one of the important areas where various devices interact together which is known as a **global village**. Here are procedures on how to connect your PC to the internet:

- **Step 1**

Go to *"Start menu"*, at your left-hand side you will see *"settings"*, double click it.

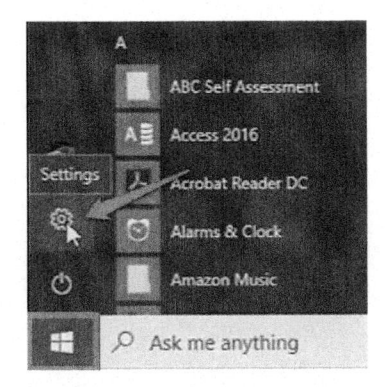

- **Step 2**

Then you will see in the middle *"Network & Internet"*, double click on it.

- **Step 3**

By your left-hand side, look for *"Wi-Fi"*, double click on it.

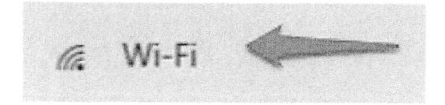

- **Step 4**

Go ahead and click on *"Show available network"*.

- **Step 5**

A dialog box will pop up; you will be shown available Wi-Fi, select on your Wi-Fi, then click on *"connect"*.

- **Step 6**

Enter your password and click "Next".

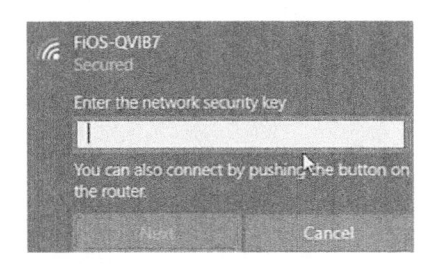

- **Step 7**

It will be verified, once this is completed it will connect completely.

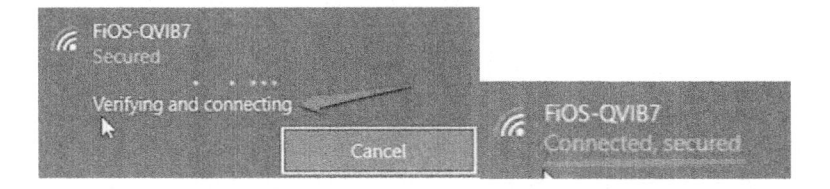

You can easily access your Wi-Fi connection by clicking on your system tray on the taskbar.

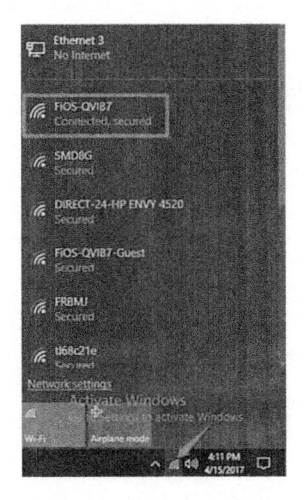

225

Connecting to Another Computer

Windows has made it possible to share items from one PC to another by connecting through the same wired or wireless network.

The easiest way to get this done is by going to your *system tray* and click on your Wi-Fi icon, a box will pop up, click on *"Network settings"* or you can type Network settings in "start menu" it will also locate it.

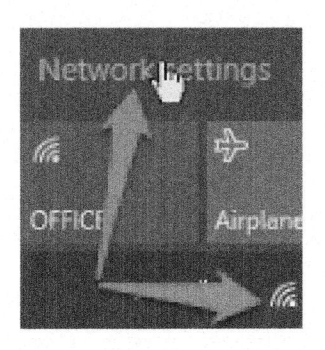

You will be brought into Network settings, make sure both computers are connected on the same network, then go to *"Advanced options"*

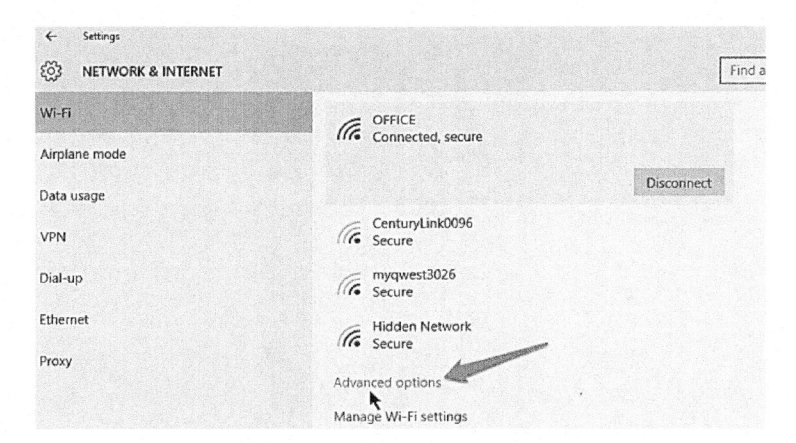

Make sure this feature is turned on for visibility of other devices; note that it is only advisable to **turn it on** while at home or work (a private network) not for other places (public network) for security reasons; make sure it is also turned on in the other PC.

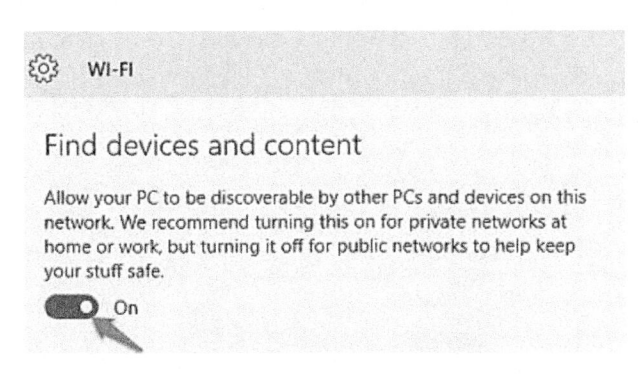

Next, go down to "file explorer" and click on it.

Then, on your left-hand side, click on **Network**.

Once you click on **Network**, you will see all connected devices on your network which you can access.

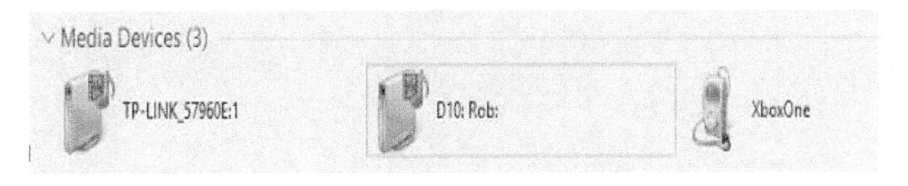

How to Add a Printer to Windows 10

A computer has a lot of inbuilt features and tools such as DVD ROM, Hard disk storage, cooling fan, and lots more which are the internal framework for efficiency and effectiveness. External support component has to come in such as Printer for printing document, Scanner for scanning documents to compliment a PC. We are going to be looking at how to add a printer to your PC:

Search on start menu "Printers & scanners"

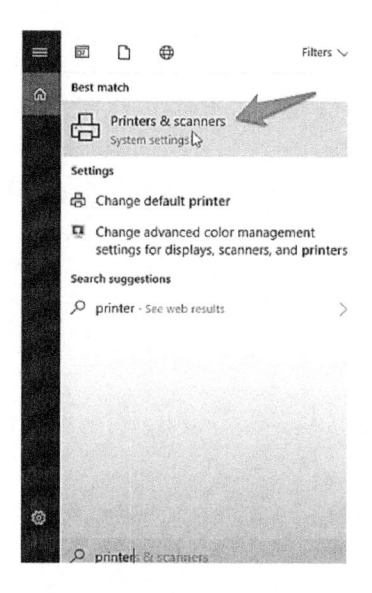

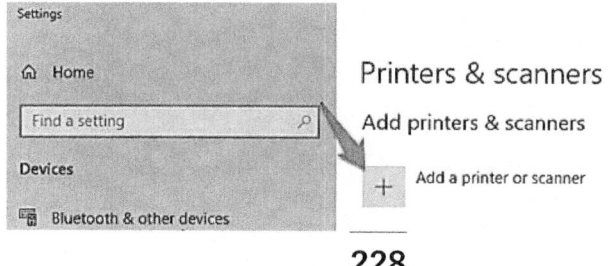

It is important to know that not all printers have "auto-recognize". If you are unable to discover your printer after connecting it with your USB port, get the printer drive online by searching for it. Assuming it is a canon printer drive, type it online and also be sure it is a canon link.

Make sure your "operating system bit" is the same as the software by checking your *"System Properties".*

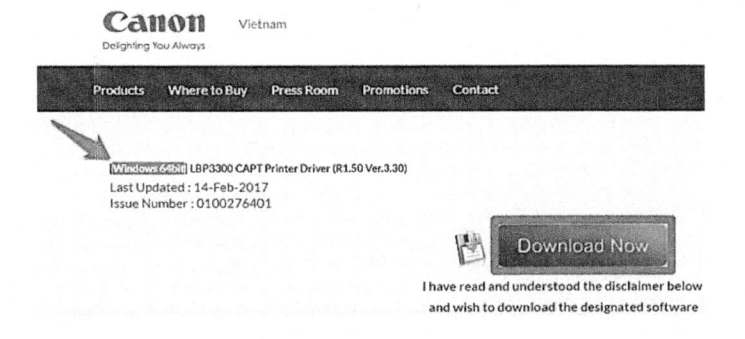

Go to your "Desktop" and select "This PC" right-click and select "Properties".

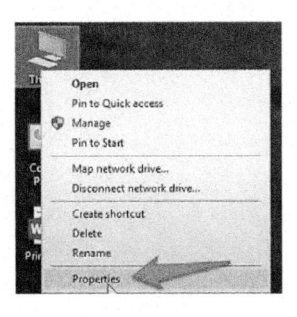

There, you will see your "System type".

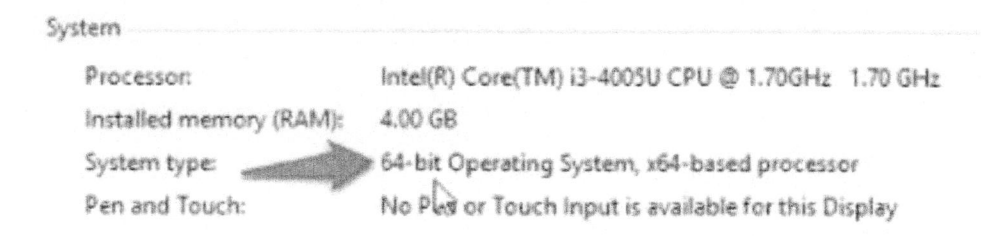

Once you are sure about your system type, click on **download**, a dialog box will pop-up to locate where you want the "printer drive" to be saved, once done, click "Save".

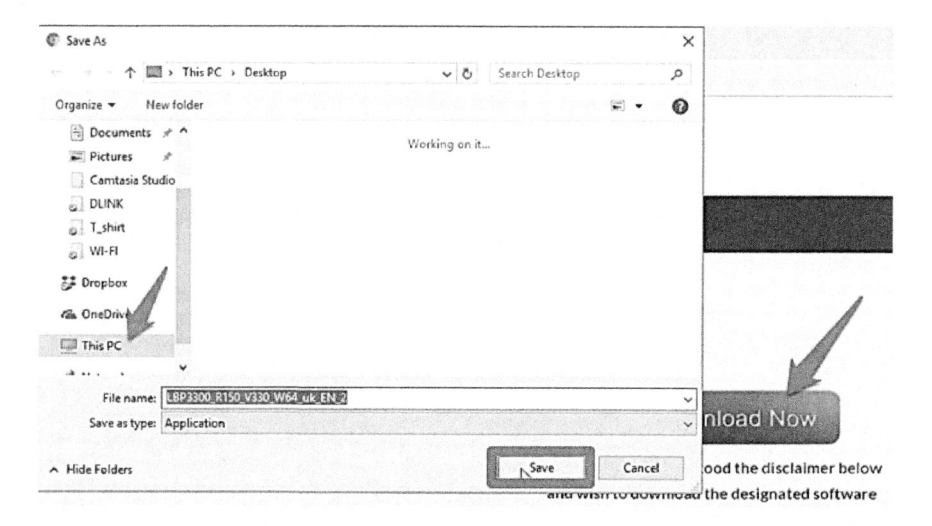

Downloading kick starts immediately; once it is completed, it can then be extracted as illustrated below.

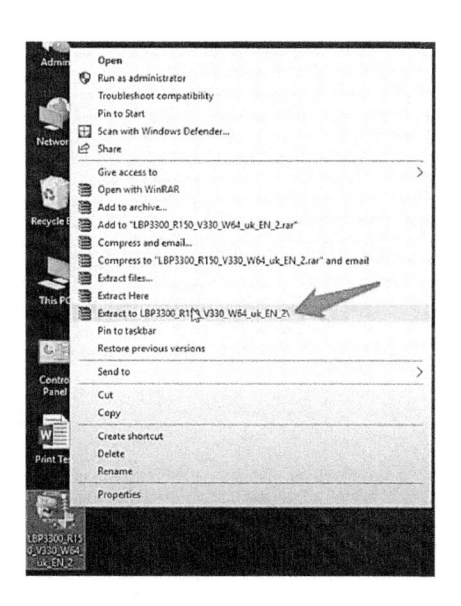

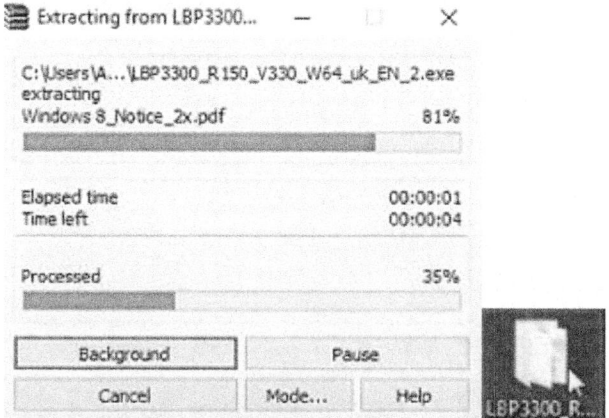

It will be extracted as a folder with the same name on the same directory. Then let's go back to "Add a printer or scanner"; double click on it.

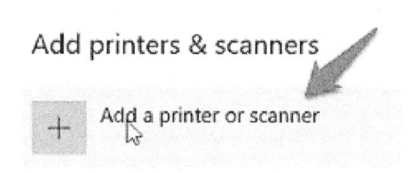

231

Click on *"The printer that I want isn't listed"*.

You will be brought here, click on *"Add a local printer or network printer with manual settings"*, then *"Next"*.

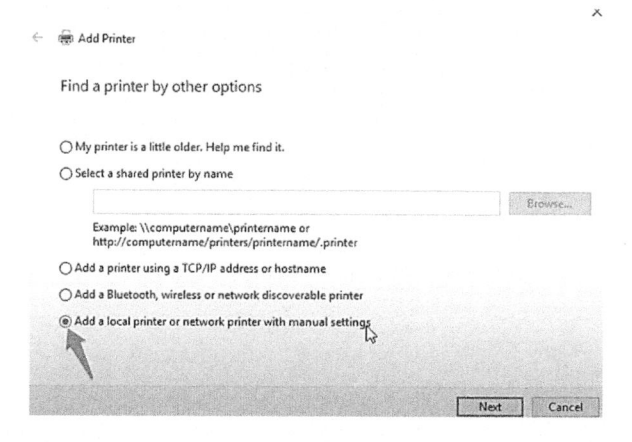

Select *"USB (Virtual printer port for USB)"* then click on *"Next"* to proceed.

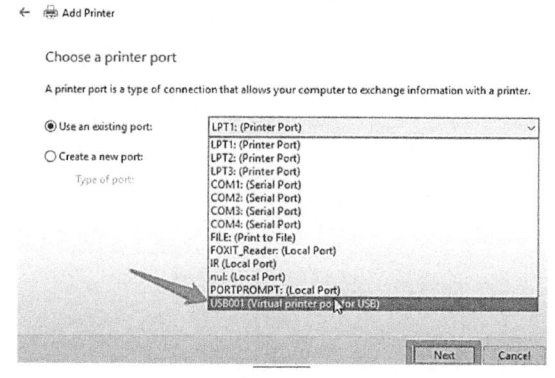

Windows will retrieve a list of all devices.

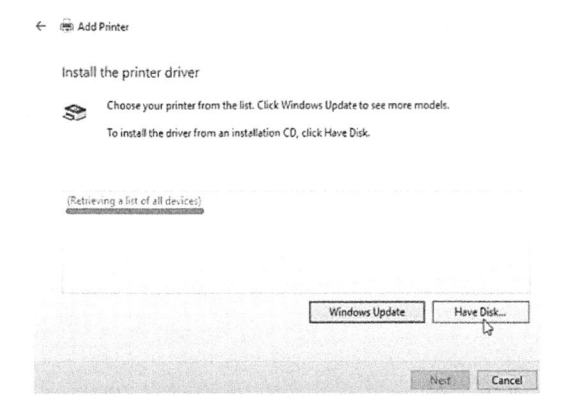

Once retrieved, click on *"Have Disk"*.

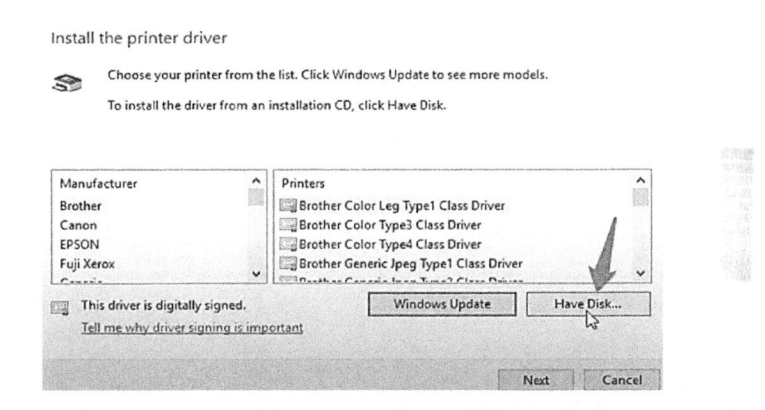

You will be prompted to install the disk; click on "Browse" to locate, for me, I saved the Canon on my desktop which is where it will be locating.

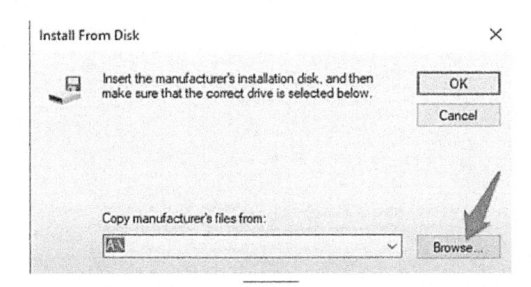

233

Below is the extracted Canon printer drive, open it and see the drive setup itself.

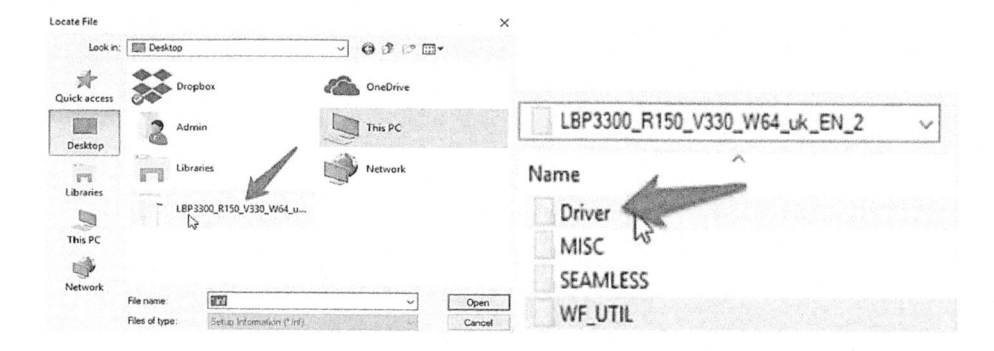

Highlight it, then open.

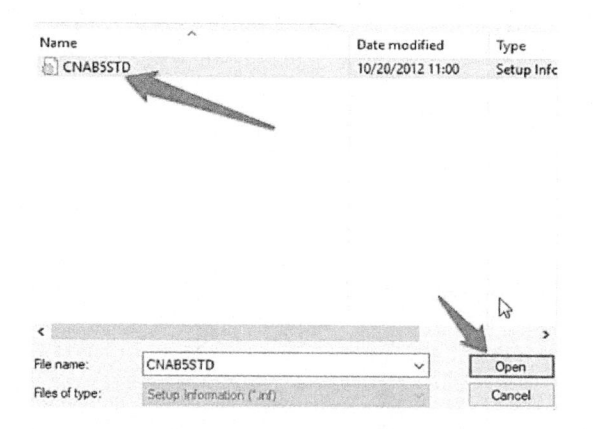

Once it has been verified below, click **Ok**.

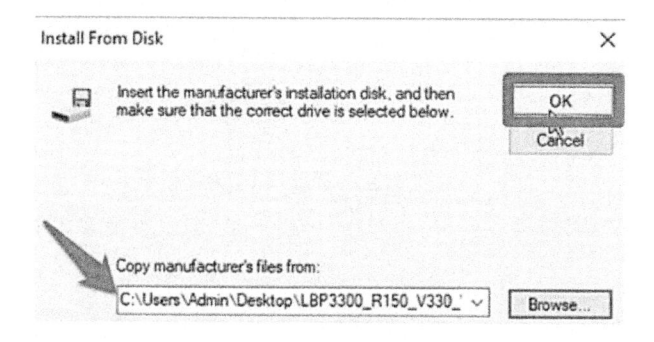

Immediately it reflects Canon, highlight it, and then click on "Next".

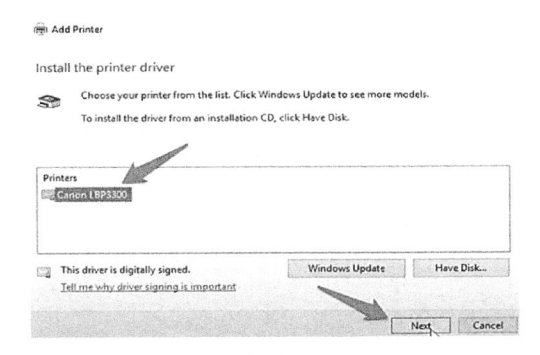

A notification will pop up saying *"This printer will be installed with the Canon LBP 3300 driver",* click "Next" to continue.

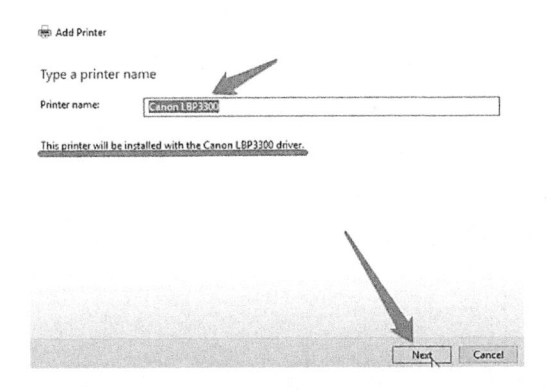

Once it is fully installed, you can now click "Next".

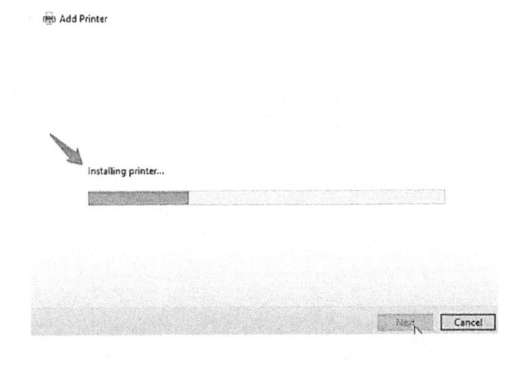

If it is for personal use, click on "Do not share this printer", if otherwise, click on "Share this printer so that others on your network can find and use it".

Next, click on "Print a test page" to test your printer by default, your printer will print out its configuration settings on a page, then click "Finish".

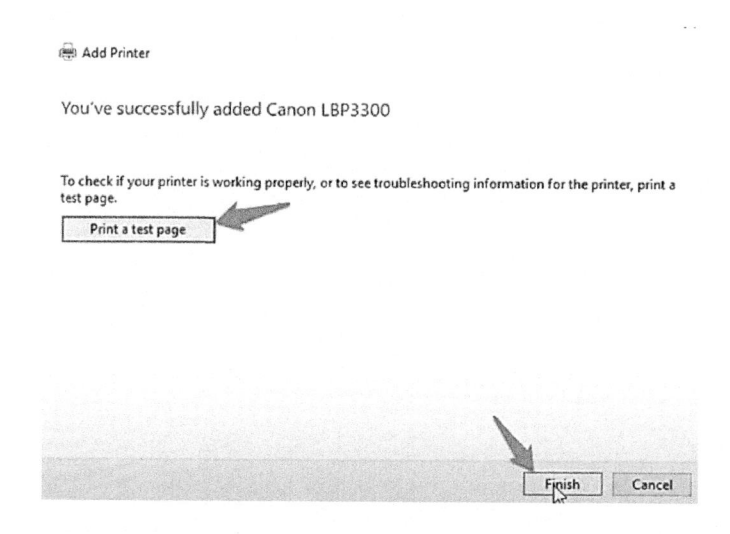

You will now be able to see your added printer.

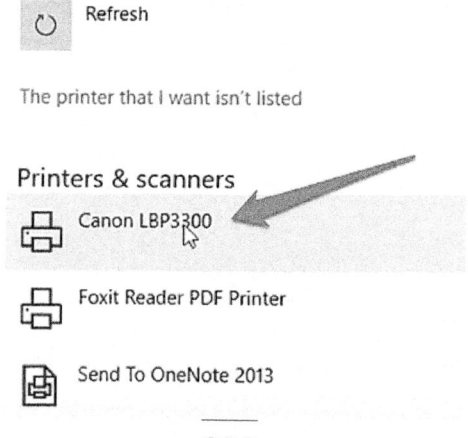

How to Scan a Document or Image

Scanning of document or photo image involves external connection which might be set up before you can scan any document, it is important to note that external scanner varies but printing procedures are similar. I will be focusing more on your PC procedure.

By default, **Windows Fax and Scan** comes with Windows operating system, turns your computer into a fax machine—potentially big money and time saver. Before you can start faxing, your computer must be properly equipped.

What you need

If you're planning to send and receive faxes at home, you first need to outfit your PC with a fax modem.

A fax modem is a relatively inexpensive piece of add-on hardware that allows your computer to communicate with a fax machine over a standard phone line. The devices are sold at major computer stores and come in two varieties; internal and external.

Internal fax modems plug directly into your computer motherboard, similar to a video or sound card. External fax modems are small devices that connect to the serial or USB ports.

If you're at work, another option is to see if your employer has a fax server—a dedicated computer equipped with multiple fax modems. Sending a fax using a fax server doesn't require you to add any special hardware to your PC. You just set up a connection with the fax server and proceed.

Setting up Windows to Fax

Once you've picked up a fax modem or found a fax server, you still need to do a little setup.

To set up a fax modem;

Before you begin, make sure that you've properly installed your fax modem, and that it's plugged into a standard analog phone line.

Click the **Start button**, click "All Programs", and then click **Windows Fax and Scan.**

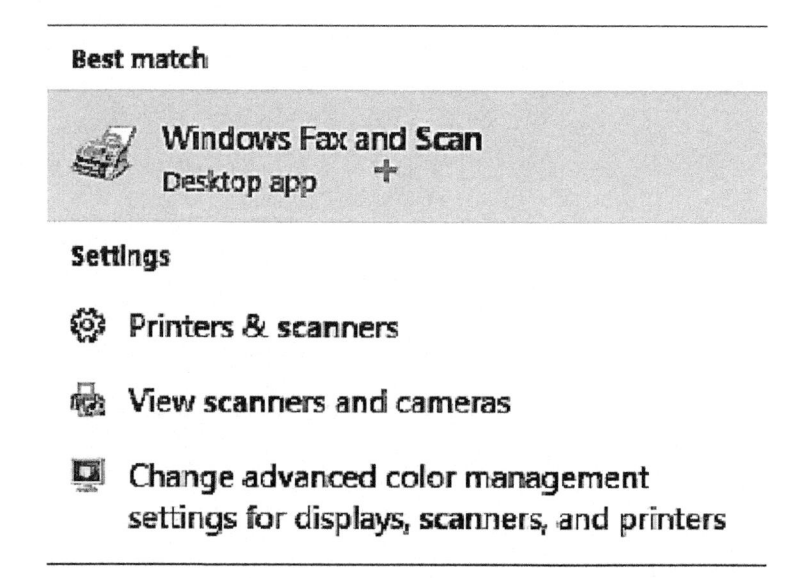

Best match

- Windows Fax and Scan
  Desktop app

Settings

- Printers & scanners
- View scanners and cameras
- Change advanced color management settings for displays, scanners, and printers

At the bottom of the left pane, click **Fax**, and then click "New Fax" on the toolbar to launch the Fax Setup wizard. Until you launch the fax setup wizard, you won't be granted access, but rather a notification indicating "No fax account is configured" will be shown as illustrated below.

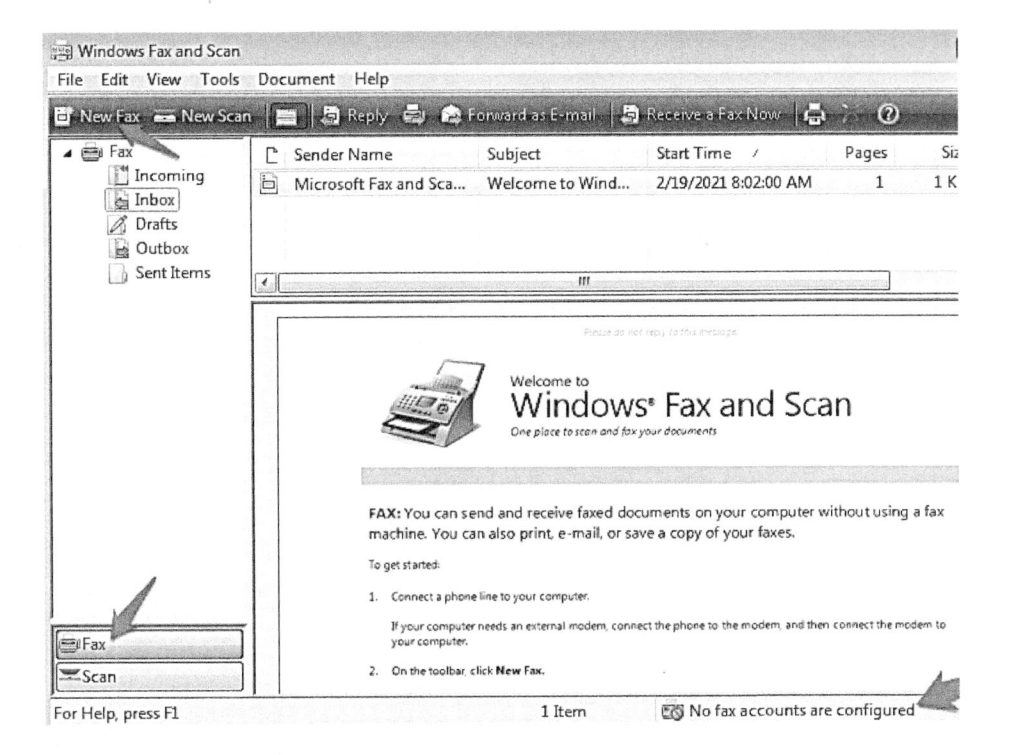

- **File menu** guides you on printing, saving, and opening a new fax scan.
- **The Edit menu** is framed to delete, select, invert and mark items.
- **View menu** is structured to show preview, status bar, toolbar, and also to arrange.
- **Tool menu** is designed to input the sender's information, cover page, fax settings, and other features.
- **The document** is a feature that gives room for a reply, forward, pause, resume and restart.
- **Help** is a guideline on how to navigate more on fax and scan features.

Click **Connect to a fax modem** and follow the instructions.

Note: To set up your computer to send faxes only, click "I'll choose later; I want to create fax now in the Fax Setup wizard". Keep in mind that by choosing this option, you'll be able to send faxes but not receive them.

CHAPTER THIRTEEN

INSTALLATION OF SOFTWARE ON WINDOWS 10

Applications Installation & Uninstallation of Software Programs on PC

You can uninstall a program from your computer if you no longer use it or if you want to free up space on your hard disk. You can use Programs and Features to uninstall programs or to change a program's configuration by adding or removing certain options. For more information about uninstalling programs, see "Uninstalling programs: frequently asked questions". To learn more about installing programs on your computer, see "Install a program".

Steps on Uninstalling an Application

It is important to note that many methods can be used to uninstall applications.

Method 1

- Go to your "Start menu", type the name of the application you want to uninstall, let's assume we want to uninstall "WhatsApp" from your PC

- Above your search bar where you typed WhatsApp, you will see the WhatsApp icon

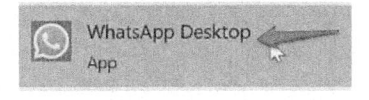

- Right-click on it; a dialog box will appear showing you multiple options, look for "Uninstall" and click on it

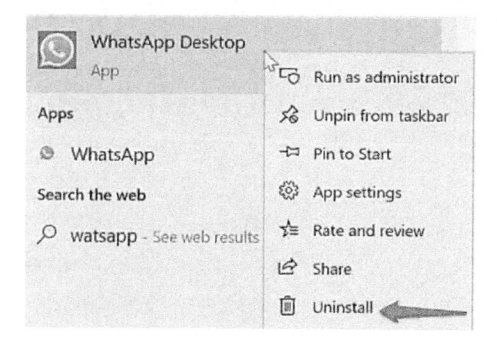

- A dialog box will pop up informing you about your action and its consequence; after clicking on "Uninstall" it will disappear from your PC.

- **Method 2**
- Click on your "Start menu", when the start menu opens up, type "settings" in your search bar.

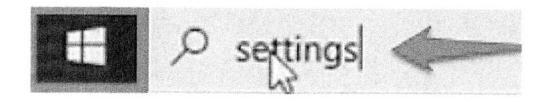

- "Settings" features will appear above your search bar, double click on it

- Locate *"Apps"*, double click on it

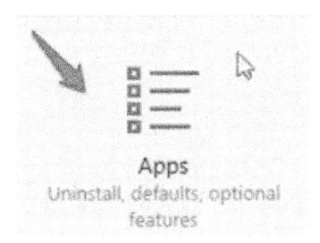

- Make sure you are on *"Apps & features"*, scroll down, you will see all apps on your PC.

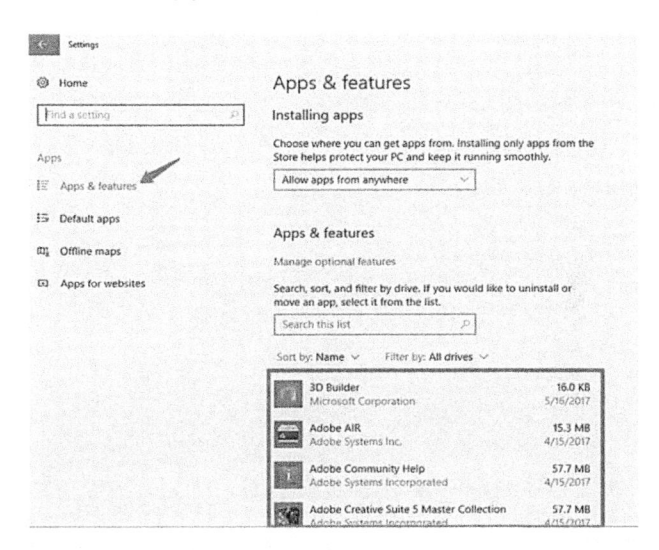

- When you find the one you want to uninstall, click on it, "Uninstall" option will display, then you can click on **uninstall** to remove the application.

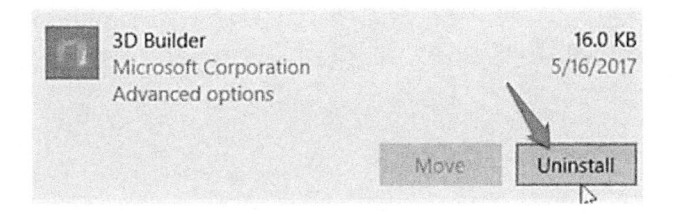

Method 3

- Go to *"Start menu"*, type *"control panel"*

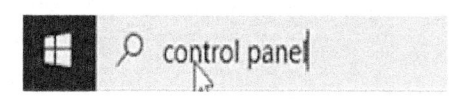

- The Control panel will display above, double click on it

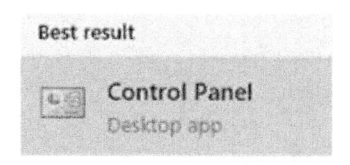

- A dialog box will appear titled "Adjust your system's settings", at your right-hand side you will see *"View by"*, make sure it is on *"category"*.

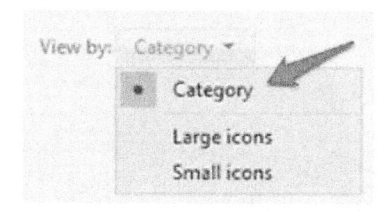

- Also, check below you will see *"Programs"* double click on it.

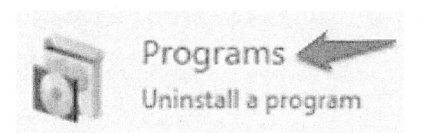

- Now double click on *"Programs and Features"*.

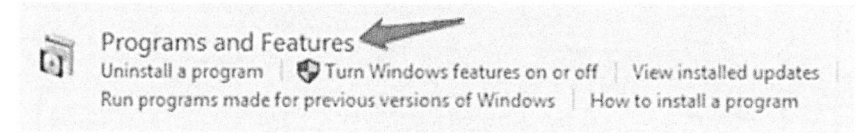

- Select a program, and then right-click on it which will give you the *"Uninstall"* option. Some programs include the option to change or repair the program in addition to uninstalling it, but many simply offer the option to uninstall. To change a program, click **Change** or **Repair** if you are prompted for an administrator password or confirmation.

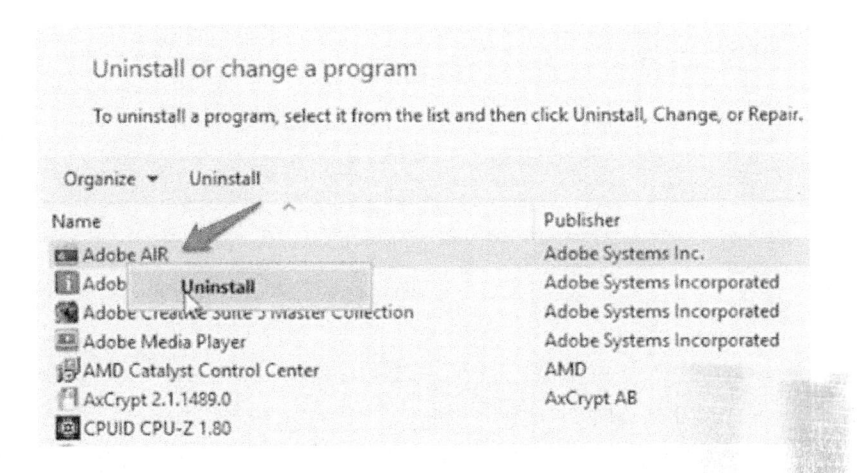

How to Recognize If an App Is Safe or Not

The fear of all humans is security & privacy of personal data; once a wrong application is installed, this can lead to attackers having full access to your PC without your permission as long as you installed the wrong application without knowing much about it. Here is a simple method of knowing which application is safe and which one is not safe.

- Go to your browser, type **www.shouldiremoveit.com**

- To recognize the status of the application; *red* indicates high risk, *yellow* indicates medium risk, *green* indicates safe.

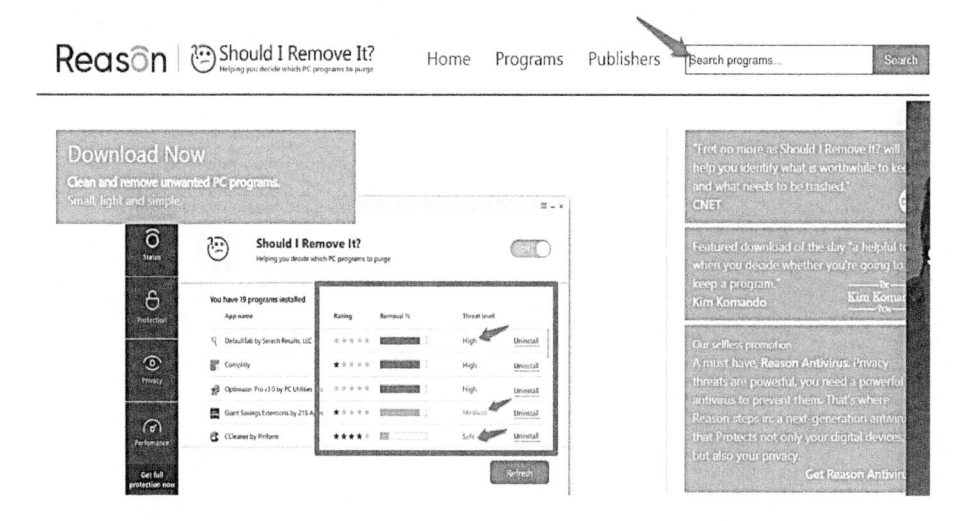

- On the website, at the right-hand corner, you will see *"Search programs"*, type the name of the program you want to verify to verify it. Assuming we want to verify "Microsoft Edge", type it in and click on "search"

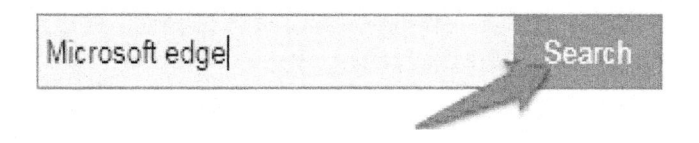

- Below is the result of "Microsoft edge" which indicates safe.

How to Download an App from Microsoft Store on Windows 10

As a result of vulnerability online and offline, Microsoft finally launched a built-in app where different apps can be downloaded securely. This new app is called *"Microsoft Store"*. Here are simple steps on how to go about it.

- Go to your taskbar below, locate "Microsoft Store"

- If not there on your taskbar, go to your "Start menu", on the search bar, type *"Microsoft Store"*

- Related options named Microsoft will pop up; choose the right one which is *"Microsoft Store"*, double click on it.

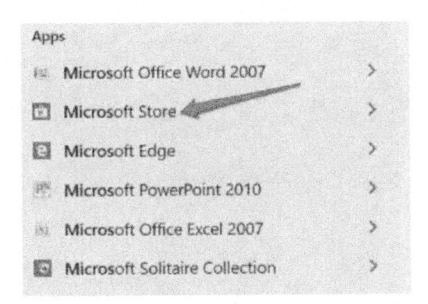

- You will be brought into "Microsoft Store", at your right-hand, side click on "Search" to locate your preferred apps.

247

- Let's assume, I want to search for "WhatsApp", it must be typed inside the search bar box; once done, click on "Enter key" on your keyboard or click on **the search icon**.

- The search result will pop up with other similar apps; the first is what we want to download. Make sure you know what you want before visiting Microsoft Store in order not to be confused with a multitude of options.

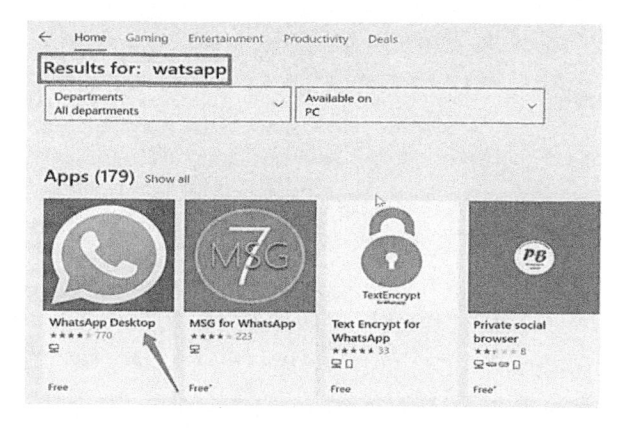

- Below the result, you will see "Available on PC", which grants you access to know if also available on mobile, Xbox, and other devices.

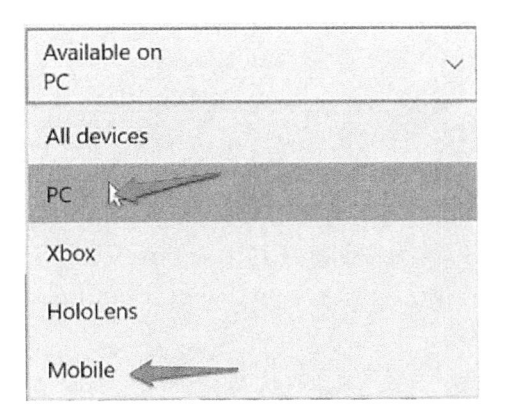

- Then double click on the WhatsApp desktop application to proceed on downloading it.

- Next, look at your right-hand side and click on "Install".

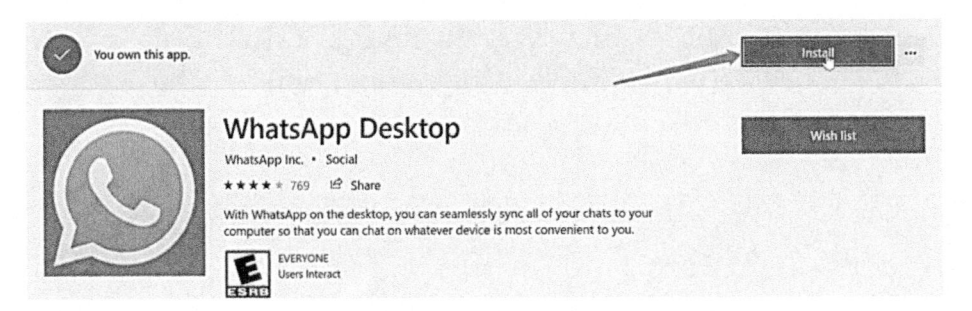

- You can click on the three dots as shown below to be sure of where the app is going to be installed. Clicking on "Install on my devices" will automatically install it on your devices.

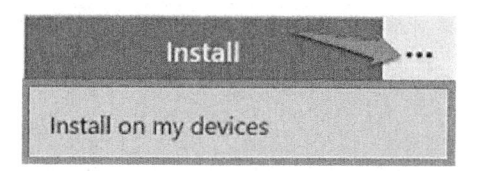

> Install ...
> Install on my devices

- Once you have clicked on Install or Install on my devices, the downloading process kick starts automatically.

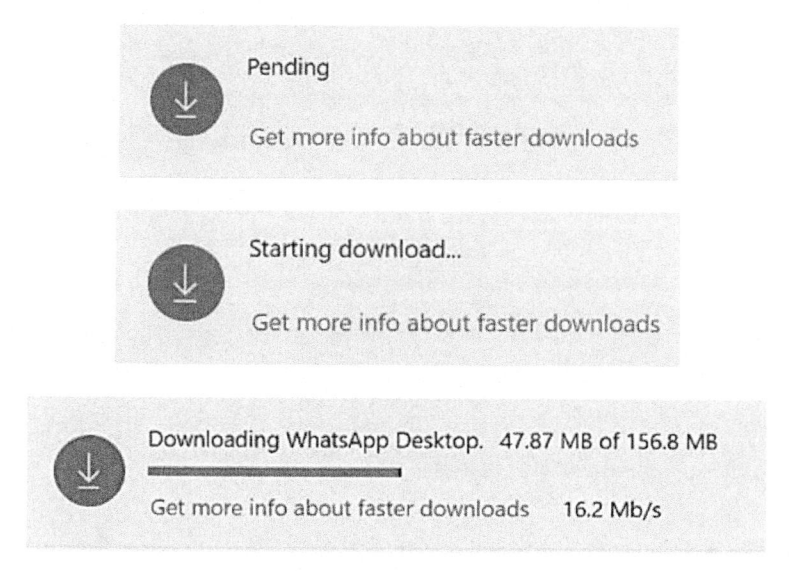

> Pending
> Get more info about faster downloads

> Starting download...
> Get more info about faster downloads

> Downloading WhatsApp Desktop. 47.87 MB of 156.8 MB
> Get more info about faster downloads   16.2 Mb/s

- After successfully downloaded, installation on your PC begins immediately. Once done; you will be informed that the *"product is installed"*.

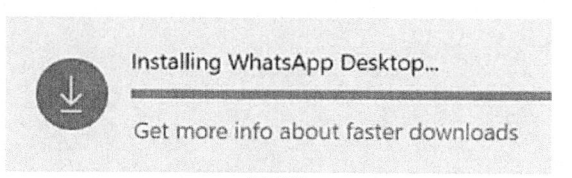

> Installing WhatsApp Desktop...
> Get more info about faster downloads

⬇ This product is installed.

- On your right-hand side, you will see "Launch"; beside launch, there are three dots, click on it and you will be told to "pin to start menu" or "pin to taskbar". Let's assume we want to pin to the taskbar,

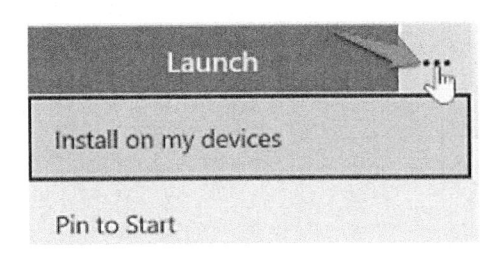

Launch ...
Install on my devices
Pin to Start

- you will be asked to confirm your request to pin WhatsApp desktop to your taskbar, click "**Yes**"

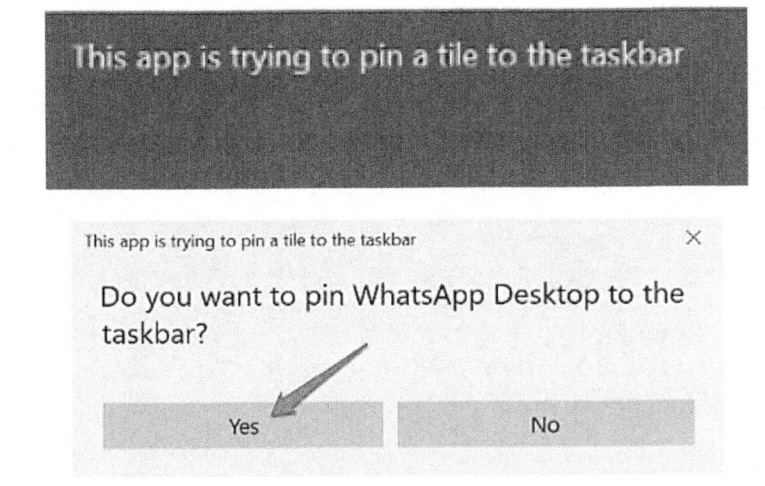

This app is trying to pin a tile to the taskbar

This app is trying to pin a tile to the taskbar   ×

Do you want to pin WhatsApp Desktop to the taskbar?

Yes   No

- It will then be added to the list of icons below your desktop interface known as *"taskbar"* double click on "WhatsApp" on your taskbar to launch it.

- It will open and ask you to open WhatsApp from your phone to activate it on your desktop by following the instruction in the illustration, then you can start using your desktop to WhatsApp freely.

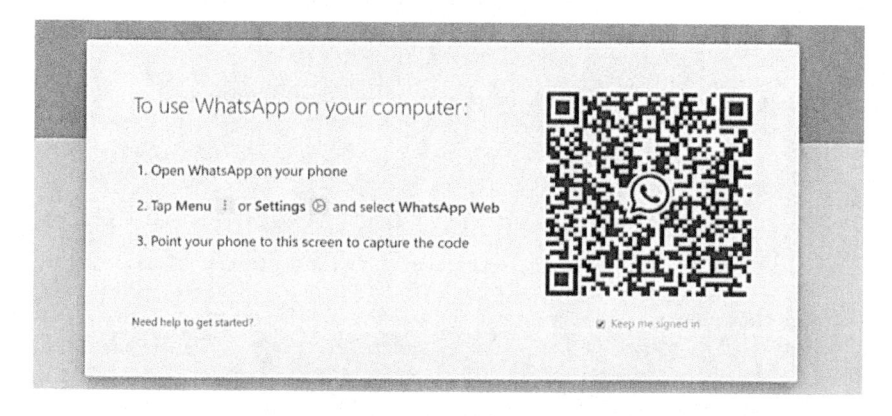

- You can also search for WhatsApp on your start menu by typing "WhatsApp".

- You will be shown "WhatsApp Desktop" double click it to open.

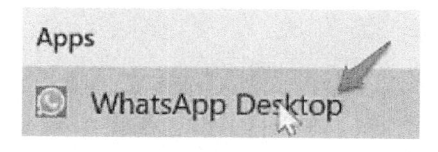

- The app will automatically open.

CHAPTER FOURTEEN

WINDOWS 10 TIPS AND TRICKS

Hiding of Desktop Items

Grip your mouse, place it on the desktop interface.

Then right-click (make sure your mouse is not placed on any item).

Select "View"; another dialog box will appear beside the "view", look for "Show desktop icons", it will automatically hide all your items on the desktop environment.

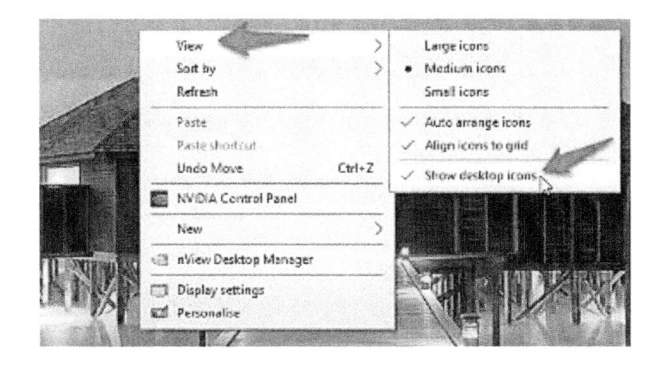

Displaying Back All Hidden Items

Go back to your desktop environment.

Right-click on your desktop interface (do note, your mouse must not hover on any item to get these tips).

255

Select "View", another dialog box will appear, click on "Show desktop icons", all your items will be back immediately.

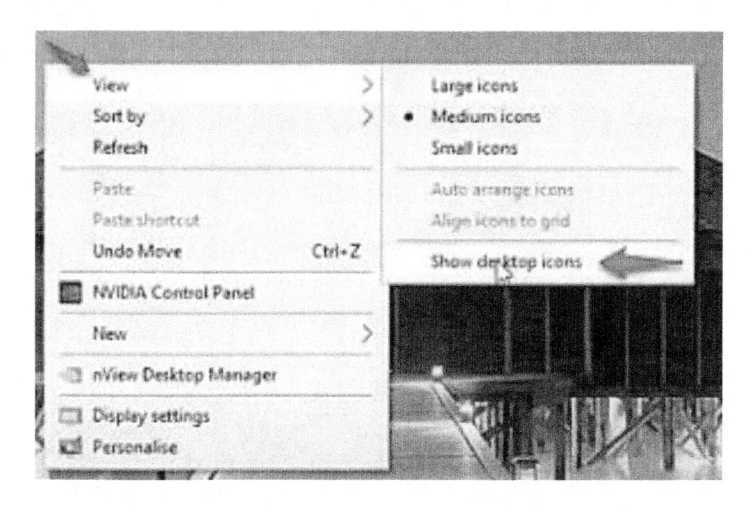

Enabling Clipboard History

Clipboard history is useful when you copy and paste often which gives you the privilege to view recently copied items. To enable this, go to "Start menu".

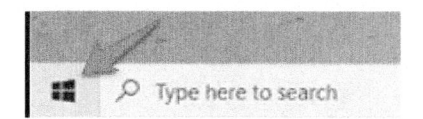

Click on "Start menu" and select "Settings".

"Settings" dialog box will display on the search bar; below search for "Clipboard settings".

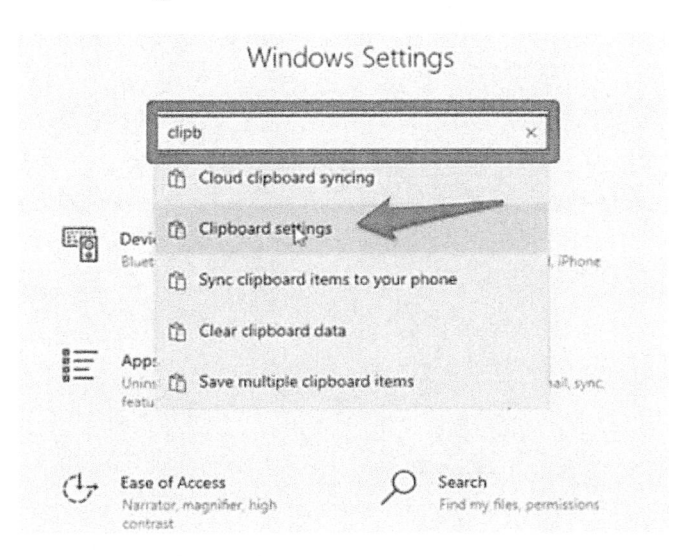

Or you select the "System" option and double click on it to open.

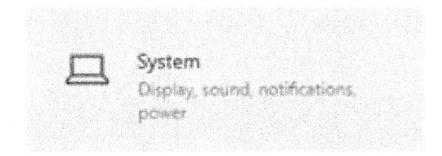

Under "Settings", scroll down at your left-hand side and select "Clipboard".

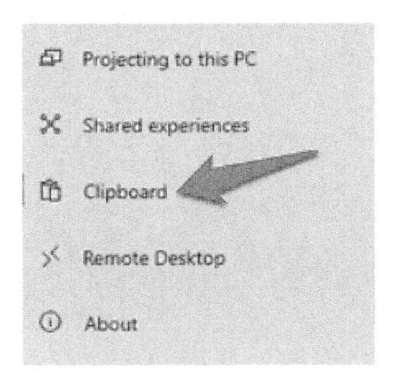

Once selected, Clipboard features will display on your right-hand side. Look for "Clipboard history".

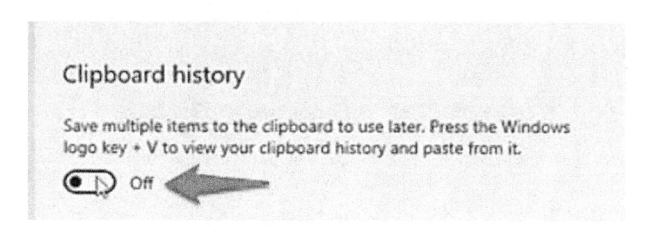

Turn it on if it's turned off.

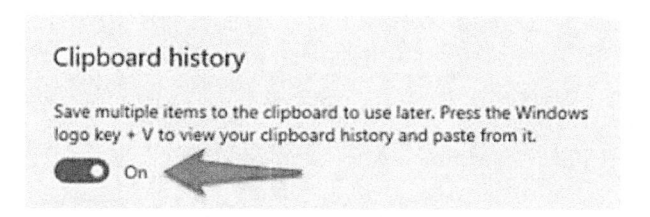

Once done, open any text editor for you to see how it works. For understanding purposes, let's practice with this; search for "Notepad" and type *"why did the chicken cross the road?"*; in another paragraph on a different line, type *"I don't know, it wrote it on this power but it's in Spanish!"*

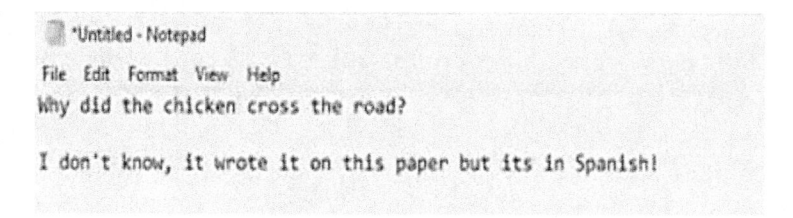

Now, highlight the first statement of the text.

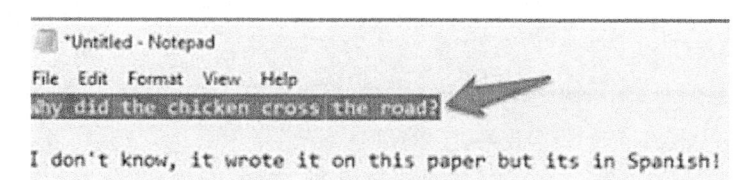

Right-click on the highlighted text, a dialog box will pop up, select "copy".

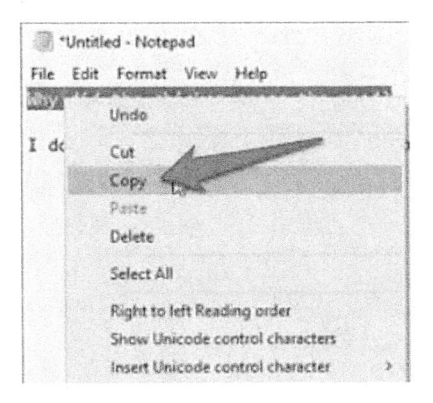

Do the same to the next statement; highlight it,

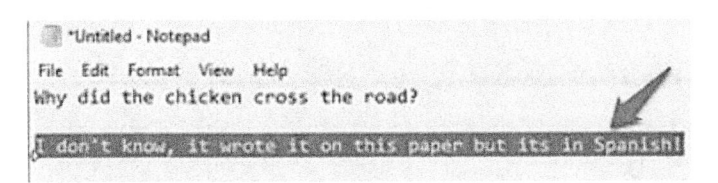

right-click on it (make sure it is still highlighted while right-clicking) a dialog box will pop up, select "copy".

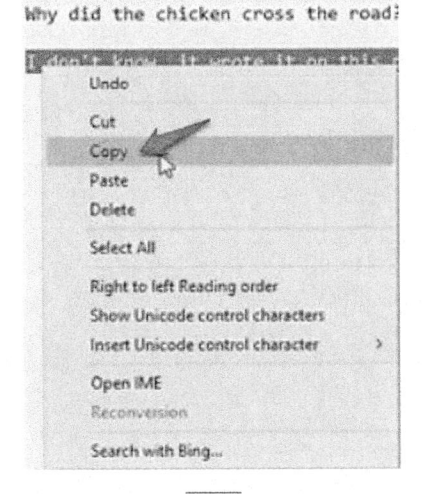

Now, to activate or to see the clipboard at work, using Microsoft shortcut keys, press **WINKEY + V,** a dialog box will pop up which is your clipboard history showing you recently added items. You paste what you once copied by clicking on your preferred option, and it will be pasted immediately.

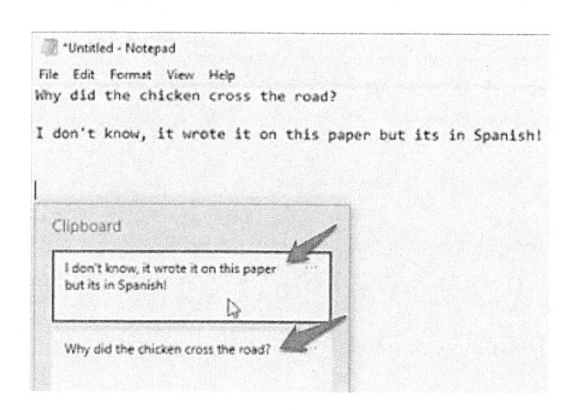

How to Delete, Pin & Clear Clipboard History

Whenever you copy various items on any text editor, press **WINKEY + V** to display your clipboard history. At the right-hand corner, there are 3 dots where the arrow below is indicating, once you click on it, you will be given an option to **delete** a specific item, and another option to **pin** a specific item above other items, and the last option to **clear all** copied items on your clipboard. This can also be applied to other clipboard histories.

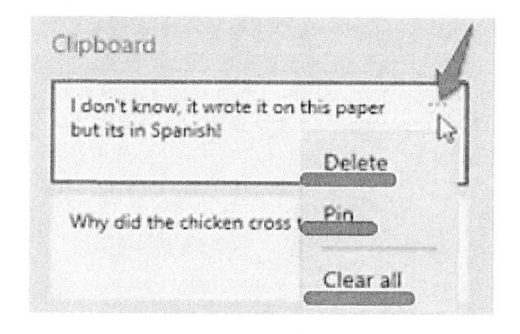

Splitting Windows App on Windows 10

Splitting Windows app on Windows 10 is a great way of rightly dividing your screen display in case of multiple applications. All you have to do is to grip an open application and drag it to the left or right-hand edge of the screen.

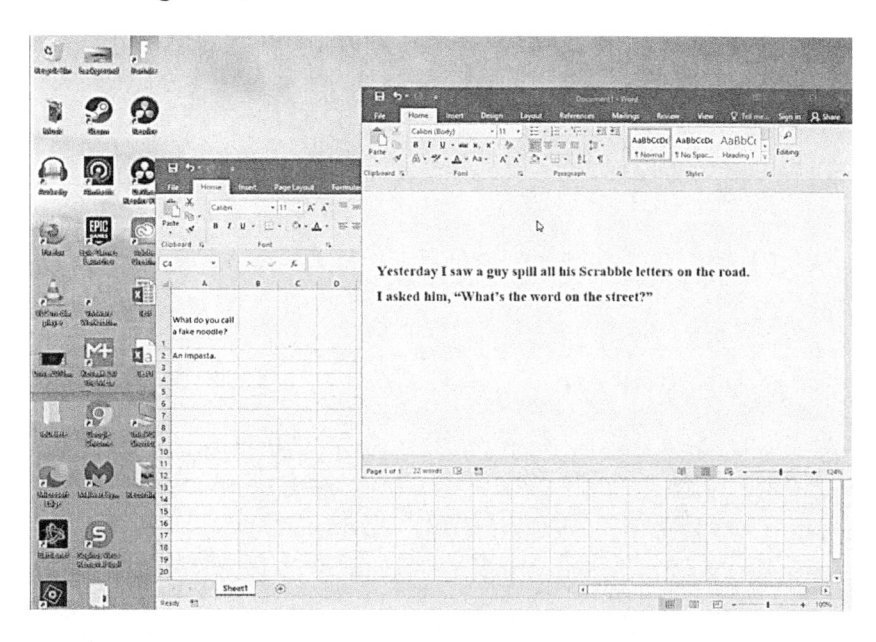

By default, the dragged application will cover half of the desktop interface and allocate the rest half for other opened application

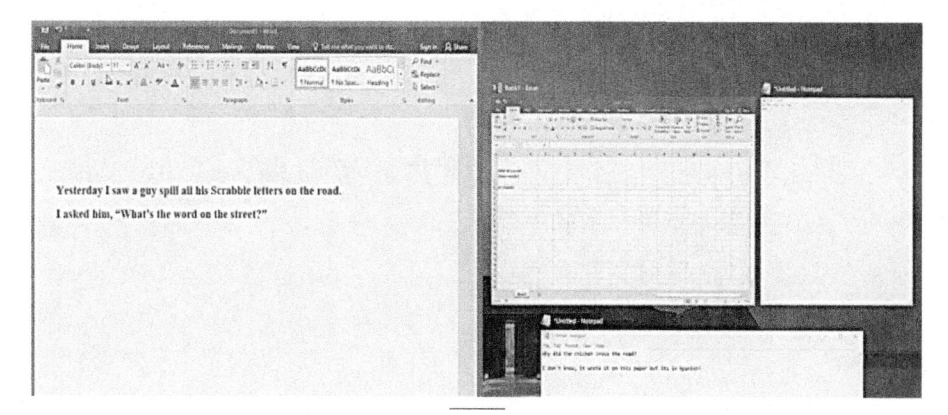

Clicking on the Excel application by your right will override the other apps and both Word and Excel will occupy the full screen in a half-divided way.

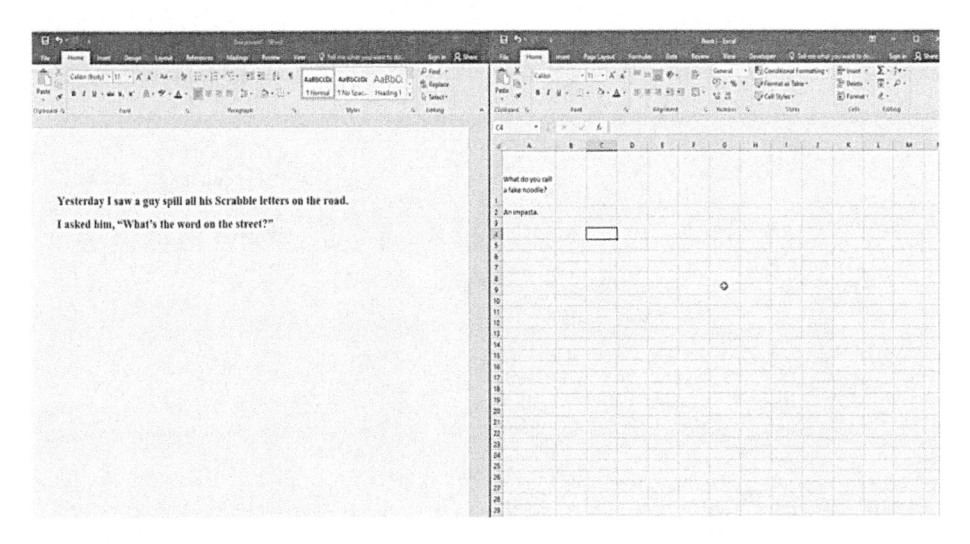

You can also bring up the overridden apps (here, it is "Notepad") by clicking on any of the two applications that are occupying the full screen by pressing the **WINKEY + Up arrow key.** By doing this you are automatically adding another application to share the screen with the overriding apps.

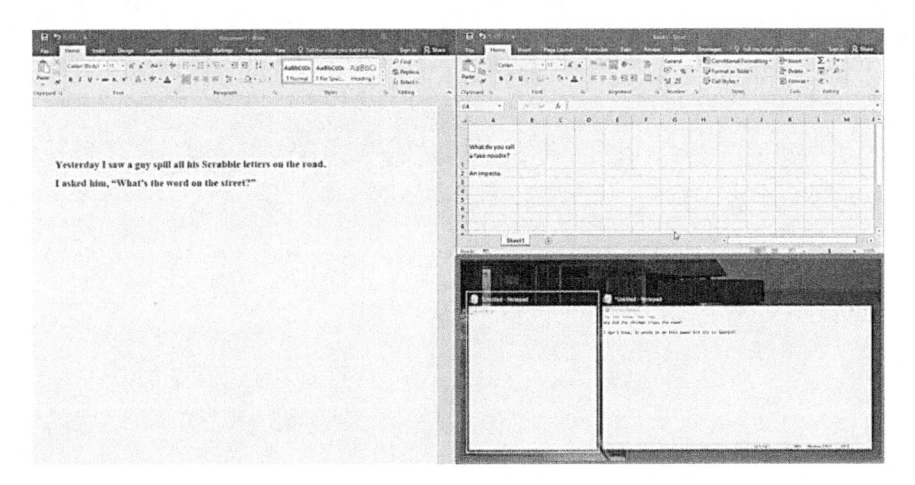

By default, all the remaining apps will appear beside the application you selected before pressing the shortcut keys; the newly added or remaining apps, once you click on one of the remaining ones displayed, you can also bring it back to the other side of the desktop edge by using the same method above and you will get the below result. You can also move them around by holding on to the app to be moved and pressing the **WINKEY + Arrow** to move it around as you wish.

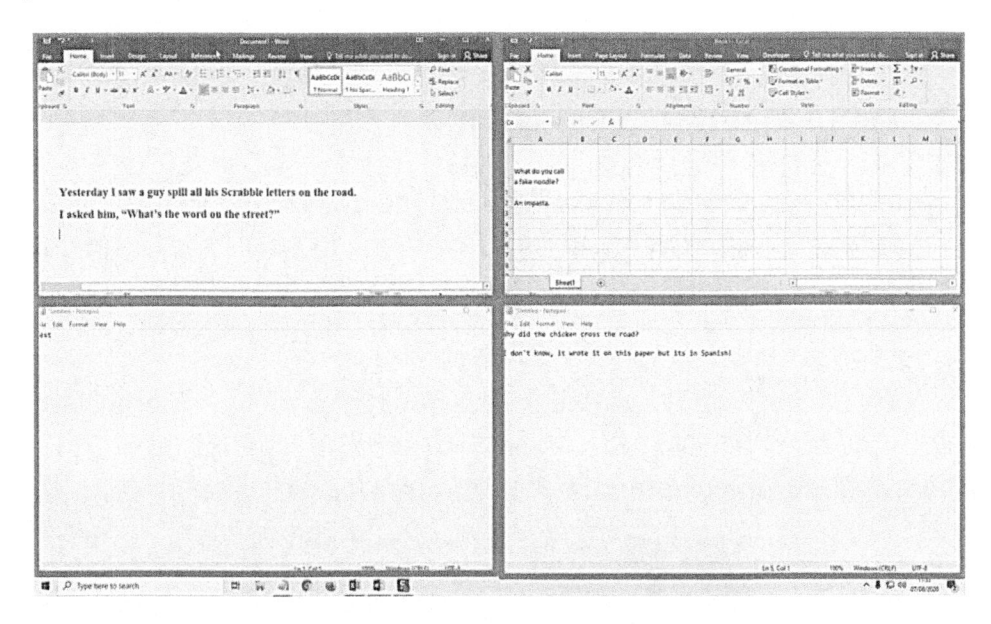

How To Make Use of Emojis on Windows 10

Emojis on Windows 10. Everyone likes emojis and Windows 10 gives you multiple options.

Before you can use emojis, make sure you are in a text or typing environment such as search box, word editor, or any other typing zone, then you can press "**Windows + ;** (semi-colon)" or "**Windows + .** (dots)" to open your emoji keyboard for multiple options, for use and selection.

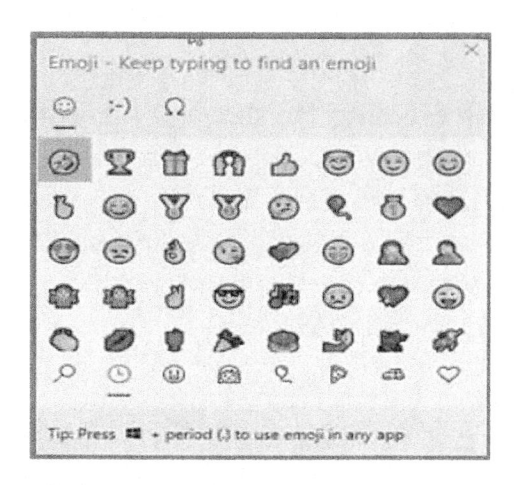

Speeding up Windows Start time

If your computer system is slowing down while booting, it is advisable to check which apps are launching in your PC startup and if there is an app you don't need, you disable it to avoid slowing down your PC.

Go to your "taskbar", right-click on your **taskbar**. A dialog box will pop up, select "Task Manager". Otherwise, search for "Task Manager" from your search bar then open it by clicking on it.

Once the task manager opens, click on "Start-up" which will show enabled apps and disabled apps.

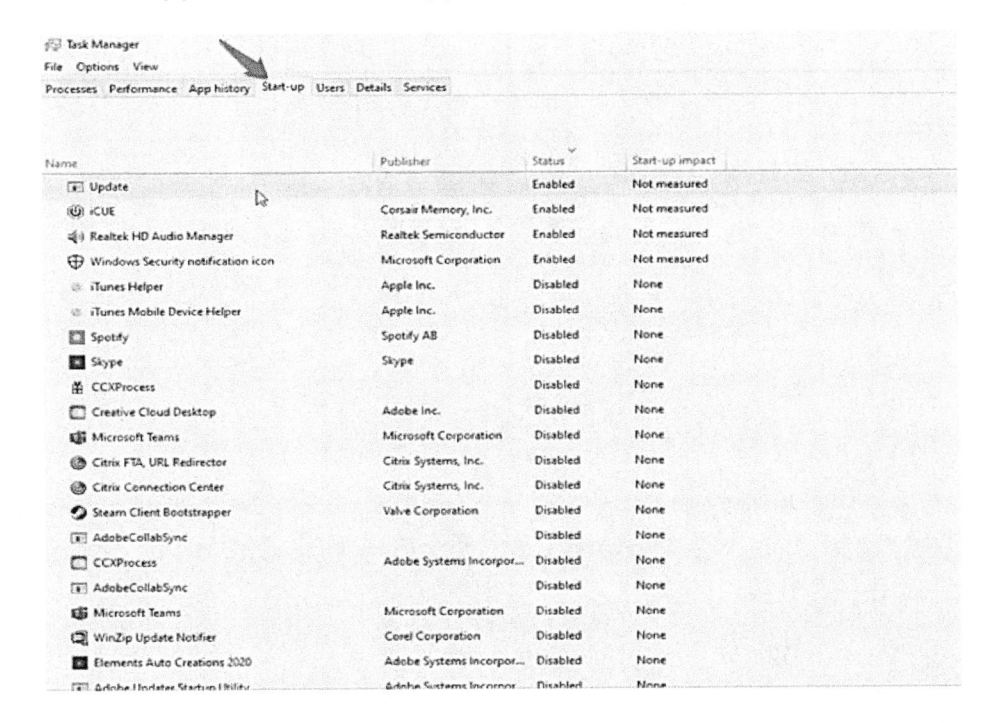

To disable, right-click on the application name you want to disable, then you will be given the option to disable.

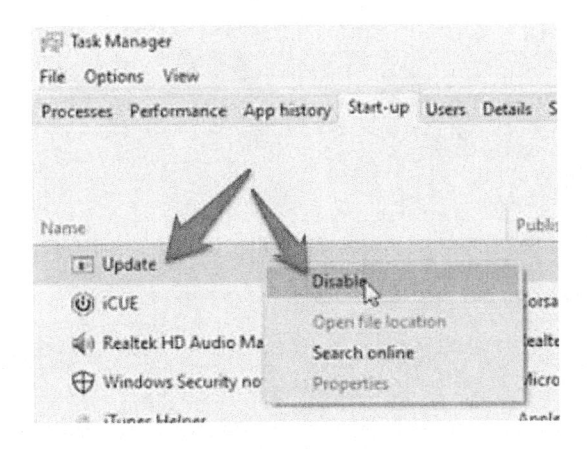

To enable, right-click again and enable it.

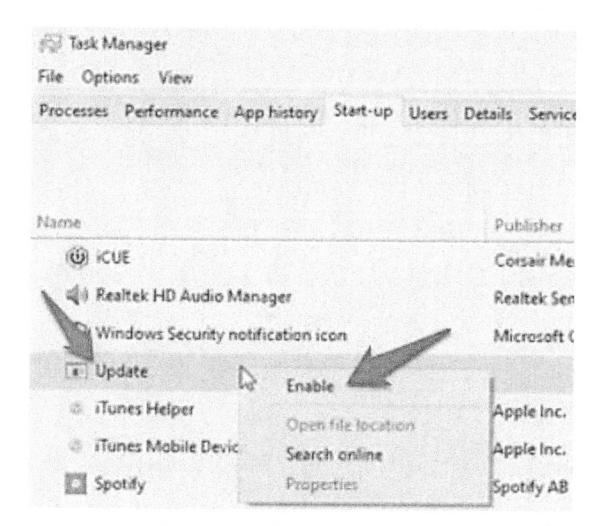

In case you are not sure what an app is all about, right-click on it and select "search online" before performing any activity on your task manager.

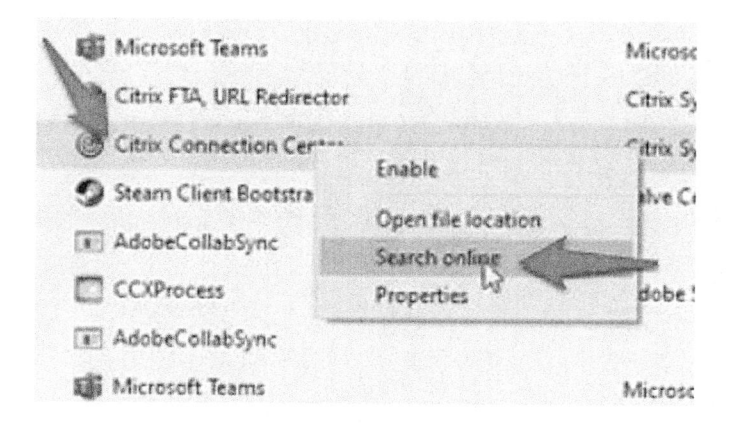

Customizing Your Search Box

It is important to note that the search box can be customized, especially when it is taking too much space on your taskbar. It can be removed or customized, see below on how to go about it.

266

How to Hide Your Search Box

Go to "taskbar", right-click on any free space, a dialog box will pop up select "Search",

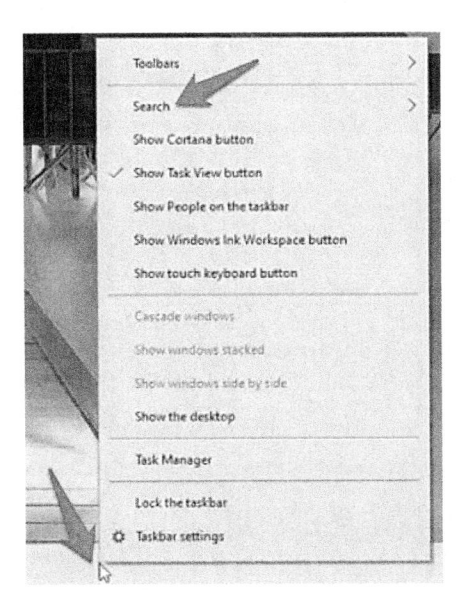

beside search, another displayed box will appear, select "hidden".

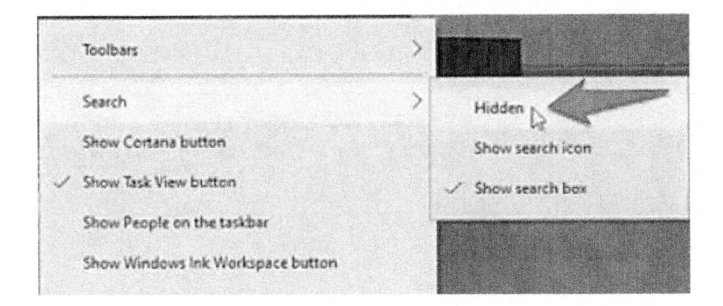

And the search bar will disappear.

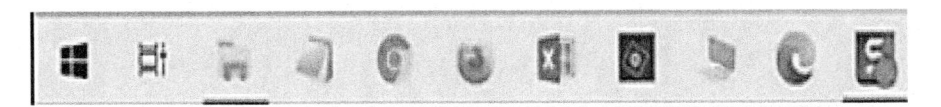

How to Display Your Search Box

To bring it back, go to your "taskbar", right-click on any free space on your taskbar, a dialog box will pop up, click "search" and select "Show search box".

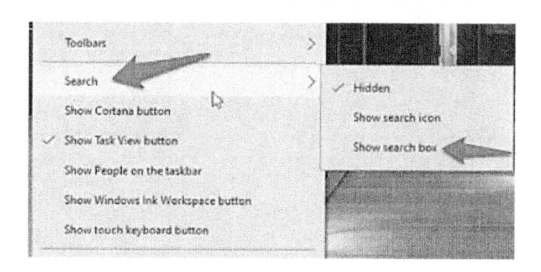

It will bring back the search box.

How to Display Only Your Search Icon

Go to your "taskbar", right-click on any free space, a dialog box will pop up with multiple options, select "search", another dialog box will appear beside your "search" option, click on "Show search icon".

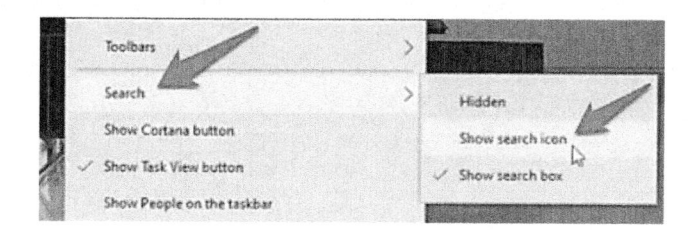

Immediately, the search box will display its icon.

How to Show File Name Extension

The file extension is a unique identifier of various applications. For example, any extension that shows "doc" represents Microsoft Word application, "pdf" represents Adobe reader, while ".bat" represents batch file that comes with your operating system which can be manipulated by hackers to pass viruses into your PC. It is important to know and recognize what different extension represents. How do you recognize file extensions?

On your desktop interface,

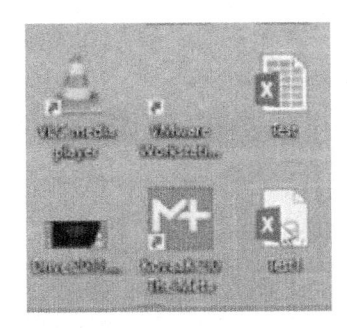

Open up a file explorer Windows by clicking on the file explorer icon or press **WINKEY + E** to display your file explorer.

Select "View" as indicated in the illustration below, then also tick "File name extension".

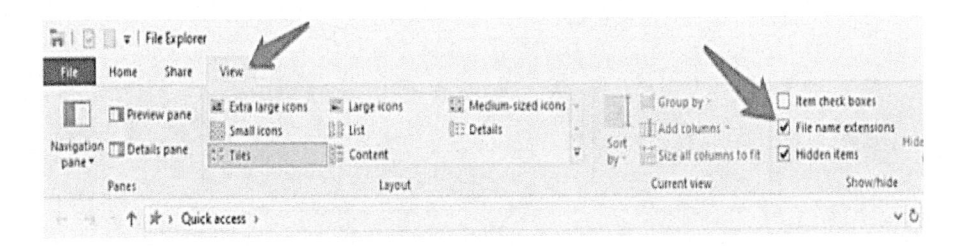

Once you tick on "File name extension", such files on your PC will start showing their unique identifier. According to the illustration below, the first one is an excel extension, while the other one is also an excel application extension that was used and converted into a contact list. Any extension you do not understand, search for it online to gain more in-depth knowledge on your PC files.

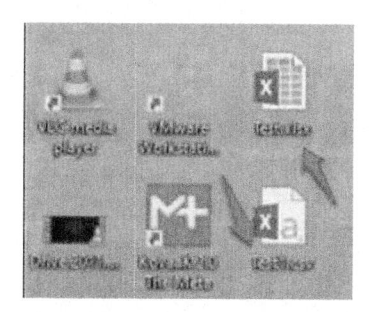

If not displaying, click on "Options".

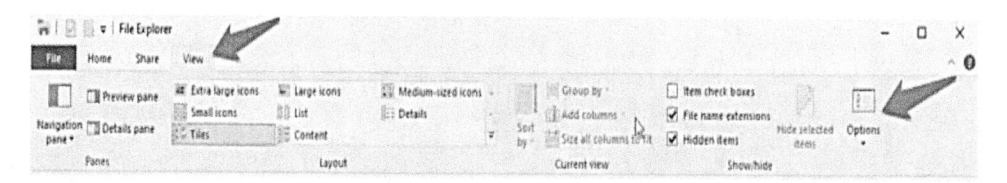

A dialog box will pop up, untick "Hide extensions for known files types" and also tick "Show hidden files, folders, and drives" then press "Ok" to take effect to changes.

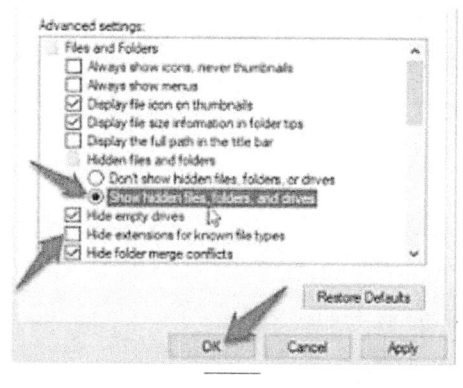

By default, every item will appear with its extension.

Minimize All Opened Applications

It is important to note that there are three (3) different ways to minimize your multiple opened applications.

i. **Aero Shake of application**.

After opening different applications, to minimize them all and be focused on one, hold the opened application and use your mouse or laptop cursor to shake the app like a polaroid picture (shake it left & right until other opened apps disappear).

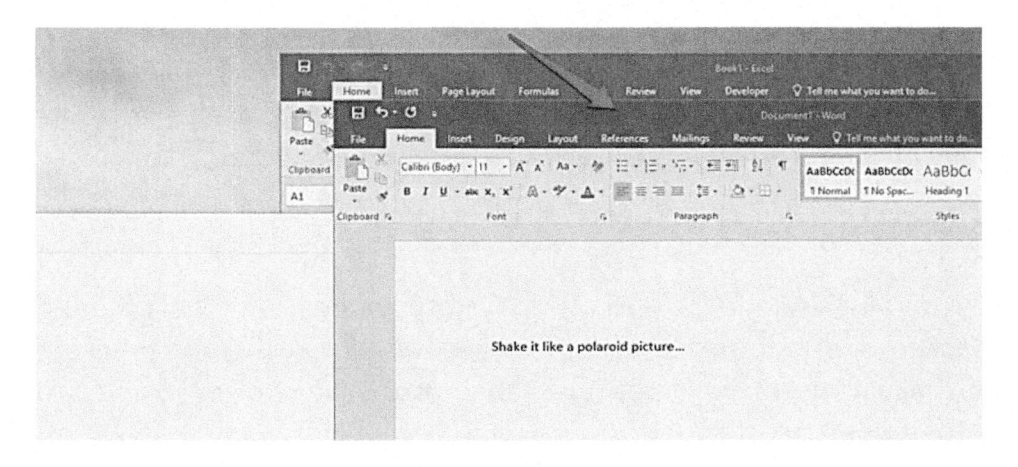

This should be the outcome.

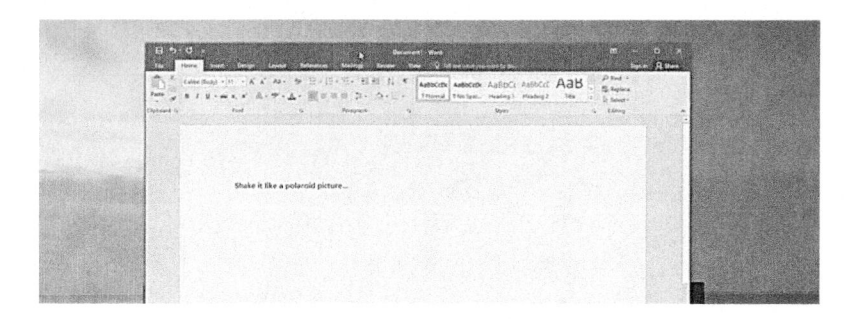

ii. Clicking method

In the clicking method, you have to click on the **last edge** on the right-hand corner in your taskbar beside the system tray. Once you click it, your desktop will minimize every opened application, clicking it again will return all opened applications.

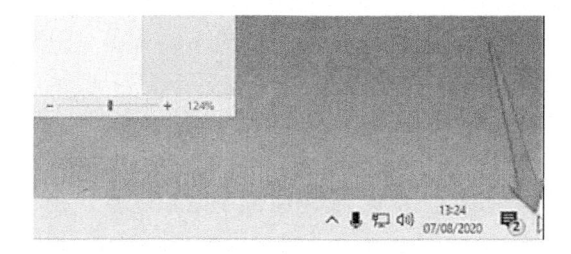

iii. Shortcut method

This is the fastest and easiest way out of all, it is a command key. Simply press **WINKEY + D**, this will automatically bring you to your desktop interface and minimize all opened applications, pressing the command again will display every minimized application.

Activating Dark Mode

By default, Windows operating system comes with a lightened background, but due to other reasons, Windows give the privilege to make its users decide to select their preferred choice. To activate dark mode;

go to "Settings".

Select "Personalization" under "Settings"'.

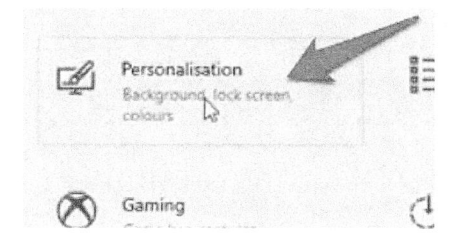

Under "Personalization", at your left-hand side select "Colors"

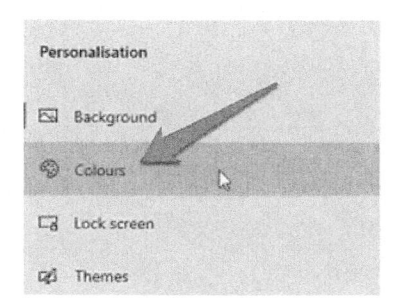

On your right-hand side, you will see your default color if not yet changed.

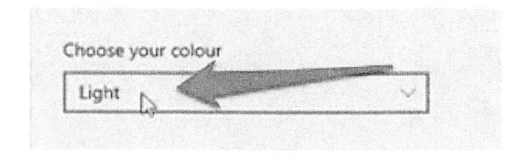

Click on the dropdown and select "Dark".

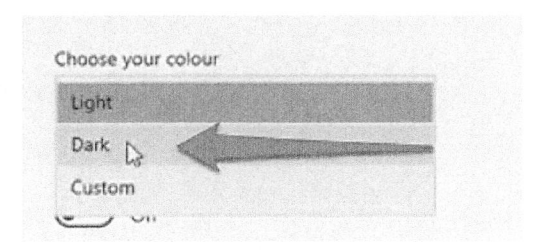

Below is the result.

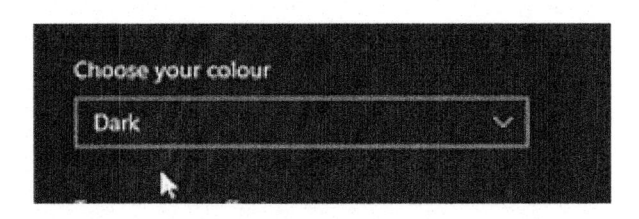

Determining What Your File Explorer Opens First

File explorer has two major opening choices which are: "This PC" & "Quick access"

- This PC

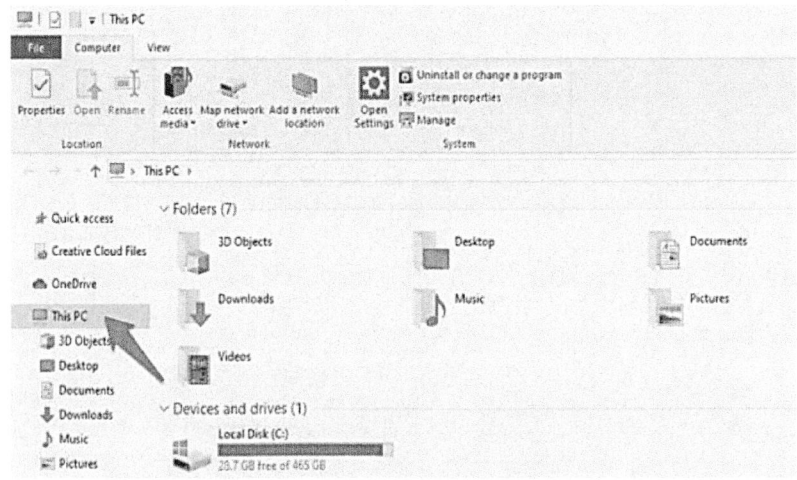

- Quick access.

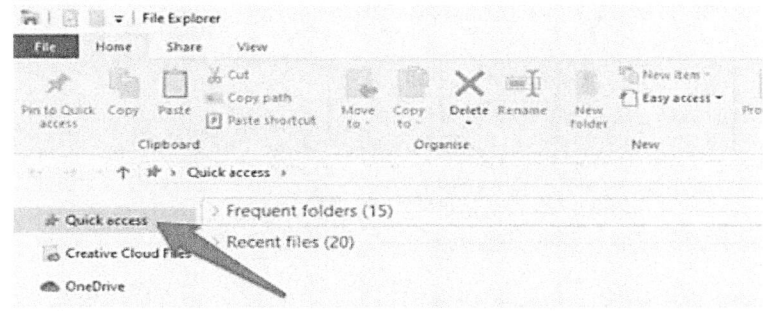

How to Switch and Determine What File Explorer Should Open By Default

Click on file explorer from your taskbar or simply press **WINKEY + E**. Whatever your file explorer display first, either "This PC" or "Quick access",

as illustrated below simply select "View" and then click on "Options".

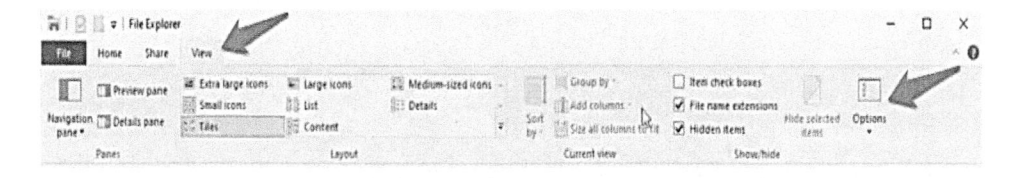

A dialog box will pop up, beside "Open File Explorer to" that is, where you want File Explorer to open to

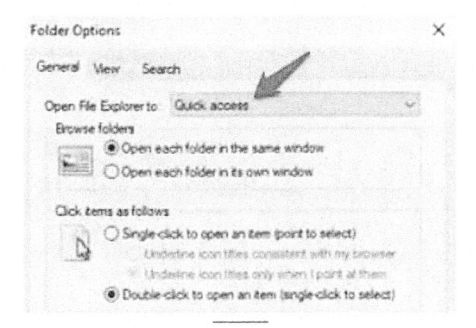

Click inside the "Open File Explorer" to switch between "This PC & Quick access" depending on your choice.

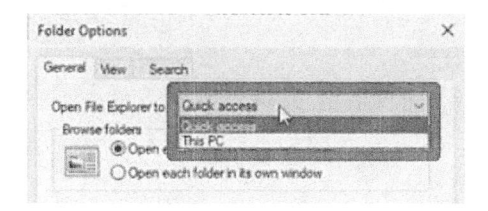

Once done, click "Ok" to effect the changes.

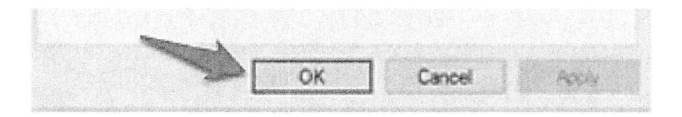

Factory Reset

To factory reset Windows 10, navigate to the "Start menu" and select "Settings".

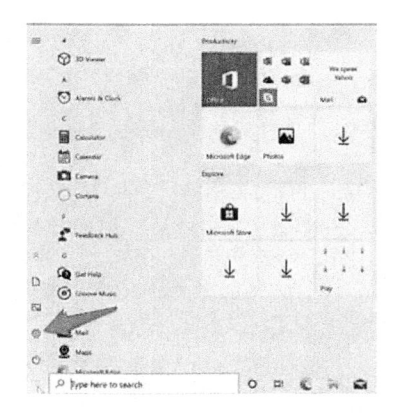

Under "Settings", select "Update & Security".

On the left side, click "Recovery".

A dialog box will pop up by your right-hand side, click on "Get started".

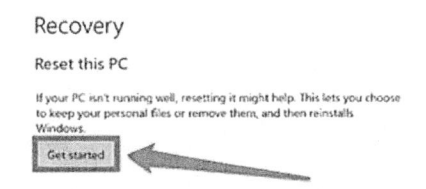

Another dialog box will appear with two options; option one will help you to reset your PC without losing your files, "option two will help you to wipe out everything both files and app", this option is only advisable if there is an external backup. For vital files without any external backup, it is advisable to choose option one *"Keep my files"*.

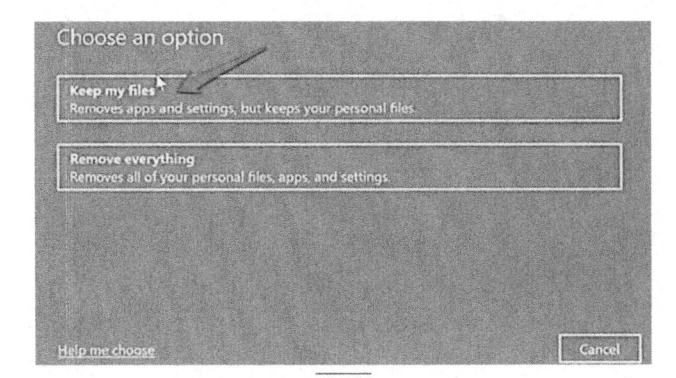

On the next page, Windows will confirm your action either to "Reset" or to "Cancel". Click on **Reset**.

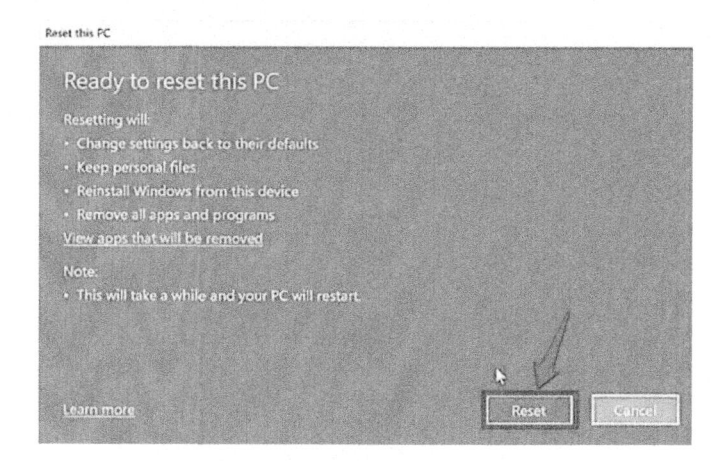

Then the initialization process will take over.

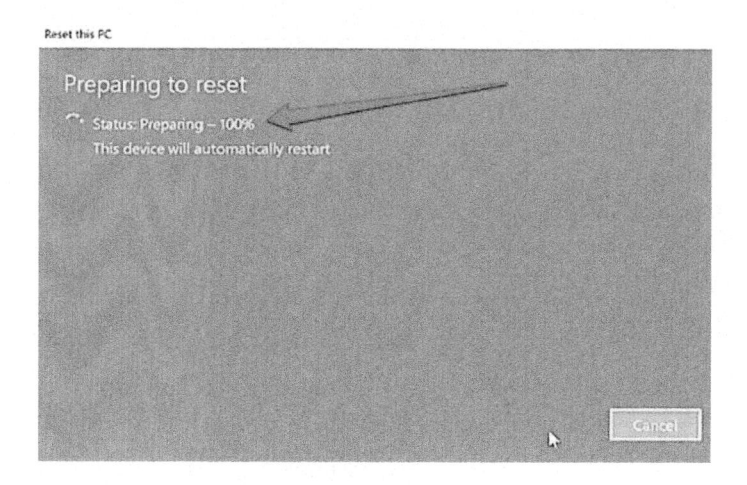

After the reset is completed, Windows will bring you back into your desktop interface.

Turn On & Off Background Apps

Navigate to the *"Start menu"*, select *"Settings"*.

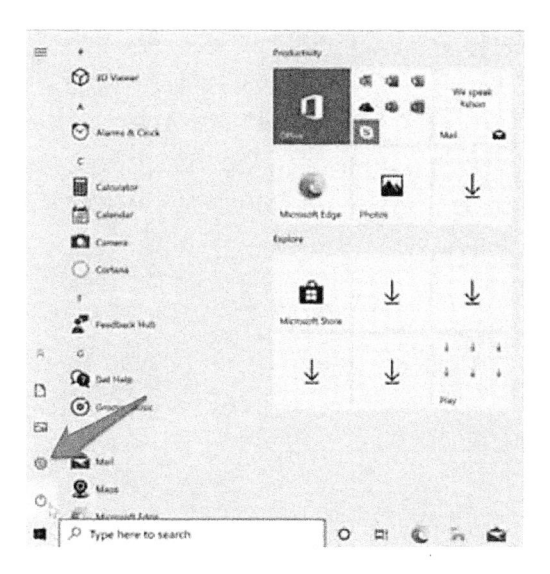

Under *"Settings"* Select *"Privacy"*.

Under *"Privacy"*, scroll down and select *"Background apps"*.

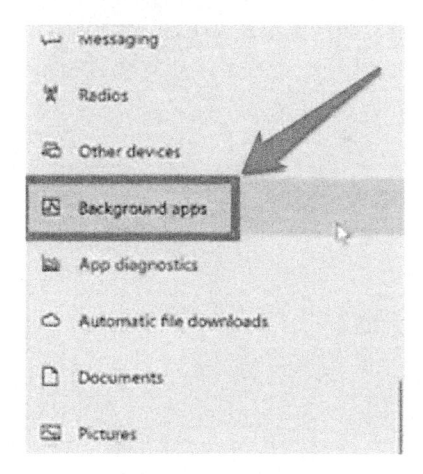

279

On your right-hand side, you will see all the background apps running on your PC. You can turn everything off automatically by turning off the on button titled **"Let app run in the background"** or specifically turn off the ones you do not need to run on your PC background and turn on the one(s) you want to give permission.

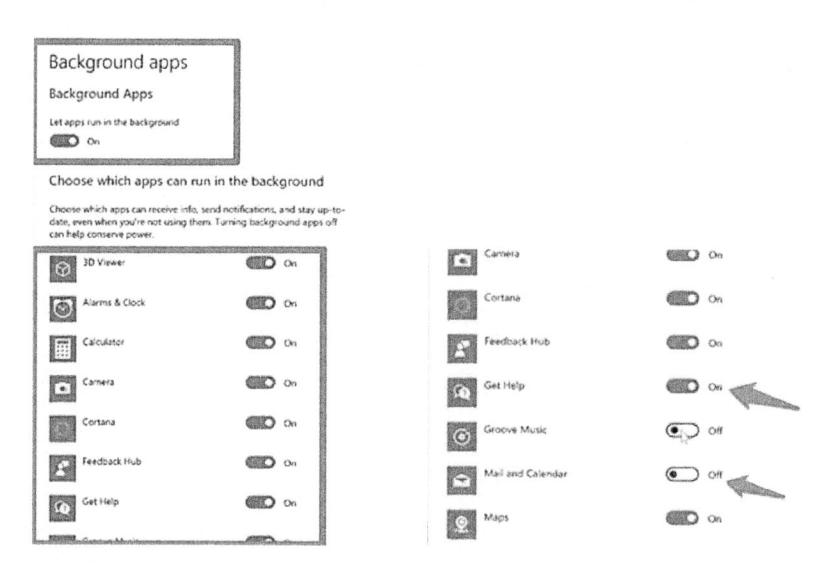

Dictation

Open any of your text editor, for understanding purpose, let's make use of an inbuilt app which is "Notepad". Search for it through the search box and open it.

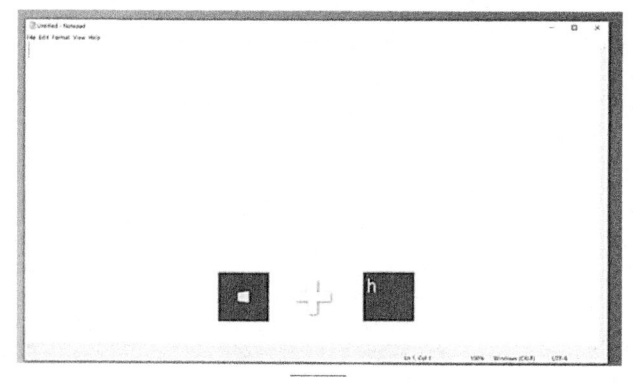

With your text area being active, press the shortcut, **WINKEY + H** on your keyboard to start the speech & text ability. Speaking to your PC, microphone and dictation will convert your words to text.

God Mode

God mode is a headed feature that compels an array of functions into one menu. To enable God mode, navigate to your desktop and right-click on **space**, a dialog box will appear, select "New", another dialog box will appear beside it, select "Folder" to create one.

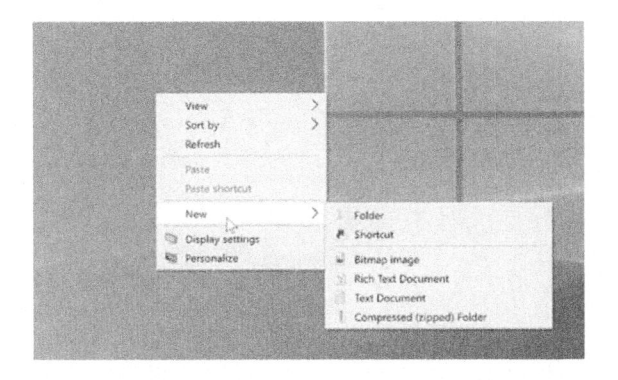

Rename the folder with {ED7BA470-8E54-465E-825C-99712043E01C}.

Once you rename the folder, icon will change to the control panel icon and the name will disappear.

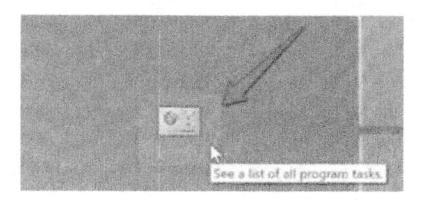

When you click on it, it will bring you into "God Mode" where we have a mass array of PC control's customization ability.

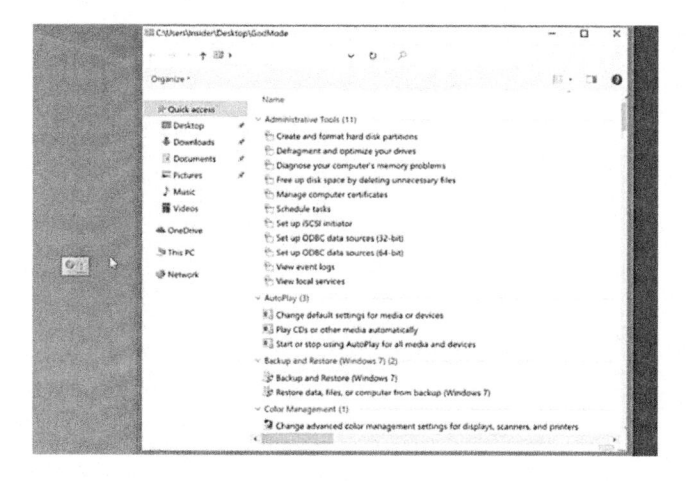

The search bar on the top right corner helps us to quickly type and search needed PC items, and at the same right-hand side is the scrolling bar.

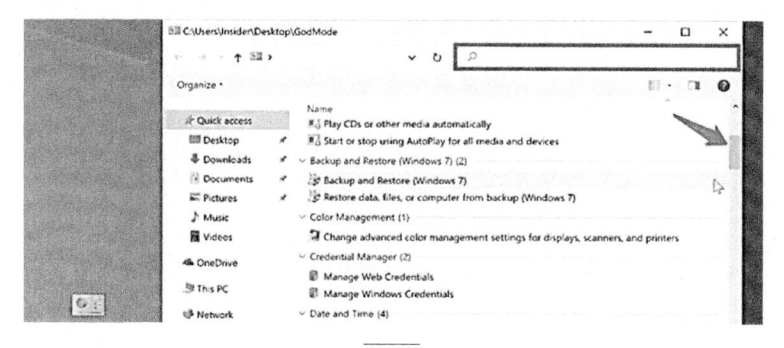

Snip & Sketch

The simple way to take a screenshot in Windows is called "Snipping & Sketch". To make use of it, open the items to be captured, then from your keyboard hold down **WINKEY + Shift + S** key.

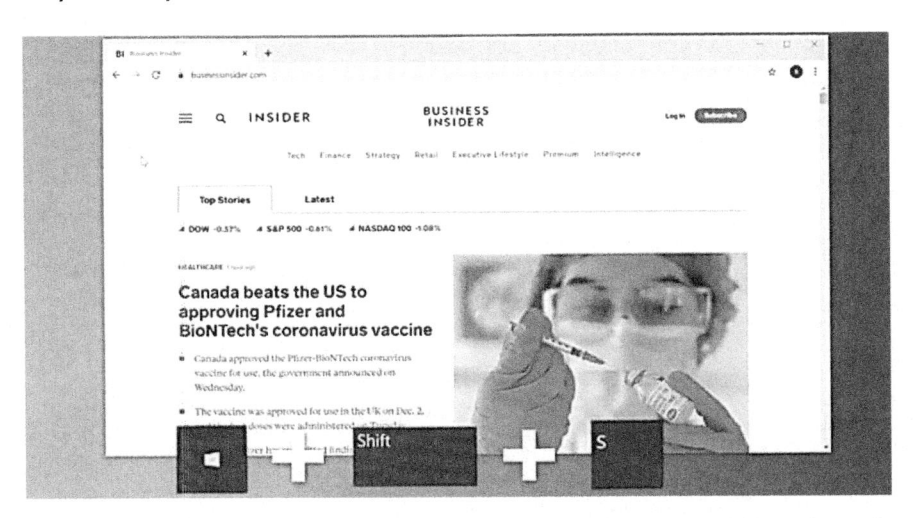

This will dim the screen, then a menu bar containing icons will appear on top, hovering on them shows "Rectangular Snip", "Free from Snip", "Window Snip" & "Full-screen Snip" select your preferred choice. For this teaching, I will be making use of "Rectangular Snip"

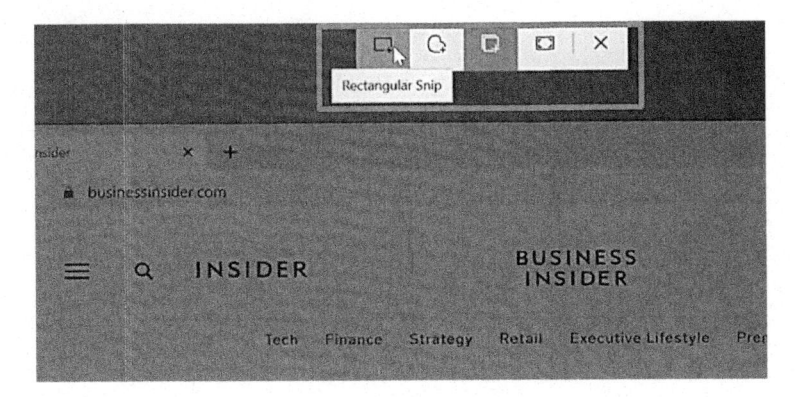

Once "Rectangular Snip" is selected, you will highlight the portion to screenshot.

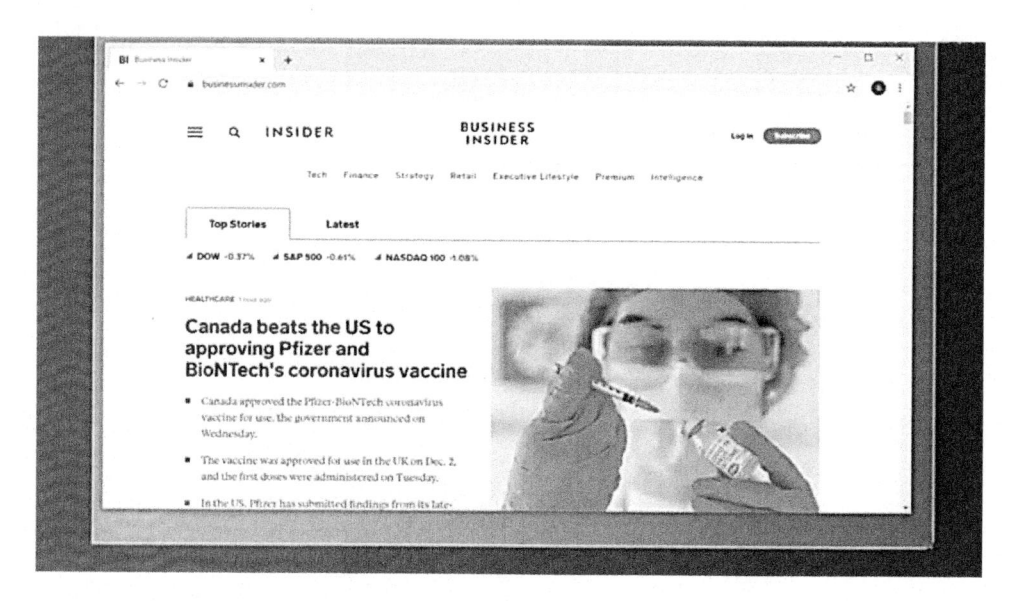

And it will affect it automatically.

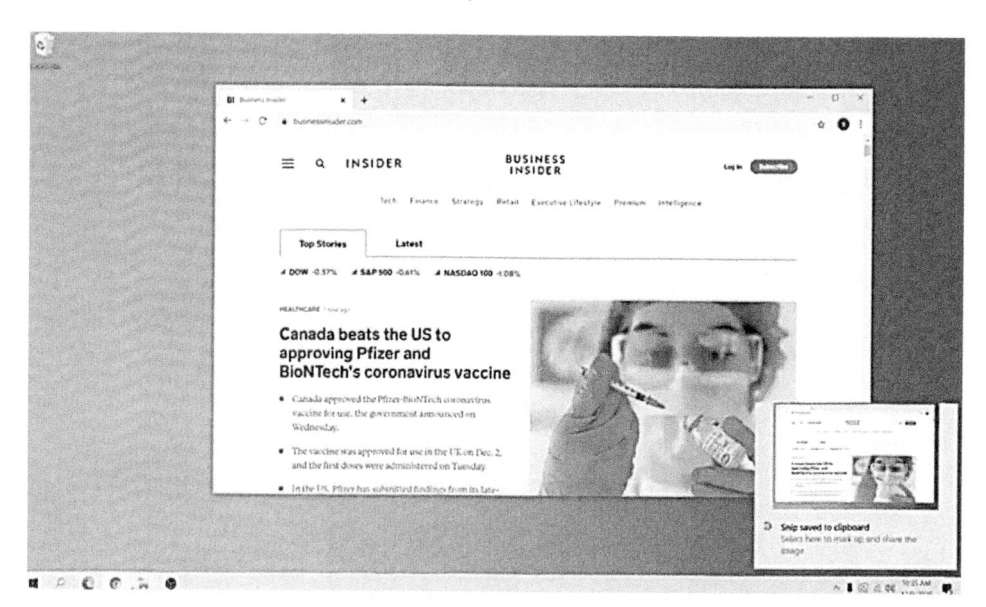

284

Windows Sandbox

Windows Sandbox is a virtual disposable environment that allows you to run applications in isolation. Once the sandbox is opened, all the data files and applications you created are permanently deleted.

Sandbox Requirements

To check out if your PC can run "sandbox", go to your "start menu" and type "System Information", double click on it.

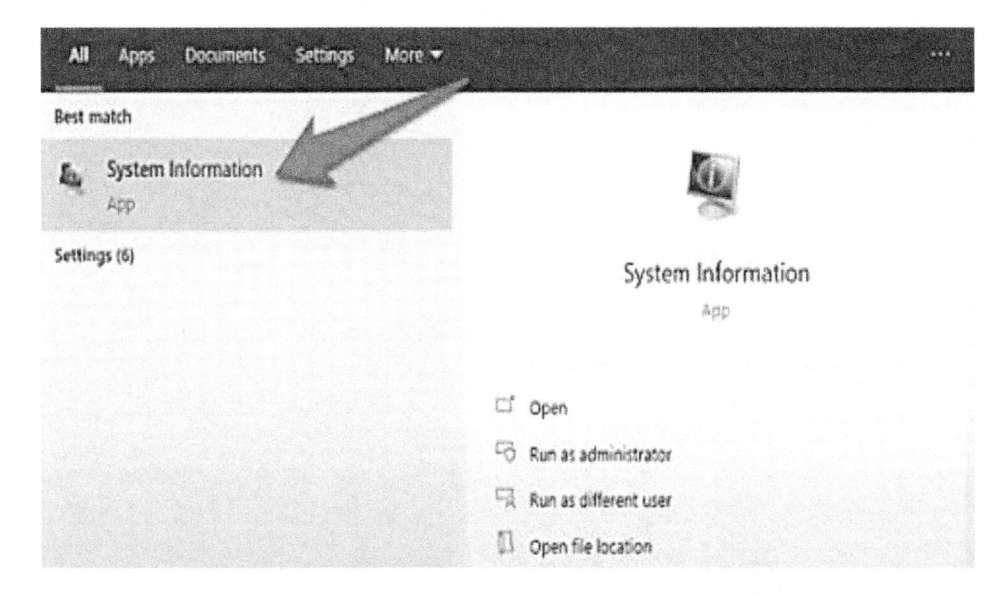

Under "System Information" at your right-hand side, check below and see if your "Virtualization enabled in firmware" is enabled, if not, you need to go to your UEFI file configuration and make sure virtualization is turned on on hardware. Also, make sure your PC is running a 64bit operating system and has at least 4G RAM capacity. If your system is not advanced enough, you might not have this option to run Windows sandbox.

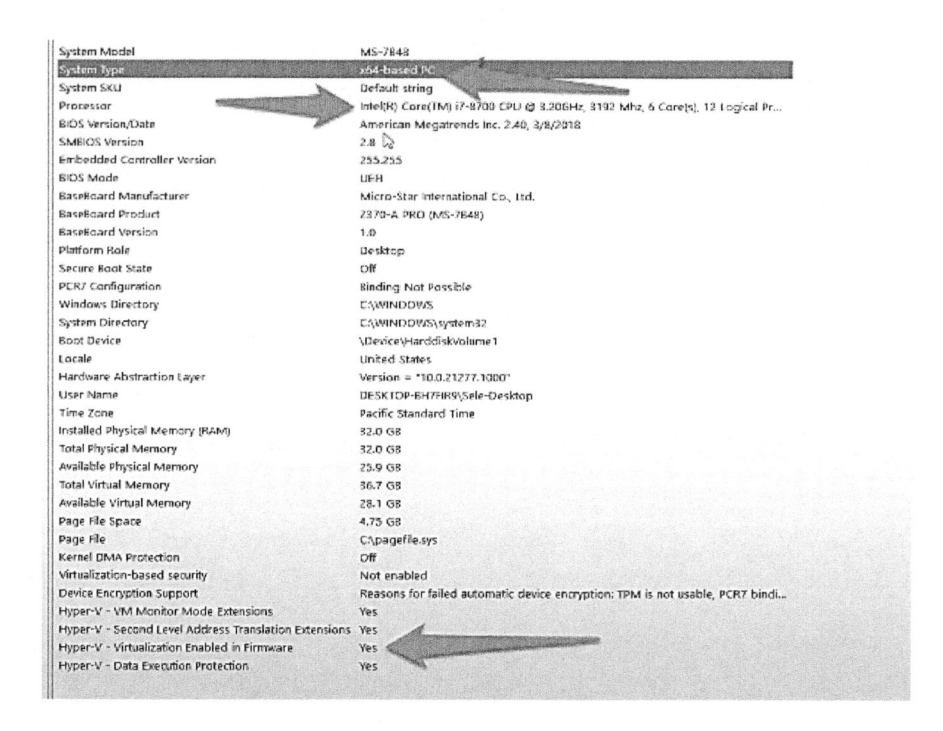

System Model	MS-7B48
System Type	x64-based PC
System SKU	Default string
Processor	Intel(R) Core(TM) i7-8700 CPU @ 3.20GHz, 3192 Mhz, 6 Core(s), 12 Logical Pr...
BIOS Version/Date	American Megatrends Inc. 2.40, 3/8/2018
SMBIOS Version	2.8
Embedded Controller Version	255.255
BIOS Mode	UEFI
BaseBoard Manufacturer	Micro-Star International Co., Ltd.
BaseBoard Product	Z370-A PRO (MS-7B48)
BaseBoard Version	1.0
Platform Role	Desktop
Secure Boot State	Off
PCR7 Configuration	Binding Not Possible
Windows Directory	C:\WINDOWS
System Directory	C:\WINDOWS\system32
Boot Device	\Device\HarddiskVolume1
Locale	United States
Hardware Abstraction Layer	Version = "10.0.21277.1000"
User Name	DESKTOP-BH7FIR9\Sele-Desktop
Time Zone	Pacific Standard Time
Installed Physical Memory (RAM)	32.0 GB
Total Physical Memory	32.0 GB
Available Physical Memory	25.9 GB
Total Virtual Memory	36.7 GB
Available Virtual Memory	28.1 GB
Page File Space	4.75 GB
Page File	C:\pagefile.sys
Kernel DMA Protection	Off
Virtualization-based security	Not enabled
Device Encryption Support	Reasons for failed automatic device encryption: TPM is not usable, PCR7 bindi...
Hyper-V - VM Monitor Mode Extensions	Yes
Hyper-V - Second Level Address Translation Extensions	Yes
Hyper-V - Virtualization Enabled in Firmware	Yes
Hyper-V - Data Execution Protection	Yes

Launching Sandbox

Once your system meets the criteria, go to your "start menu" and type "Turn windows features on and off" double click on it to open it.

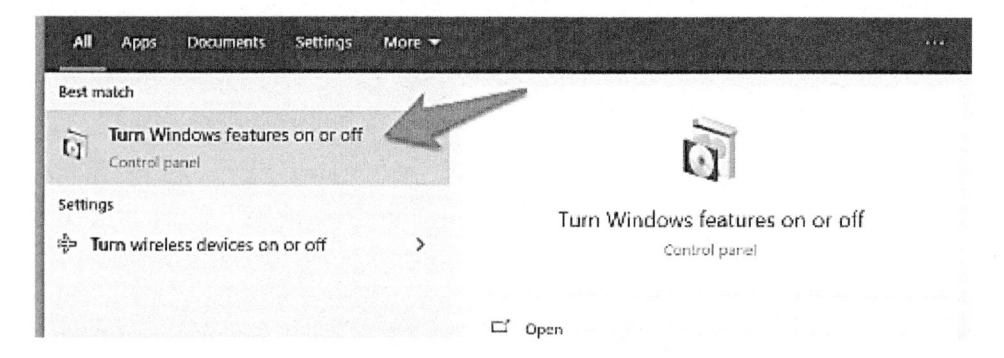

Scroll down to Windows Sandbox, tick (mark) the box, and press "Ok".

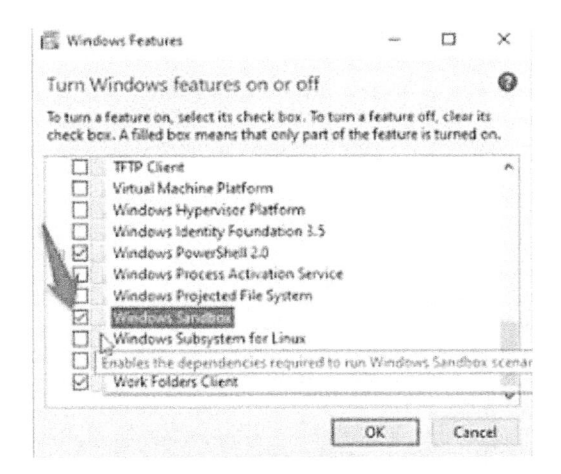

It applies the changes.

After the changes have been applied, it requires a restart, click on **Restart**.

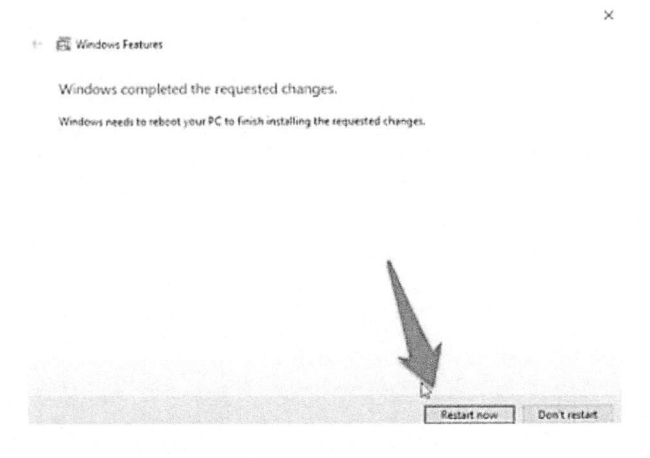

After the PC restart has been completed, you can now go to your "Start menu", scroll down to locate, and open your sandbox.

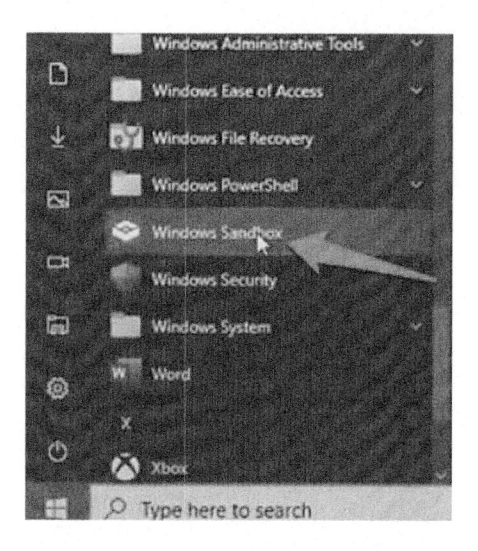

This will open your sandbox virtual environment.

Anything that makes you close your sandbox environment, all activities will be disposed and it won't be retrieved back but rather open afresh on a plain page again.

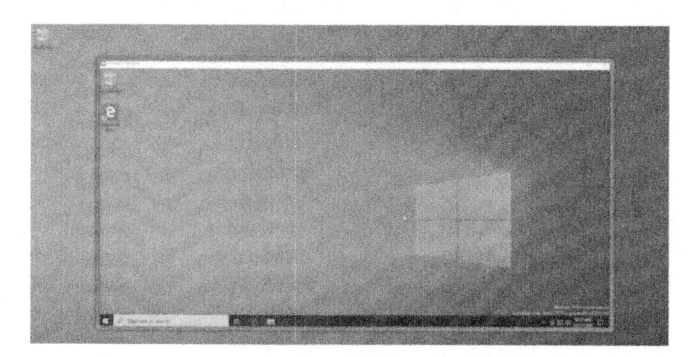

Calculator

The Windows 10 calculator has been improved dramatically.

Take a look at the options that are now available on the improved Windows 10 version such as "Standard", "Scientific", "Graphing", "Programmer", "Date Calculation" and a bunch of other commands.

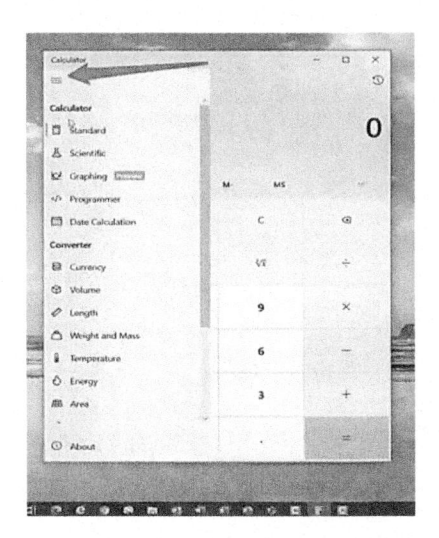

Storage Sense

Storage Sense is a feature designed to monitor your device and free up space automatically.

You can access it by going to the "start menu", select "settings"

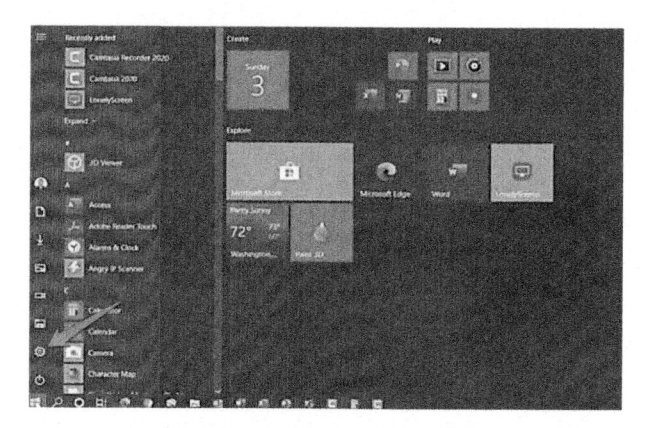

Under "settings", select "system"

Under "System", select "Storage" on your left-hand side

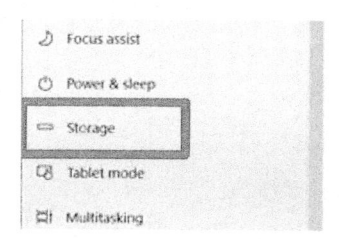

Once you select "Storage", on your right-hand side, turn on your "storage sense" to get rid of unwanted files; you will also be shown your storage usage.

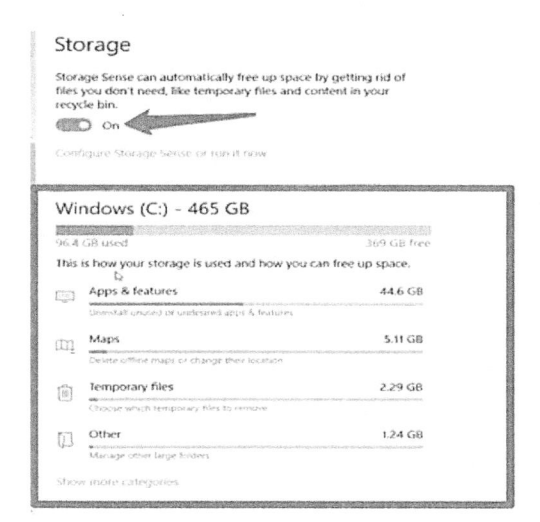

You can click the "Configure Storage Sense or run it now" to configure your storage usage.

Kindly change the configuration to your preferred choice.

You can also scroll down to clean up your storage by clicking on "clean now".

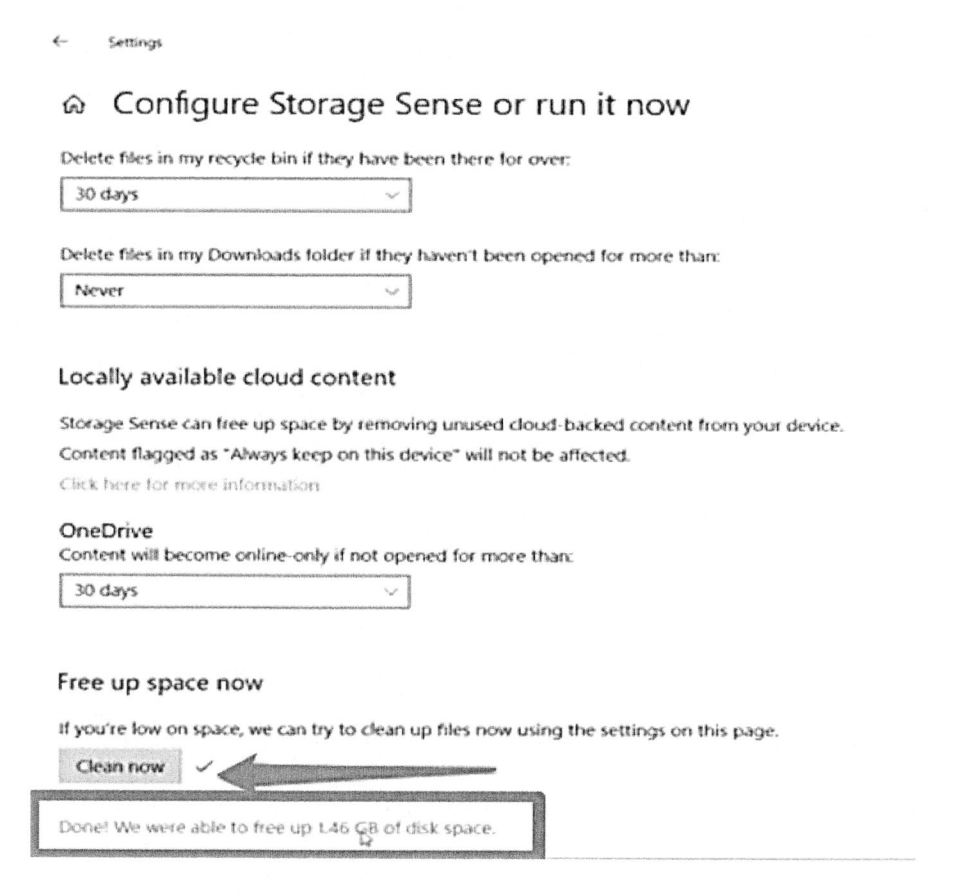

![Configure Storage Sense settings screen with Clean now button highlighted and message "Done! We were able to free up 1.46 GB of disk space."]

Once done, you will be notified below of the amount of number that was automatically freed up.

How to Use Inbuilt Video Editor to Edit Videos

Like I have said earlier, there is more to Windows 10. Windows 10 comes with a free video editor.

Go to your "start menu", type "Video editor" and open it.

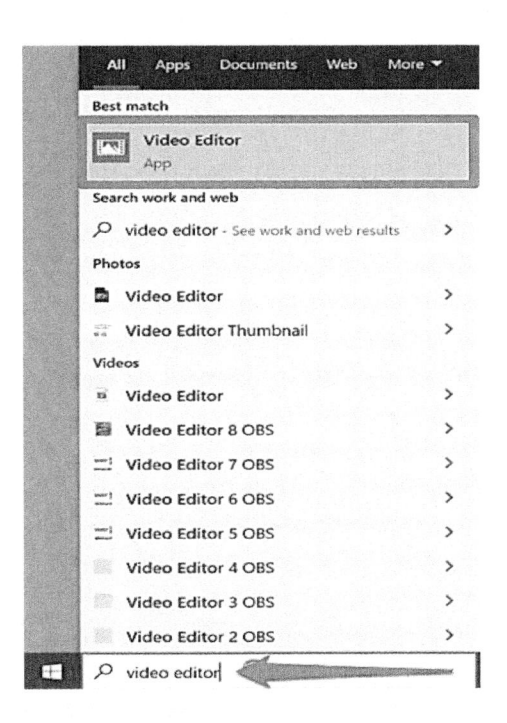

The video editor is built-in into the photo apps, below, you'd see "Welcome back to Video Editor", yours might not be welcome back if you haven't made use of it before, panic not just click on "New video project".

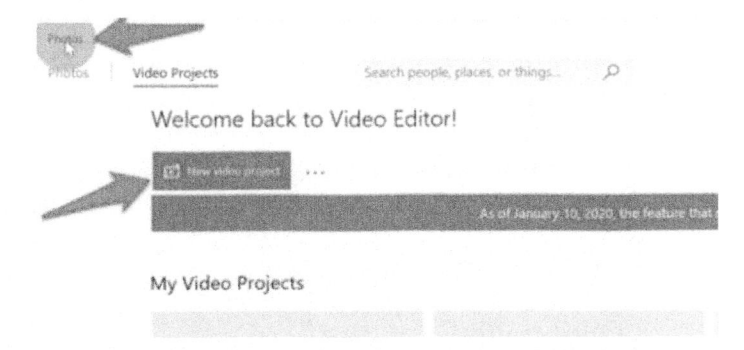

Once you click on "New video project", a dialog box will appear asking you to "Name your video". Name it according to your purpose of creation. Once done, click on "Ok".

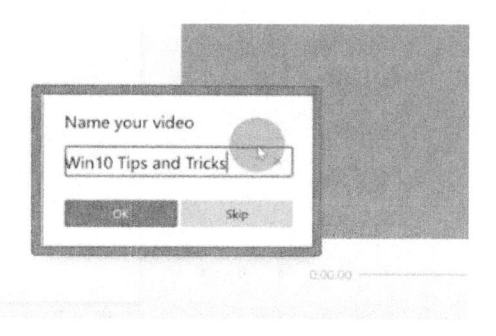

You can start editing your video on the left-hand side by clicking on "Add" to import your items.

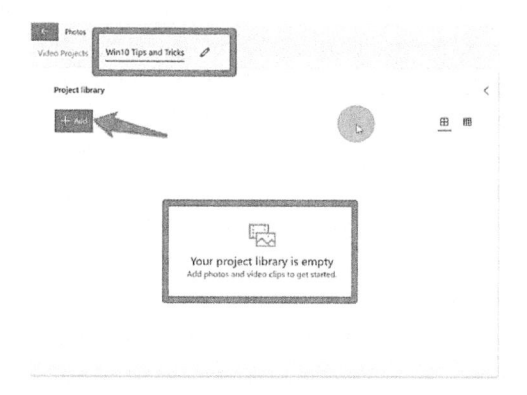

At your right-hand side is where the preview of your work will be shown to you; you can add "background music", "custom audio" & "finish video" for completion of your video editing project.

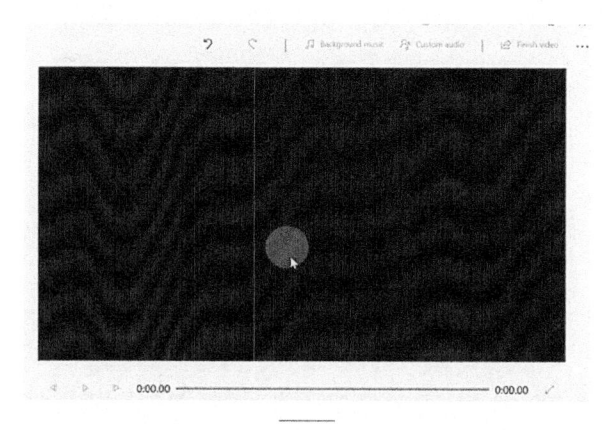

Below is your storyboard where all your items can be added for analysis.

Magnifier and Read Aloud

Windows has made it possible to zoom your screen and also make itself read your text on your behalf. To see how it works, let us open a "Notepad" and type "Magnifier and Read aloud Windows logo key ++", once done with the text, make sure your mouse censor is active in your "Notepad".

On your keyboard, press **WINKEY + +**, it will automatically start reading all your text from beginning to the end.

Windows Insider

And lastly, Windows Insider is a built-in software testing program by Microsoft that allows its users who own a license of Windows 10 to register for a pre-release version of the operating system.

295

To be part of this, make sure you are running a valid licensed Windows on your operating system.

Go to "Start menu", type "Windows Insider".

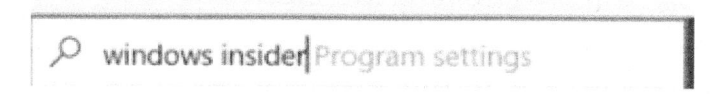

Once you see the feature as illustrated below, kindly double-click to enter.

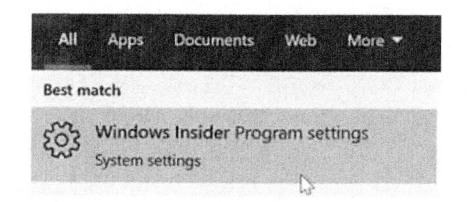

Once you are in the Windows Insider program, if you are not yet enrolled, kindly enroll; once you do, you can choose what channel you want to be part of.

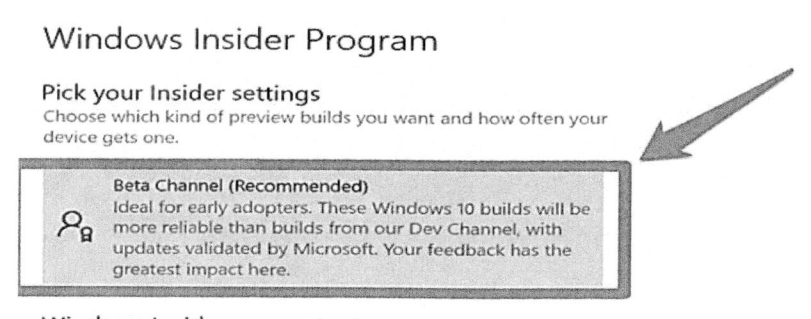

There are three (3) options channels to pick from:

- ***Dev Channel***

Dev Channel gives the latest features of Windows 10 earlier.

296

- **Beta Channel (Recommended)**

Beta Channel (Recommended) provides more reliable features than Dev Channel with updates validated by Microsoft.

- **Release Preview Channel**

"Release Preview Channel" comes with access to any upcoming release of Windows 10 with advanced quality updates and certain key features.

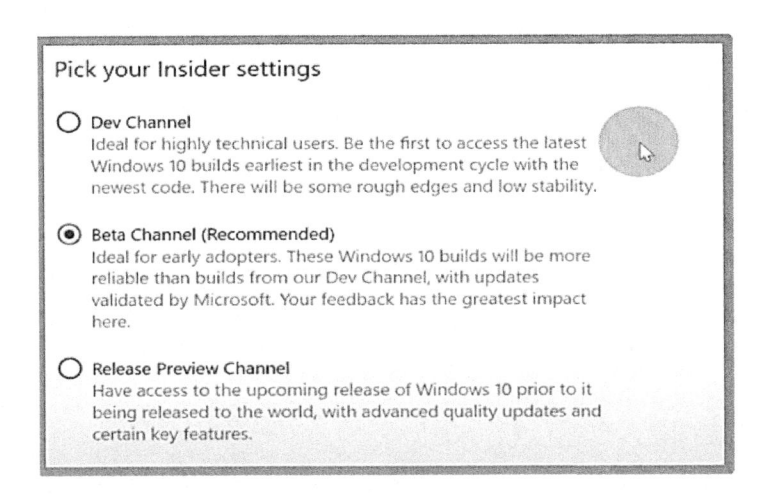

Pick your Insider settings

○ Dev Channel
Ideal for highly technical users. Be the first to access the latest Windows 10 builds earliest in the development cycle with the newest code. There will be some rough edges and low stability.

⦿ Beta Channel (Recommended)
Ideal for early adopters. These Windows 10 builds will be more reliable than builds from our Dev Channel, with updates validated by Microsoft. Your feedback has the greatest impact here.

○ Release Preview Channel
Have access to the upcoming release of Windows 10 prior to it being released to the world, with advanced quality updates and certain key features.

CONCLUSION

There is numerous simplicity that comes with Windows 10, with this guide you can be fully employed as a Microsoft pro. It is of no doubt that the world at large is advancing in a blink of an eye, and not learning about technology improvement tools won't give you an exception out of life, but your willingness to study and understand the terminologies of technology tools which are irresistible demands in Microsoft Windows operating system.

No organization with an operating system can do without Windows. If you are still using previous versions of Windows, here is the time to step up and be updated about the global trend against security vulnerability and the latest Windows simplicity.

Am glad that you have seen the hidden secrets of Windows 10 features. Don't forget to check out our other eLearning books, I will be glad to hear your testimony.

INDEX

3
3D Object, 77

A
Accessing Your Files from Anywhere via the Web, 84
Accounts Settings, 159
Activating Dark Mode, 271
Administrator account, 137
Advance System Settings, 166
Aero Shake of application, 270
Airplane mode, 154
All Apps, 104
Allow, 210
allowing a program to communicate through the firewall" mean, 216
Apps & features, 158
Apps & games, 142
AutoPlay, 151

B
Background, 155
Benefits of OneDrive, 79
File Backup, 79
Beta Channel (Recommended), 296
Bluetooth & Other Devices Settings, 149

C
Calculator, 37, 288
Calendar, 37
Can I undo the changes System Restore makes?, 202
CD or DVD Drives, 86
Change account settings, 105
Changing an Account Type, 136
Changing Your Background Displayed Colour, 105
Choosing an advanced recovery method, 204
Clicking method, 271
Clock, 37
Color, 146
Colors, 156
CONCLUSION, 297
Configuring Cortana, 62
Connecting to Another Computer, 225
CONNECTIVITY, 222
Cortana, 38, 161
Creating Different Document Format, 84
Custom Scan, 212
Customizing Cortana, 64

Customizing Your Search Box, 265

D

Data usage, 154
Date & Time, 160
Default apps, 158
Delivery Optimization, 184
Desktop folder, 75
Determining What Your File Explorer Opens First, 273
Dev Channel, 295
Dial-Up, 154
Dictation, 279
Difference Between CD & DVD Drives, 86
Difference between Settings and Control Panel, 110
Disc Cleanup, 181
Display settings, 145
Displaying Back All Hidden Items, 254
Document, 238
Documents folder, 76
Downloads folder, 76

E

Ease of Access, 161
Edit menu, 238
Enabling Clipboard History, 255

ENHANCING YOUR PC PERFORMANCE, 164
Essential Frameworks, 17
Ethernet, 153
Exploring File Explorer, 67
Exploring OneDrive Storage, 79
EXPLORING SETTINGS FEATURES, 145
Exploring Task View, 53
Exploring Windows 10 Desktop Environment, 31
External Backup, 206
External drive, 87

F

Factory Reset, 275
File Explorer Default Folders, 75
File menu, 238
files changed during a system restore, 203
Firewall, 213
Flash drive, 88
Frequently asked Questions about System Restore Point, 200
Full Scan, 212

G

Gaming, 160
Get OneDrive Cloud on PC, 80

God Mode, 280
Graphics Performance, 171

H

Hardware, 17
Help, 238
Hiding of Desktop Items, 253
Historical Background of Windows Operating System (OS), 10
How Can I Backup My Files Against Loses of Data?, 205
How do I choose a restore point?, 203
How does System Restore work?, 200
How long are, 204
How to Add a Printer in Windows 10, 227
How to Add a Shortcut into your Desktop Environment, 112
How to Adjust Screen Resolution, 108
How to Block a Program With Windows Firewall, 216
How to check all application programs?, 49
How to Connect Your Windows 10 PC to the Internet, 222
How to Create a New User, 132
How to Create A Tiles Group, 50
How to Delete, Pin & Clear Clipboard History, 259
How to Disable Cortana, 60
How to Display Apps List on the Start Menu, 52
How to Display Only Your Search Icon, 267
How to Display Your Search Box, 267
How to download an App from Microsoft Store on Windows 10, 246
How to Enable Cortana, 56
How to Ensure Windows Security is up to Date, 89
How to hide Apps list on the Start Menu, 51
How to Hide Your Search Box, 266
How to Locate Your Firewall, 214
How To Make Use of Emojis on Windows 10, 262
How to Make Use of Task View, 54
How to Recognize If an App Is Safe or Not, 244
How to Remove a User, 135

301

How to Rename Tiles Titles Bar, 44
How to Resize Your Desktop Application, 121
How to Scan a Document or Image, 236
How to Show File Name Extension, 268
How to Sign Out or Switch Users, 143
How to Speed Up Your Windows 10, 164
How to Switch and Determine What File Explorer Should Open By Default, 274
How to switch from Local Account to Microsoft Account, 129
How to switch from Microsoft Account to Local Account, 127
How to Treat Windows Unexpected Issues, 187
How to Use Inbuilt Video Editor to Edit Videos, 291
How to use Quick scan, Full scan, and Custom Scan, 211

I

Importance of Installing Windows on your Computer, 12
Inbuilt Apps on Windows 10, 31
INDEX, 298
Installation of applications, 240
INSTALLATION OF SOFTWARE ON WINDOWS 10, 240
Installing Windows 10, 21
   customize, 23
   upgrade, 23
Internal Backup, 206
Internal drive, 87
INTRODUCTION, ix

L

Launching Apps with the Start Menu, 48
Launching Sandbox, 285
Left Portion of the Start Screen, 41
Local account, 122
Lock, 105
Lock screen, 156

M

Magnifier and Read Aloud, 294
Mail, 34

Managing User Accounts, 138
Memory card, 89
Microsoft account, 122
Microsoft Edge, 33
Microsoft Store, 32
Minimize All Opened Application, 270
Mobile hotspot, 154
Mouse, 150
Moving the Tiles Icon, 46
Multitasking, 148
Music folder, 76

N

Network & Internet, 153
Night light, 146
Notepad, 31
Notification, 146

O

OneDrive, 38
OneDrive Cloud Storage Features, 81
   Always keep on this device, 83
   Free up space, 83
   Share, 82
   Version history, 83
   View online, 82
OneDrive Files & Folders Visualization, 86
OneDrive Status Icon
   A person icon, 81
OneDrive Status Icons, 81
   Blue cloud icons, 81
   Green marked icons, 81
   Sync icons, 81
Online Backup, 206
OVERVIEW OF MICROSOFT WINDOWS, 10

P

Paint, 33
Parental Controls, 138
Partition, 207
PC User Account Name, 105
Pen & Windows Ink, 151
Personalization, 155
Phone, 152
Pictures folder, 76
Pin to Taskbar, 42
Power & Sleep, 147
Printer & Scanner, 150
Privacy Settings, 162, 180
Procedures for Downloading Windows 10, 20
Process in Copying of Files & Folders to a CD or DVD, 88
Projecting to this PC, 149
Proxy, 154

Q

Quarantine, 210
Quick Access, 77

R

Real-time protection, 208
Recent activity, 141
Region & language, 160
Release Preview Channel, 296
Remote Desktop, 149
Remove, 210
Remove Desktop Shortcuts, 183
Renaming a Folder, 78
Resizing the Start Screen Tiles, 45
Resizing the Tiles Icon, 47
Restart, 104
Right Portion of the Start Screen, 41

S

Sandbox Requirements, 284
Scale & Layout, 146
Scanning options, 209
Screen time, 143
Searching on OneDrive cloud storage, 84
Setting up Cortana to be your Personal Assistance, 65
Setting up Windows to Fax, 237
Settings Features, 145
Share Experiences, 149
Shortcut method, 271
Shut down, 103
Sign Out, 105
Sign-in Options, 125
Sleep, 103
Snip & Sketch, 282
Snipping tool, 35
Software, 17
Sorting of Files on OneDrive Cloud Storage, 85
Speech, 160
Speech Recognition, 35
Speeding up Windows Start time, 263
Splitting Windows App on Windows 10, 260
Spyware, 211
Standard Account, 137
Status, 153
Steps on Uninstalling an Application, 240
Sticky Notes, 32
Storage, 147
Storage Sense, 289
System Configuration, 175
system protection, 201
System Restore, 200

T

Tablet Mode, 148
Task manager, 36
Taskbar, 157
The Power Key, 103
Theme, 157

Time & Language, 159
To Undo System Settings and Files to an Earlier State, 191
Toggling Between the Tablet Mode and Desktop Mode, 98
Tool menu, 238
TROUBLESHOOTING WINDOWS 10, 187
Turn On & Off Background Apps, 277
Turning Off Tiles, 47
Types of CD or DVD drives, 87
Types of Scanning, 212
Types of User Accounts, 122
Types of Windows Security, 126
Typing, 151

U

Ultimate Performance, 164
Understanding Windows Defender Real-Time Protection, 209
Uninstallation of Software Programs on PC, 240
Unpin from Taskbar, 43
Unpin Tiles Icon, 46
Update & Security, 162
Uploading Content on OneDrive, 85

USB, 152
User Account Settings, 123
User Accounts, 122
Using OneDrive Cloud in File Explorer, 80

V

Videos folder, 77
View menu, 238
Voice Recorder, 35
VPN, 154

W

Weather, 34
Web browsing, 142
What if System Restore doesn't fix the problem?, 204
What is Windows 10?, 11
What Should I Do When My PC Refuse to Give Me Latest Update?, 91
What's New About Windows 10?, 13
WIFI, 153
Windows, 30
WINDOWS 10 ACTION CENTER USER, 93
Windows 10 Editions, 15
Windows 10 Hardware Requirement, 17

Windows 10 Shortcut Keys, 114
WINDOWS 10 STORAGE, 67
WINDOWS 10 TIPS AND TRICKS, 253
Windows Defender, 208
Windows Defender Offline Scan, 212
Windows Insider, 294
Windows Sandbox, 284
WINDOWS SECURITY, 208
Windows Update, 163

Windows Various Versions, 10
WordPad, 32
Working on Tiles, 43
Working with Cortana, 55
Working with the Start Menu, 39

X

Xbox, 33